I0838806

Part of the 'Life Without A Laughter Track' Series

Erroneous Facial Nerve Rewirings

and Other Stories

First Edition 2021

By

Christian Frank

Additional material inspired by **Jamie Morgan & Simon Asker & Dan Walton & Paul Miller**

For Cana

CONTENTS

Christian:	I was shouting at my son about clocks, you know about 'to the hour' and 'past the hour.' And I'm really not a good teacher is what I learned. I get a bit stroppy when he doesn't understand that the short hand is for the hour and the long one is for minutes, then you say to him, 'Put the short hand onto that number.' And he uses the minute hand, I mean, that's just a sin.
Jamie:	If the minute hand is next to the hour hand, what's the seconds hand to?
Christian:	I don't like the seconds hand. We don't need them. What do you need a seconds hand for? Only if you're doing a stopwatch.
Jamie:	We're exactly a minute into the show.
Christian:	Now we need a seconds hand watch. Other than that, you don't need one, get rid of it. You only need the hour hand. If I place the hour hand between a number, you should be able to gauge whereabouts it is. Yeah, half past is easy between numbers. If I placed the hour hand, maybe closer to the three you're going to say maybe it's about 10 to three. Do you see what I'm doing?
Jamie:	If I say 'no,' you'll shout at me like you did your son? I'll just throw away the seconds hand from my watch. It was a gift, but I want an easy life.
Christian:	I was on early shift this morning, so I'm very tired. I might have caffeinated coffee later on and we'll review it. We've got a brand-new vending machine at work. And it tells you the number of your order. Let's say you like plenty of sugar in your tea, make

it strong, and give it some milk. It'll say your order is 1879. So, if you remember that number and someone takes your mug or thermos flask to the vending machine, you can simply say mine's an 1879 or a Rorke's Drift if you work with history buffs.

Jamie:

So, you just have to remember a famous historical event that happened. It could be difficult if my drink happens to be a 282. I don't know what happened unless it's 1066.

Christian:

Wikipedia is there isn't it? You could find out and say, 'Hannibal crossed the Alps with his elephants.' That could be 282. Let's just say it was. Otherwise, you're only ever drinking a Battle of Hastings and it could be plain hot water for all we know.

Amelia Lily – 'You Bring Me Joy', is midweek chart number one. With only a hundred days till Christmas people have gotten mad. Buying them as stocking fillers, that's what it is. I've noticed the charity Christmas cards are out now it's September. You're best to check how much the contribution really is, as only some of the money from the sale of each pack goes to help good causes. Sometimes they list about 10 different charities, meaning they all get a tenth of a penny once the card makers clawed back their profits.

Middlesbrough's finest Amelia Lily. We wish her all the best. We've been very supportive since she went through the first auditions. And that's an utter lie by the way. I mean, she's not evil. We don't wish anything bad on her, but your music…It's not even generic. It was awful. I've played generic music before and enjoyed it. But this potential future number one - I couldn't go for that.

I charge you Jamie, what have you done this week?

Jamie: Well, I've got this presentation to present. It's to do with the college taking advantage of technological benefits aimed at students over the next five years.

Christian: Are you sending these people to sleep? Well, what do you think's going to happen when it comes to education?

Jamie: It's all on mobile phones now. That's where it's headed.

Christian: Oh, is it? No one's told me. I could have done this show from home on my phone. Instead, we're sat in Studio B. Studio B is normally where I leave my laptop to record the output from Studio A, which we always feel most comfortable presenting in. But as we live and breathe right now, I don't know what any of the levels are. Jamie's a bit more fidgety than normal. Have you had your fish oil today? That's probably what you need to calm you down.

Jamie: My Mam gave me cod liver oil years ago to try and cure my epilepsy. It actually brought the fits on. It was my Dad who suggested to stop taking it to see what happens, and the fits stopped. Bizarre!

Christian: My advice is to stick with what the doctor says. Regardless of Jamie's holistic approach or whatever his Dad said. I'm sure it was for the best, it was probably costing him 8 quid a bottle from Holland and Barrett, so he told you to stop self-medicating with his money. But he's not a doctor is he, like Dr. Dre? He's a real doctor.

I'm handing you a bag of Haribo Starmix, to take only one sweet, which one are you going for? It's not difficult because everyone's got a favourite. If you try and get more than one, I'm going to nip your little fingers when they're still trapped inside the bag, so you won't get any out then. I'm not a nice guy.

I had a bit of a nightmare when we went camping, because I kept a bar of chocolate for my evening treat secretly tucked away in my sleeping bag. Well, you don't need me to tell you what happens to chocolate stashed away in a hot stuffy tent during Summer. I wanted to cry. What a waste of chocolate. There are many things that I won't cry about.

Jamie: Spilled milk?

Christian: Did I tell you about the kids with their cheeks getting nipped while they're eating their Frosties? I was telling them to just eat it, until I sniffed the bottle. It was like tangy butter. I'm going back to the Starmix question. You haven't chosen one yet.

Jamie: I'll go for the jelly ring. The wedding ring, just so I can wear it a bit.

Christian: Did you know the small gummy bears use those as rubber rings if they ever fall overboard.

Jamie: I did not.

Christian: Do you eat the end slices of a loaf of bread? I didn't realise so many people don't eat the crusts, the bookend slices of your loaf of bread. None of my family do which is good news for me. I have no problem with eating them. I'll pick up the bag of bread and there's only two slices left in there. And

it's the crust. That's great. But when I said this at
work, 'Can you believe my family are like this?'
They agreed with them, they don't eat crusts either.
And so, it got me thinking this is more common
then we first thought. Chances are the listener
doesn't either. They're now thinking, 'Shut up.'
And you can imagine their feeble hand coming out,
wired with intravenous tubes drugging them up,
trying to reach out and turn us off. And they can't.

Jamie: Pull the nurse cord. They'll come and turn us off.

Christian: I prefer for a nurse to turn us on. Sounds like a
perfect strap line for our show here in the hospital.
So, is Dr. Dre a real doctor? We can ask the nurse
before she turns us off, 'You know Prof Green? Is
he a real professor?'

Are they allowed to bear false witness to having
these qualifications? Could you call yourself Dr.
Morgan? Can rap artist put letters at the end of
their name and become a Bachelor of Science,
Snoop Dogg BSc? You can use your stage name
and incorporate a little bit of certification, Cliff
Richard, PhD.

Jamie: Christian Frank, NVQ level 3.

Christian: Jamie Morgan, O-levels, no grades A to C. I just
think if you do that, and they're getting away with
it, they should be put in prison. What kind of
punishment should that crime carry? 'You see this
Dr Dre, who's not really a health care professional'
Mr Dre will be thrown into some molten lava to set
an example to other rap artists. 'Dr Dre wishes to
call his first witness – big props to Prof Green.'

Jamie: 'Is Major Morgan really a Major?' No relation.

Christian: This is a heart clutching story at the moment.
                    When your chest gets a nasty pain. Joanne said to
                    me, 'We've bought Calvary a pair of shoes for 50
                    pounds.'

Jamie: What? He's gonna grow out of them though.

Christian: Exactly. You understand my heart palpitations.
                    However, I've been won over with maths. We were
                    buying a pair of say 10-pound shoes which didn't
                    last. And so, we probably bought about five pairs a
                    year. Because he kicks and scruffs his shoes so
                    much they start talking. I don't know what he does
                    with them, but it's a false economy to keep buying
                    the cheap pair of shoes every six weeks or so. If we
                    buy him a better pair, I might even be able to hand
                    them down.

                    Have I told you the story of my older brother and
                    how he bullied me at school? We weren't rich, and
                    we were on free school meals for a while. And we
                    had an auntie whose husband's father had died. Sad
                    story, but for me it gets far more tragic. He left
                    behind a pair of shoes that he'd barely ever worn.
                    Literally brand-new shoes that he'd probably wore
                    the once trying them on in the shop.

                    After the death the family were clearing out the
                    belongings and getting rid of stuff. And as is
                    completely normal in society, offering quality
                    items to good homes. They said, 'By the way,
                    there's a pair of shoes here that have never been
                    worn. If you fit them, they might be of use.' Of
                    course, my Mam said, 'Yes please. I've got a child
                    who'll fit them.' Okay.

I'm walking to school with my friends and my older brother is walking there with us. And he decides to tell those friends, who were in my class, 'Christian's wearing dead man's shoes.' Well, needless to say, I didn't want to wear them ever again. It's weird, but the moment a 12-year-old in your class finds out you're wearing a pair of dead man's shoes, they tell everyone.

Jamie: What's that about?

Christian: Yeah, strange. It's almost like kids want to find fault with other kids so they can have fun by ridiculing them. But it was my own brother, who knew just how poor a family we were. Retelling that tale as an adult, I actually feel more humiliation for him.

We got a letter by the way on the third day of Trinity at secondary school. 'I am disappointed that you are taking your child out of school for holidays during term time.' It was a very generic letter. It didn't say, 'And you were off to Butlin's half board to enjoy the splash pool.' It didn't go into detail, but it was definitely a pop at me as a parent. I actually replied, I sent a letter back. They need to know it happens every year.

It's a double-edged sword. The school are always wanting money, always on the scrounge for any extra cash. They use the words 'voluntary contributions' when asking for £8.50 for your child to go on a day out. I searched on the internet and this place they're going gives free meals to the teachers. I'm beginning to work out how they can afford to subsidize their meals.

I can't talk about children like this, because as you know I have experience of a frugal childhood. But

I can certainly talk about the parents. Some of the parents will read the letter and go, 'Voluntary? Then they're not getting owt.' And they still expect the school to provide the same experiences with less and less budget. You'll know these parents because they're the first to complain if the school doesn't pack little Chardonnay a free lunch box when she's on a trip to an Outward-Bound centre that was also free. They can't even provide a snack for their child for just one day. They feel entitled to every benefit under the Sun. I'd deduct any of these costs from their support allowance.

Jamie:

I completely agree with you. But can you imagine the uproar with people getting this bill?

Christian:

There are some lazy parents that don't want to contribute anything to their child's education, not even a pound a term.

The other side to this, is that schools are always on the lookout for cash, but as soon as you can't afford to take your child on holiday in August, because it's almost £1000-a-week to stay at Butlins, they're quick enough to denounce you. So, hold on a minute, I'm trying to save cash, so I have disposable money left over to be better financially prepared to assist with your 'voluntary contributions.' Yeah, I should have put that in the letter. 'Don't have a go at me - I'm doing this for you Mr. Headmaster.'

Speaking of shoes, you know my school shoes were obtained after an elderly adult had died. He obviously bought the shoes just before passing. Sounds awful. But when he bought the shoes, he was buying children size shoes, right? Now you don't pay VAT on children's clothes or shoes based on the size measurements. So, this old man had never paid VAT on his footwear.

On the flip side there are plenty of larger children having to wear adult clothes and shoes, paying tax on them. Why should a child have to pay tax just because their feet are too big? Or equally why should fully grown dwarves avoid paying their shoe VAT? Although in their defense, don't they actually make the shoes when the cobblers asleep? But if you can always fit into a pair of kids shoes, you can save about 20% on the retail price for the rest of your life. And most times the kids have the better designs on their shoes like Peppa Pig and Batman. It's all a bit footist.

Foot binding that the Chinese people do, sorry the Japanese. I don't want to be called a bigot by Nick Clegg. Perish the thought of other people's thoughts. But what I could do is bind my feet. You know, like the Geisha girls did and walk around in ceramic collectable slippers, you know the ones old people buy from the back of the Mothball Monthly magazines in porcelain and keep them as ornaments? No tax for me. Clever plan eh?

Books also aren't charged a 20% sales tax. Jamie is sat there staggered because some books cost an arm and a leg. I mean, they can easily be £25 and that includes no tax. That's huge. When it comes to kindle or eBooks there's still a reading tax even though technically, they're still books. I heard the expression, 'the dead tree version' this week.

Jamie: Is that like dead man's shoes?

Christian: Say you've got the Jaws novel on Kindle, 'I didn't want the dead tree version.' 'Oh, you mean book.' We still call them books.

Now that raises the question; when in the future
will it not become a book? Yeah, like TV, it's now
HDTV. Didn't the analogue signal get pulled today
as well? If you're trying to tune in to Cbeebies
you'll have just seen a black screen. It's gone. It's a
thing of the past. It's HDTV but people are still
saying 'telly.' I guess screened entertainment will
always remain as the telly. even if it comes out 3-D
or hologram.

One day we may have smelly-vision and it'll be
called a 'smelly', that's for sure. And a news
article you would not watch on the smelly was the
auction of Elvis memorabilia. Some weirdo was
selling an authentic pair of soiled Elvis Presley's
underpants. If you were a surviving relative to the
Presly estate, you would buy them from the auction
house just to dispose of them. Although there's got
to be some DNA in there.

They were worn in the same year he died under a
blue jumpsuit during a concert. A very sweaty
concert from the looks of it. The unwashed
underwear did not meet the £7,000 reserve price
with the headline, 'Return to sender.' Imagine if I
walked to school wearing those dead man's pants,
my brother would have had a field day, 'They're
dead mans pants.' 'Shut up!' 'He paid 7 thousand
and they're not even washed.' 'But they were
specially chosen by the King. Look, there's no
visible lines.' LUNGE!

The auction house did sell his personal Bible which
Elvis received from his uncle during his first
Christmas at Graceland in 1957. It went for
£59,000. You would think his treasured holy book
would have been kept within his own family,
would you not? But they're into Scientology all of

the others. The sales room manager said, 'The winning telephone bidder who did not want to be identified was an American man based in the UK.'

Jamie: It was Elvis Presley.

Christian: Yeah, he's alive and well buying back his own Bible. He just didn't want his kecks. You can't blame him. You think the people who couldn't get the Bible might have wanted the auctioneers to revisit his undercrackers again? I suppose not until cloning technology can extract the forensic evidence needed to create your very own hip swiveling pop star. Simon Cowell will be bidding like crazy.

I have a story about things you find in the toilet. Joanne my better half was using the toilet brush and noticed it was in real need of a clean. And of course, they're quite cheap to replace. So, rather than struggle to freshen up the brush, we decided to sling it and buy another one when we were next in the shops. You can buy them from as little as a pound. Don't need it – sling it. Made a mental note, 'Need a bog brush.'

Now I have five children. Okay. So, they wipe, they put it in. They don't always flush. They wipe, they put it in. They don't always flush. They wipe, they put it in. You get where this is going? Yeah. Eventually I look in and go, 'Has no one flushed?' FLUSH! FILL! SWIRL! LIFT! And I'm standing there thinking, 'That doesn't look too nice.' And 99% of the time you cross your fingers, and it starts to go back down. Sometimes it goes down quite fast – phew! But on Saturday it didn't, it didn't move at all, not even a slow seepage.

I had to get a carrier bag to wrap up my arm to the elbow and I went in. I can confirm carrier bags are not waterproof, there's holes in them to prevent suffocation. I put my hand into the bag and went into the brimming toilet and the plastic clings around your arm. It's got that kind of condom property, that you can feel everything, you know, I could feel everything between my fingers. There was only me and probably a charity shop bag protecting my fingers from the objects floating around in there. I could feel it all. And I thought, 'How dare they?'

I had to scoop it up and then pull the bag from off my elbow, over my hand. I had to pull it back inside out to keep whatever was in there - in there. Then hold it till it stopped dripping over the toilet and take it out the house. Then it flushed. But just so you know, on Saturday, ironically the day of the week that contains the word 'turd' stuck in the middle, we went and got some toilet brushes. We've even invested in some extra ones as back up. I'm not doing that again. It was horrendous. Never throw out a dirty brush unless you have a replacement one already to go. Lessons learned.

Oh, speaking of lessons. I learned about Jason Donovan and 'Jason D.' When he was in his interview, he said when he was a kid, his name helped him know the months of the year from July. July, August, September, October, November, December. And I thought, 'Can't wait to tell Jamie about this, it might finally help him crack the whole struggling with a calendar thing.'

<table>
<tr><td>Jamie:</td><td>I thought it was January, August, May, after my name.</td></tr>
</table>

Christian: Done some bell ringing at St. Nicholas church. I don't know about this, but can you spell Guisborough? I spelt it wrong, without the first 'u'. But surely everyone spells it wrong because it's the ancient capital town of Cleveland and it should have the first 'u' missing. Most people would have been illiterate back then and written the name phonetically.

Jamie: Middlesbrough is spelt wrong. It should have an extra 'o' in it, so the brough sounds more borough. It should be that, but it isn't. So, we all misspell it. I think that's why we call it 'The Boro', you can definitely hear the two 'O's', which is closer to the original sounding name.

Christian: I've been enough times to Guisborough to spell it right. Anyway, there's a guy who's been bell ringing for over 40 years at St Nicholas. And in all that time Calvary was the only one who didn't listen to him. My four-year-old child was bell ringing which was excellent. However, the bell is the weight of a small car. And once it swings, it uses its own momentum and then the skill is to just pull on it lightly. There's a real talent to it, I didn't realise.

Calvary pulled down on it, and as it went down, you know, you get that coloured holding cloth along the rope? Well, he decided to grab the next bit above that. So, as it went back up, he went up with it. I've never seen his face go so white. I thought he was gonna rocket up to the belfry. As the bell went down, the rope went down. He just, without thinking, grabbed the next portion, ignoring the place holder of where to safely grab the rope. I think his arm nearly came out of its socket. He got grabbed quickly by me. I think he may have experienced a kind of whiplash, but certainly more fright than anything else. I think the guy who was doing it, a senior citizen, thought, 'Oh my, we're gonna end on this. A child going through the stained-glass windows.'

I'd never seen a church clock or how it works. It still gets wound up. And the people who installed it over 100 years ago, the company still exists, and they go around maintaining these clocks. Anyway, there's a disc with grooves in different parts. And they're not all uniformly done. So, when it's one o'clock, there's only a little gap so the hammer is released, gongs, then goes back into its slot.

When it's two o'clock the gap is slightly bigger, say twice as big. So, the hammer is free to knock the bell as it moves for that limited time. Only when it's back in its slot it can't hit the bell and every hour depending on which hour it is, that slot is bigger, so it bounces 10 times for 10 o'clock. I thought that was pretty clever. I didn't know that. I thought the vicar was out there at midnight, with a night gown over his cassock jumping over tombstones. You know what they're like.

I went jogging and took the two eldest children with me, because Trinity, who's 12, is now in secondary school. I thought I'd take her jogging on Sunday morning, but then Calvary who's 10, wanted to go as well. Then the thin end of a wedge became a wedge, Cana wanted to go who's not quite 8. I said, 'Not yet.' But that's false hope. I thought, 'No, I'm making my mind up. You're not going.' To be honest, I only wanted to take Trinity. Now I had two of them and they about managed.

Later during the day, when we were walking through Guisborough forest Cana didn't stop running. He kept running up and down the walkway going, 'Dad, look at me, Dad, look at me. I'm just as good at running Dad.' So, the next time I do a run, he's going out. It was heartbreaking to see that. 'Look, did you see how fast I was there Dad?'

I've seen something that I thought was really nice. I normally don't mention things on Facebook, but somebody had posted what they've done after their father died. She'd took her father's dressing gown, like Terry towel cloth, and had it made by some company into cuddly bears for all the children. And they posted a picture of them all on Facebook. And I thought that's quite a touching thing. Not sure my clothing would be hugged that close to my children if I passed away. 'Mam that smell is still there.' 'But I've bleached it ten times already sweetheart.' Hey, Lisa Marie Presley could fashion a cuddly from her Dads skiddy marked knickers.

Cana asked his Mam this week, 'Where's my blue bear?' And his Mam went, 'He's in the bin.' It was the way he took it, because you don't realise just how young they are. He had a little cry, you know, because that was his bear, and he was telling me that he used to talk to him at night. And then Joanne said, 'Well, you should have really looked after him a little bit more, because when I found him, he was a bit matted and shoved down the radiator.' I think some of his fur had melted away because it had gotten so hot.

I may have been insensitive by saying, 'He's dead now. Your bears gone. He's in bear heaven. We'll replace him. We'll get another one, a better one.' Of course, sometimes gallows humour is the only recourse you have in situations like that. Children know you can't replace the irreplaceable. It's one of life's hardest lessons. His Mam said, 'Oh, well, we'll go up in the attic tomorrow and there's other bears up there. We'll have a look. See which one you want to choose to bring down into your bed.' And Cana said, 'Oh yeah, because maybe the blue bear is still up there, and you didn't really throw him away.' We don't learn the lesson first go. It's difficult grasping the cold reality. I said, 'You're not listening to Mam, he's gone, he's in the bin.'

Do you still have your childhood bear tucked away somewhere?

Jamie: Mum made me get rid of them because they were taking up too much room.

Christian: Too much room? How many cuddly toys did you have?

Jamie: Three.

Christian: They were either very big bears or that's just mean.

                Chunky Monkey news. *An obese woman who didn't wear a seatbelt because it wouldn't fit around her large frame has told how an on the spot fine prompted her to shed half of her body weight. She weighed 408 pounds when she was pulled over by the police and in little more than a year, she's managed to shift 190 pounds.* If you're that fat do you need a seatbelt? Wouldn't the stomach act like an airbag anyway, to protect you on impact with all those layers of fat.

Jamie: It's your head that needs holding back from crashing through the window.

Christian: So, if she put a bicycle helmet on, she'd be fine?

Jamie: Oh, God yeah.

Christian: She now weighs 218 pounds. She says that the combination of healthy eating and exercise is responsible for her trim physique - I would say 'trim', but she lives in South Carolina so maybe that's 'trim' to that locality. Have you tried doing Zumba? We should do some in Studio B, because it looks like it should be used for that, rather than a radio station.

Some local Chunky Monkey news here, *Fitness Instructor Kevin Hayes 44 from Saltburn smashed the Guinness Book of Records for eating three pickled eggs in the fastest time of 52.6 seconds.*

Eggs are all different sizes so technically it's not the same for each contestant.

They weren't all eating pickled ostrich eggs and he got to choose quail. That would be a little unfair. You can eat duck eggs, and I'll have sturgeon, just suck them straight from out the fish. And to be honest, it depends how much vinegar has been used on them. There was a corner shop where my grandparents lived when I was little. And in 1983, the shop owner had a big jar of pickled eggs placed on the front counter. It must have been there for years. You know, full of brown malt vinegar and you caught a glimpse of the egg when it came close to the sides. An oval white sphere brushed against the glass and you'd know something was in there. There's an egg in there.

It would have fermented over years. The amount of vinegar would make your eyes stream. So, there would be a difference between the ones soaked in brine for years and a jar you've bought today from the supermarket. For a fair competition the eggs

should have been soaked for the same amount of
time. The longer the better to make the yolks acidic
and less dry. Yeah, that doesn't sound like a
choking hazard. Anyway, great story, no training
involved just a guy walking in the market, steps up
on stage, eats three eggs, gets crowned, all within
under a minute. Can happen to anyone. It must
have been like winning the lottery. Well, except
without any of the money and not receiving any
World Record verification yet. Still, a close
second.

You know we were talking about getting a new
toilet brush. Well, in the same shop they had one of
those innovation TVs on a shelf, advertising
pointless labour-saving devices, like lint remover
gloves or nonstick Tupperware or something. And
my kids were gathered around it listening as if it
was the sermon on the mount. It just goes to show
what happens when children don't have TV. Any
TV will do. Eyes wide open, mouth dropped as the
infomercial demonstrates lint being removed from
someone's suit. All my kids just standing in the
aisle completely oblivious to anything happening
around them. I did think, 'This is great, it's like a
babysitter.' We can go around and do our
shopping. But I ended up joining them, watching
the non-static duster that comes with a five-year
guarantee. 'Only the price is shocking.'

I've made my first DVD, not with me in it. I mean,
I've actually used my DVD burner. It takes almost
real time to write to disk. A 3-hour movie takes
just as long again to transfer. And while I was
doing this painfully slow process, I looked outside
and there were kids in the street playing hide and
seek using my garden. We have a tall hedge which
must seem ideal to those hiding.

I did look out the window and gave them one of
my I-want-you-out-of-my-garden-stares. Okay, I'm
gonna try it here in the studio and see how
effective it is on Jamie. I'm tightening my lips up,
my nostrils are gonna flare.

Jamie: They didn't move, did they?

Christian: No, they didn't. They looked at me and then went
to hide behind the tree. Clearly not interested. I
thought to myself, 'Well, you know, me going to
the door and telling them to leave my garden is
going to result in exerting a lot of unnecessary
effort here.' So instead, I went, 'Meh!' and just
stopped looking out of the blinds and sat back
down waiting for the DVD player to finish burning
my disk.

Jamie: They're gonna think they can do it anytime they
want now.

Christian: It's like the Oscar Wilde story, isn't it? The Selfish
Giant, when he chases the children from his garden
and one of them is Jesus. I don't want to chase
Jesus out of my garden. Would he be the ginger
kid?

Jamie: I don't think you need to worry about Jesus coming
to your garden to play. You'd be asking for him to
perform miracles on your hedge for a start.

Christian: And to speed up my DVD writer. And to stop the
local riff raff trespassing on my property. And to
be rich enough that I could afford a car that doesn't
keep failing its annual MOT.

Jamie: Is this what you pray for?

Christian: More like a wish list. I'd also like to get electrolysis all on my face. I'm fed up with shaving. I've got to a point where I can't be chewed anymore. If I can't be bothered to go into the garden and shout at kids, I mean, that should be fun, I certainly don't have the energy to keep shaving for the rest of my life. So, when I do eventually look like Grizzly Adams, it's because I've got to an age where I've put in so many hours already into shaving, I think, now you can all just leave me alone. But maybe one day I'll want to look like Kenny Rogers, and have a big beard grow back again. Can you reverse electrolysis on your face? Jamie will have to go and do his homework on the internet and find out for me.

Jamie: I didn't do the last homework you set for me about lemon top ice-creams only being sold in Redcar.

Christian: You just google the question. Although it has a tendency to auto fill with predictive text based on the most popular searches. 'Do Salmons… eat humans?' On a production level Jamie circumvent the internet and just respond with a confident lie that sounds completely fit for broadcast.

Jamie: No, no it doesn't.

Christian: And that's how you do homework.

Christian: They always say, 'Hey Joe' by Jimi Hendrix is one of the best guitar tracks ever, but I've just gone and faded it out after the first 10 seconds. If Jamie had arrived on time, we may have heard a bit more of the classic tune. Would you like to explain where you've been during the last 10 minutes? It wasn't a penny you were spending was it? It was closer to 100 quid converted into Zimbabwe money. It would be phenomenal. Enough to fill my skip, which has been in front of my house for days. The hire company are so inconsiderate to move it, I have no place to park my car.

A big fat guy dropped the skip off. What's with it? As soon as the weather gets nice, all the fat men are in shorts. And their T-shirts get taken off, and you see the marks where the skin doesn't tan. I like to call them the stripes, it's where the sun doesn't shine underneath their flab falls. Anyway, there was a younger skinny whippet lad perched on the top of the truck that he dropped the skip off with. I kid you not, I mean, this fat guy was big built but only collected the money, and the little lad that was with him had welders boots on and was flipping the skip from side to side with his arms and feet to wherever he wanted it placing.

'Where do you want it?' If that fat guy said, 'Oh, you put it there.' FLIP! FLIP! FLIP! Then they left? And I thought to myself, 'That skip isn't right in front of the garden gate where I'd be best to place my rubbish into it.' So, I thought, 'Well, if that rake thin lad can do it, it won't be a problem for me.' I mean that lad must have been 17 years old, and he was physically jostling the skip along the road. And I thought, 'If he can do it, there's nothing stopping me.' I grabbed the back of it and pushed. Then I thought, 'Maybe it wasn't because he was pushing from the back, I'll try the front.' I put my fingers, like clawed under it and that's not good, 'It's still not budging.' It was about then, that I decided it was probably all right where it was.

I was kind of hoping that the neighbours weren't looking out the window, 'It looks like he's having trouble.' I was a little upset. If it had been the big guy that had moved it, I would have thought, 'Well, you know, I'm not fat.' But the fact was, he was scrawny. He needed feeding up with pie. But he clearly had lots of hidden muscle. I ask this hypothetically, would that have impressed you? Jamie, if you were a 17-year-old girl, would you go for a bit of rough or would you be looking to mate with the more intelligent nerd types? You've only got two choices.

Jamie:	From your description of this lanky lad, it sounds like he could push my skip anytime. No, I'll go for the pen pusher.

Christian:	Not into the masculine type? I suppose that would explain the lack of physical chemistry on our show. So, what did this lad do to make you reject him?

Jamie:	Dating anyone with a penis is usually reason enough.

Christian:	No, that's not the question. That was never the question. It was hypothetical. It was more pathetical I admit, but what was your answer though? You're going for the lad who might achieve something in the sphere of labour as regards solicitor, lawyer, doctor, rather than someone who nick's brass plaques and melts them down for cash.

Jamie:

Well, there we go. you've answered your own question.

Christian:

Some girls do. What is it about women? This is so sexist, but what is it about women? They do, they're attracted to thugs. Also, this is a question for the listener tonight. Men with long hair. Does it make them look like an ugly girl? Or does it make them look quite attractive? To give you an example think of Jamie with long hair. Ugly girl is winning so far.

The security guard spotted Jamie's doppelganger this week. I saw a doppelganger of another friend in New Zealand and he was Chinese. He was his oriental twin; I couldn't believe it. My goodness, it spooks me even today. 10 years ago today, I was celebrating my 24th birthday, on this exact day, and I was exploring Auckland City, mooching around in New Zealand. And it was there I seen this Chinese guy and I thought 'Wow, that looks like my friend Foxey. But it's not because he's not Chinese.'

Imagine if I spoke to him. Would you do that? I mean, loads of people do these days. You know, your phone acts as a video and camera. Would you say, 'Don't take this the wrong way. But I've got to have my arm around you, and I want to take a photo because you're weird looking.' Or would you say that you look like a friend rather than a freak? 'Look, look, look what's growing on his head. Quick! Get a picture.' But you've got to be in it. You can't just have a picture of a man who's got something that's growing on his head that looks like a hat. 'It's a hat.' 'Awww! Swizz!'

The reason why today is special, is because 10 years ago today was my birthday. I'm 10 years older and it's my birthday. I would be nowhere else. Well, except with my family.

You know I've got my five children, well I decided to have this conversation with my wife after having the third child and said, 'It's too much for you to cope with all these kids, I've decided to call it a day with hospital radio. You need me here more than the volunteer sector of the NHS needs me. So, I'm gonna be here.' And she looked like death warmed up. 'Oh, my God.' As if I was sentencing her and reading out the verdict. 'What have I done?' She said, 'You keep doing it. Gives me a break.' So, as far as I'm concerned, being here on my birthday is simply a fluke of the calendar this year.

Anyways, talking about my skip. The children next door were sitting in it. Do you think that's the parents to blame? Or you think it's for the kids to have a bit more sense? When you're say 10 or 11, are you old enough to know not to sit in a skip with your legs dangling towards the traffic as it passes? I think you should. Maybe we were just more grown up back then. Maybe I should have went out there and took a stick to them. Although nowadays you get into trouble if you chastise someone else's kid. It's frowned upon in these politically correct days.

You know we were talking briefly about Zimbabwe money. I want to know, ATM machines, you know, the hole in the wall in Zimbabwe banks. You make a withdrawal, and enough paper money spews out to crush you to death with just enough cash to buy a sandwich. Place your wheelbarrow next to the ATM and let it all pile up like a photocopier and as it falls out it literally devalues in those few moments as it's getting fed out.

May we be the first official Western show to congratulate Mugabe on his win. There's no one else congratulating the man. I mean, he was the only candidate running for election. Yeah, but he won. He won the title of 'Dictator' yet again.

Jamie: I'll congratulate the way he went to Egypt's African Union summit even though he wasn't invited but turned up anyway. Eventually everyone dies out, and he's 84, so we might not have long to wait. It's evil ideas that can live on a long time afterwards, just like Hitlers moustache.

Christian: Yeah, sometimes your mouth isn't designed for your cup. Mugabe's isn't. I imagine his tea goes all over his toothbrush tash.

I had a spot on my nose. It was a big white lump this morning and it was painful. But I was speaking to people at work without knowing it was there. And then later on I noticed it and went to the mirror in the toilets to check. People had been speaking to me wanting to puke from the sight of it. I mean, it was like a snow man's head hanging on my nose. I looked like a pigeon. It's not pleasant. It would have knocked Mugabe ill.

I've got some stuff here that I never knew about and I'll share with you, because we're drinking our cups of tea. Let me tell you about coffee enemas. Do you know about them? It's the procedure of inserting coffee into the anus to cleanse the rectum and small intestines. Now this procedure, although well documented, I've never heard of it. It's still considered by most medical authorities to be possibly dangerous. I assume you could burn yourself. Depends on how hot the coffee is.

A Murphy drip may be used to administer this medical procedure. While the idea of anal cleansing dates back to the Egyptians the notion of caffeine as an enema was conceived as early as 1917. Research suggests it helps detoxify cancer cells when the body is under attack. It specifically detoxifies free radicals. In mice, for example, there were drops recorded of 600% in the liver, and 700% in the bowel. What did they do? Stick a coffee bean up their butt? Squeak! Squeak!

There's a section of the large intestine that links directly to the liver called the sigmoid colon. That's at the very end of the colon and there is a special circulatory system between this portion of the colon and the liver. So instead of it being ingested and going through the stomach and the gut the liver can absorb it straight away and gets detoxified. Amazing stuff. That's the thing though, if you think about it, some filthy doctor years ago, decided to see what's up there. 'Hey, maybe there's more to this than meets the brown eye.'

The enema makes the caffeine enter the blood more quickly. So, if you wake up in the morning late for work and you're bleary eyed and still tired from a sleepless night, you can go to the local McDonalds drive through and ask for a McEnema. Wind your car window down and stick your bottom out to greet the kiosk worker waiting with a long straw. 'Quick, I've got to be at work in five.' One supersize squeeze later, 'Champion! I'm awake now. Top coffee colonic.' Blow the froth off Jamie, you'll end up with a Mugabe tash.

Jamie: It's the idea of whacking a Starbucks up my back
                passage. You could film two girls with one cup of
                Espresso.

Christian: *Insert the lubricating nozzle no more than four
                inches and release it at room temperature. Breathe
                deeply to draw fluid in as far into the large bowel
                as possible. Set the kitchen timer for 10 minutes.*
                You can hold it for 10 minutes? You should have
                seen Jamie run to the loo when we got here. *The
                caffeine triggers natural peristalsis which urges
                emptying, you'll be battling a natural inclination to
                empty out.* That explains why coffee works as a
                laxative on me.

                *On your first few attempts it'll rid the colon from
                commercial white bread and other baked grains
                and starches, donuts or cakes.* I had loads today
                because it was my birthday. My colon must be
                cover in black sticky patches of processed fibre.
                Now there's a beautiful image for the listeners. I
                took in all those sweet treats to celebrate my big
                day, but next year I'll be taking in coffee enemas
                all round. We can give each other them in the
                office. I do like the smell of coffee. I'm sure that'll
                be the over whelming smell to this very clean and
                hygienic activity.

Jamie: Yeah, like a Brazilian public toilet. Spotless.

Christian: You interrupted my gag that I was going to do
                which is just as well because you told me it was
                deeply offensive, which is great. And in a way. I
                love the idea, so I'll try again in a different way.
                The last bit of news Jamie gave us was, 'Concerns
                over the health of movie legend Paul Newman,'
                who's looking shockingly frail and in ill health.
                The tabloid story suggests he's battling lung
                cancer. Well, first of all, you mentioned Madonna

and Guy Richie, obviously having marriage difficulties. And I said, 'Perhaps Madonna and Guy Ritchie could learn a thing or two from Paul Newman.' And you say, 'Oh, because he's been happily married for a long time?' And I reply, 'No, I mean they could both get ill health.' Ba dum-chh! But I decided not to.

I've got some headlines that have come from the Times Online, probably change next week to The Daily Mail. Make sense if that's my new homepage. But anyway, evangelicals. Now I don't understand as a church goer what's happening with the Evangelical Church. It says *800 clergy and lay people have taken the first steps to setting up a stronghold against the ordination of gay people.*

So, 800 clergy are pretending that men off the cloth over many centuries have never been gay. You mean to tell me all those men who live alone and have never been interested in women have suddenly infiltrated the church? It's not news, it's been happening for years. I love the idea that these people think a big manly minister is needed in the pulpit, not an effeminate weak dainty chap. Does it really matter? I understand firefighters need to be strong and able to carry entire families down blazing stairs to safety, but the work of God doesn't require breathing apparatus and cool red engines. Ministers, vicars, priests - gay or otherwise - have been carrying the entire church and the good news of Christ's saving love from generation to generation. Leave them be.

Church of England clergy threatens mass exit over woman bishops. Oh yeah, because obviously again, it's only men who can read the Bible and spread the good news. *1300 clergy, including 11 serving bishops say they will defect if two key votes are passed at the General Synod.* What's amazing is these clergy are hypocrites. They're suffering the same persecution over their sexuality as the lady ministers are over their sex, but they're keeping up appearances. Out them. Say to the bishops, 'You're gonna love the single women priests. They're hot.' And make a note of all the ones who mince out in protest, 'Oh, no, we're out of here. People with breasts can't save souls. It's wrong, it's morally wrong. Simper!' It's nothing more than job protection. Hey, nothing wrong with that, but don't try and hide behind your penis. It's not big enough. Let's be honest, all men would if they could.

Have you seen this idea that John Prescott is gonna be a waiter? Sticking with his actual skills. People are going to bid on him, and he'll serve them drinks all night. Why don't they raise party donations like they normally do? Millions of pounds from some faceless businessmen. And then give them a title or make them a lord. It's worked for Labour so far.

I got Hungry Hippos for my birthday. The kids had said on Sunday, 'Dad can we play the hippo game?' I said, 'I don't know anything about a hippo game.' He said, 'Yeah, the one Mam bought in the shop the other day. That hippo game.' So that was one present I had to look surprised opening. Give it the old 'Oh, I wonder what's in this box. Whatever could it be?' Do you know, you get stickers and have to stick on the hippo's eyes? You have to assemble it yourself. I also got a bike pump as well and a spare inner tube.

Jamie: You never want to use it, just like a gun. You only have it for backup.

Christian: You make me laugh, but for all the wrong reasons.

Christian: You'll never guess how long it's been since I last done a show on a Sunday. In fact, my first show was on a Sunday and it was just called the Sunday show.

Simon: And why did they call it Sunday?

Christian: Because it's named after the goddess of Sun.

Simon: It is.

Christian: I was driving in and sometimes you look down your nose how the other half lives. So, not the scenic route. Why is it, everyone seems happy on a sunny day? So, what's the problem in the Middle East? It's Always sunny over there, why can't they just chill out?

Jamie: They'd fire bullets in the air just to celebrate it's hot.

Christian: You know, firing bullets in the air is a dangerous practice.

Jamie: Because they come down.

Christian: You wouldn't think that would happen? Well, you would think they'd come down, but not with such extreme force that it could still kill you.

Simon: You know, just talking about that, I watched an American TV show. It was a detective thing, one of those CSI Miami shows, and one woman was found dead in her front garden. Anyway, without going through all the investigation, it transpired that this guy had this pistol and he just fired it into the air. The bullets' velocity carried it so far, about four streets away and hit her in the chest. I mean there's got to be some bearing of truth to it.

Christian: Happens on New Year's Eve, a lot of reported cases, because people go out celebrating and shooting up into the air like Yosemite Sam.

Jamie: These guns fire at 1000 mile an hour plus when they leave the barrel right?

Christian: So, you've got this huge projectile factor when calculating the accuracy, it can't be easy for him to strike that woman. That's like a good game of scorched earth. Or dislodging a coconut from its shy on a windy day.

They're in trouble CSI for telling would-be-murderers 'what not to do.' How not to get caught? Bleach the crime scene, that sort of thing. There was something I was discussing this weekend. I thought surely the only person who is interested in this kind of programme is someone who wants to know how to make a bomb.

Simon: No, I'd watch it as an alternative to Coronation Street.

Christian: Can I tell you something? I entered a contract with Sky last year, because I got a Freeview box which picks up all the free channels. Instead of paying the 150 pounds for one in a shop, Sky said, 'Come with us for a year, 10 pound a month. And we'll give you two packages as well.' Which is great. So, I save 30 pounds. You've got to phone them up after a year to cancel it. However, when I called them on the exact date I'd set it up, they said, 'No, you've paid it now until next month. You should have phoned after 11 months as we need that time to cancel the agreement.'

I've not made that saving now. I asked about the original call when they told me 'a year,' but they've said, 'Oh, we don't keep telephone calls on record that long. It would have been deleted.' So, by the time the conversation is actually of any use and able to win my argument, they dispose of it. It's gone. I know the script they used did not include 11 months, so how many others were screwed over by them? These agents work on commission.

It's probably not just Sky, most places you're always tied in with them for a year and they always want notice, or they just renew the subscription via your direct debit. It's criminal, but they call it customer service.

Jamie: Rupert Murdoch will be rubbing his hands with glee. Simon you be Rupert, Christian give him your snotty complaint.

Simon: Strewth mate. I was just having a tinny the Sheila bought me from the supermarket, because they were on offer and I like a bit of an offer. I really do.

Christian: No wonder he doesn't record his telephone conversations.

Simon: The other day I got clamped at The Durham Tees Valley Airport. Just very briefly. I work for a chauffeur company. I went into the loo and came out and it was there. It wasn't in a disabled parking bay. And the clamper said, 'I'm sorry.' Sorry? They're on the prowl 24 hours a day. Be careful.

Christian: Jamie, you go first. How much did the penalty
                    cost? Higher or lower?

Jamie: 100 pounds.

Simon: Yeah.

Christian: I was gonna go 30.

Simon: 100 pounds plus VAT. £117.50.

Christian: That is an appalling amount for spending a penny.

                    What's been going on in the news this week? We
                    obviously try and keep our finger on the pulse. I've
                    got something here about the 2012 London
                    Olympics logo. *Apparently the 24 second advert
                    was causing issues for epileptics and received
                    complaints that they couldn't watch it to the end. It
                    cost a lot of money to do the graphic design and
                    artwork for this, 12 months.*

                    Here's my amazing fact, the *Terrence Higgins
                    Trust has said that the competition at the 2002
                    Winter Olympics in Salt Lake City, Utah, those
                    competing got through a quarter of a million
                    condoms in just 10 days.* Now it doesn't seem to
                    me that it's all about the sport, does it? I didn't
                    realise that kind of shenanigan went on.

Jamie: You're very naive Mr. Frank.

Christian: Another thing that caught my attention in the news
                    this week - it says, '*the Pope's Popemobile was
                    attacked.*' Why does it state it's the Pope's
                    Popemobile? Does someone else have a
                    Popemobile that we don't know about?

Jamie: Yeah, I saw this on TV. How in the right mind would anyone go and jump in the way like he did and expect to get away with it?

Christian: Still, he got longer with the Pope than the McCann's did. He kind of just walked past them. I think they gave him a picture of Madeleine. Perhaps he's going to circulate it around the Catholic Church to see if anyone's seen any bairns. Jamie got it. Simon's just smoking in the corner and you're not allowed as of July the first.

I'd love to buy a Popemobile, but what is it? Because it's not one of those golfing carts that candy you around the course. There's plenty of standing room on this thing. Is it one of those things that clears the slushed ice off an ice rink or something? I assume it's specifically been designed for him. A pickup truck with a disabled shower cubicle attached. Do you think there are over riding controls for driving it under his holy feet? He can make it go faster. Controls it like a skateboard.

If you were going to touch him, you would plan around his heightened security. Let's say I wanted him to bless me personally, I'm going to do it as a gang. For instance, a gang of three. First, we get Simon to jump out in front of the holy vehicle and the security are piling onto him with Vatican knuckle dusters. Jamie jumps second. And obviously the stragglers on the security team will grab Jamie by the throat and stamp on his soft head. And before they realise what's going on, I'm on top of the infallible pontiff. Don't worry though, I'll ask His Holiness to bless all of your injuries and forgive us so we can escape going to jail.

Anyone watch 'Embarrassing Illnesses'? It's on Channel Four. Well, they claim to have these people on the show who've got something wrong with say their unmentionables or their breasty-dumplings, and they're so embarrassed by it that they won't go see a doctor, but they'll happily appear on national TV. That's the irony.

Not one of them is wanting to go to a clinic and have their health concerns checked out, but the guy's got the camera filming a fame hungry idiot saying, 'I don't think my boobs are symmetrical.' They've got no shame. Yet each one in the interview says, 'I'm so embarrassed. Here have a close up of my dickey di-do.'

Simon: I once watched a programme with all these presenters of very big talk shows with real candid intensity, and they could not believe how some of their guests come on to television and they bare their souls and private lives. And are willing to talk about everything. Okay it makes the show, but the presenter is constantly left thinking, 'Have they comprehended the enormity of their honesty?' They can't work out the mentality of people.

Jamie: They have the security blanket of knowing that their parents are going to be watching.

Christian: They have an urge to confess in front of the cameras. This show is on at half past eight on an evening. Clearly for channel four, seeing a person's bits is not a problem for teatime viewing. Now, my problem is this, and I've spoken to my wife at length, and we both agree, a women's top part is not offensive in the slightest. It's almost like seeing litter of a page three newspaper blowing down the street.

Simon: Correct.

Christian: It's not socially acceptable, but we take it for what
                it is. It's when you see other body parts, you can't
                help but think, even if Channel Four has got its
                heart in the right place. That it's saying, 'Look,
                we've got to discuss this because there's young
                people out there that need to be aware, and they
                need to go and get help.' I understand that. There's
                still something very taboo and wrong about
                showing me, even if it's a mosaic, I'm not wanting
                to look at that. I've got food to eat.

Simon: Yeah, sausage and chips.

Christian: Joanne said, 'They're never going to show me
                that.' We say 'pudenda.' We're very Victorian in
                our house. I'm actually not a prude, I just believe
                some things are not acceptable to polite society
                before a certain time. I can hear the cries of
                hypocrisy now, 'and discussing it on hospital radio
                probably isn't appropriate either.' But I like to
                think we've gotten away with it, because I employ
                euphemism so the younger listeners wouldn't even
                get what we're talking about. Jamie still thinks
                we're discussing 'bashing the bishop.'

Jamie: Jumping on the Pope, wasn't it?

Christian: *The last Canadian to have fought in World War
                one is left. From the 600,000 that fought in the
                Great War only one of Canada's serving remains,
                and when he dies, he'll be given a state funeral to
                represent all the others.* So, he's like the white
                rhino now, an endangered species. Perhaps when
                the last rhino passes, they could give it a state
                funeral. Raise it up on an ivory plinth.

What's wrong with animal rights activists?
Everyone knows they've got this passion but why
do they direct it in the wrong way? What's that
about?

Jamie: Misguided.

Christian: Is that what it is? I thought it was people who can't
hold down a paid job. When I was younger, I
wished I too felt the same way about our planet,
like those who chained themselves to trees, you
know tribal hippies. But now I have no time for
them. Did I betray myself?

People complaining about seal hunts, maybe need
buying off with a free pair of furry slippers made
from seal pups. 'Hey everyone, look at my
slippers. I don't know why I've been campaigning
for so long. They're lovely.' Or a big thick warm
coat made from mink. 'This is brilliant. I'm out of
here.' Then they start telling all the other unwashed
the good news, 'By the way, you've got it all
wrong. Beatnicks, put down your placards and feel
my fluffy coat.' 'Hey, he's right it's lush. You
know that's really all we've ever been after. A new
furry jacket.' 'We've seen the error of our ways.'

They're the same mentality as the disgusting
bodies interviewees. Just like we said, point a film
camera in front of them. They just want to be
heard. 15 minutes of fame. It's nothing to do with
animal cruelty, they just want someone to listen to
them and then send them on their way with
something tangible and worth money for all their
troubles. A new pair of walrus leather boots would
do nicely for that kind of recognition. It's a good
job someone like me finally listened to their
concerns. Now they can all go home and have a
much-needed bath.

If it was a later show I could have told you about
my friends' vasectomy.

Jamie: You can off air.

Christian: What's the point in that? I'm one of those people, if
the cameras rolling and the microphones are on,
I'm chatting. I can tell you though that it put his
wife off spaghetti Bolognese for a while. She
looked. You shouldn't do that. She was there to
give him support. Like when you hold your wife's
hand as she has a baby. Stick to the top half, talk to
them, don't get a bit curious. 'Oh, Hello! What's
going on down here?'

She can still eat spaghetti Bolognese as long as it's
covered in lots of cheese. I can as well, it's lovely.
Isn't it? A bit of ketchup. Nice.

Henry Allingham is the oldest living Britain aged
111 years old. The armed services took him out for
a bit of a bash. He's one of the oldest surviving
world war one veterans. I seen it in the papers. And
they always ask these supercentenarians for secrets
to their long lives. 'Well, I've smoked 20 a day, I
have whiskey intravenously pumped through my
veins every hour, oh, and lots of unprotected sexual
intercourse.' They've probably lived essentially on
eating lettuce every day. People are annoyed
thinking, 'Oh, what a great life he's had,' when it's
just not true. He's counting his calories every meal.

Simon what's the secret to it? What's the secret to
reaching an old age? It's so far away from me and
Jamie. What age are you ambitious to achieve? I
think anyone who says they've not thought about
it, that's a lie. I think as a child, you know it's
possible you could live to be 100.

Simon: I've not really thought about it. Really.

Christian: Jamie, how long might you stay alive till?

Jamie: Oh, about 111.

Christian: Look, that's the difference between you and Jamie.
                Yeah, you're pessimistic. You told me you applied
                for a new job and you're saying, 'I won't get it.'
                My advice is to say, 'Well, maybe then don't go
                for it.'

Simon: All it was, I just said, 'With some of the
                requirements they're looking for, I may not be
                qualified enough to get it.' That's what I meant.

Christian: So, if you do get it and you're not qualified enough,
                it would go to show it's not much of a job. Clearly
                anyone can do it. That's what you could say, 'I'm
                not qualified for it and I still got hired.'

Jamie: People promoted to their level of incompetence.

Christian: Does that really happen though? The Peter
                principle. Are you aware of people who are not
                qualified in the slightest, no experience in a given
                field, who apply for something completely out of
                their sphere and still get given the role?

Simon: No, I haven't.

Christian: No. It's kind of unheard of, isn't it? So - good luck.
                No wonder Simon lacks confidence. We've got to
                try and build him up, Buttercup.

                We'll play 'Baby I don't Care' by Transvision
                Vamp for Simon.

Simon, by the way, I've got to tell you something that has happened to me. You know, we were all laughing and saying, 'When you're in a nightclub, you can remember when it wasn't a nightclub, and it was all fields.' Well with me, I actually started to burn…

Jamie: Effigy's?

Christian: I was going to say, 'CDs onto my computer,' but there's always a real possibility for me setting fire to any famous figure. Anyway, sometimes I don't know the names of the songs I like. Now I never thought I'd become this person. And instead, now I've got Transvision Vamp on the laptop and I'll listen to it and hear the lyrics, 'Baby please believe me,' I'll label the track 'Please believe me.'

Jamie will correct me and say, 'It's called Baby I don't care.' 'I think if you listen carefully you can hear the name of the song. And it's called 'Please believe me.' And that's what I've named it on the computer. So, when you don't know the actual titles of the song, you just type what you think it is. And before you know it, people look at your music folder on your computer and they know you've got an old man's collection, because none have the correct titles. You barely even know who sings it.

Try this one, Spice Girls and 'When you're alone.'

Jamie: Is it Madonna?

Christian: Emma Bunton and 'Downtown.'

Jamie: Makes perfect sense.

Simon: I have the original by Petula Clark.

Christian: On the PYE record label. See me and you in the nightclub, 'Eeee, this song! I don't know it.'

New Zealand made international news last week when a woman didn't pay her electricity bill. She was ill and on a life support oxygen machine in her own home. The electric company comes around and cuts it off and the teenage children said, 'You can't do that, she needs this to live.' 'Hey, you ignored our nasty final demand letter.' Off it went. Within two hours she was dead. What I want to know is, what stopped the children going to their neighbours and asking nicely, 'Here's an extension cable, can you keep my Mum alive?' You would have thought they'd have phoned for an ambulance or something to come and collect her.

At the funeral there was the Prime Minister Helen Clark and also the chief executives of Mercury Energy. The electricity company was there as well. Would you have invited them? I guess if they've said, 'Sorry!' A tragic and very preventable story there again with little regard for human life, all for the pursuit of greed. Sad times.

Can I tell you I watched Batman? It's called 'Batman Forever' or something. And in it, Alfred the butler, who's actually the uncle of Bat Girl, played by Alicia Silverstone, he's the one who gives her the costume, the sexy costume. So, he makes his niece or great niece this tight bondage attire. 'If you want to be part of Batman's crime fighting gang, then here's your outfit. Go on - try it on. Let me see you in it.' 'But Uncle, it's so figure hugging.' 'Aye!' Imagine if your Auntie bought you clothing and asked you to put it on. 'But they're tiny speedo swimming trunks.' 'Put them on, it's your costume. You'll fight crime in those.'

In physics, when scientists say a light year, do they include the Leap Day? Because if I went to the nearest star in our constellation, other than the sun, Proxima Centauri, and it's 4.2 light-years away, and I was expecting to get off the spaceship and the driver went, 'Ah, you know what? We didn't take into account the Leap Days. You're stuck on board for another month I'm afraid.' That would be really annoying, wouldn't it? You get all excited, take your luggage out from the stowed compartment above your head. Push up your meal tray back into the chair in front, only to be told over the intercom, 'The nerds back on Earth had miscalculated.'

Especially when you consider that some of these distant planets aren't just 4.2 light-years away, they're thousands of light-years away. You imagine all those extra days. It's taken you 50 years to arrive at your new colony outpost and then the pilot says, 'Sorry, you've still got another year.' You could understand if it was traffic or roadworks causing the delay, but for a spotty cretin not carrying over the 0.25 of a day. I'd rather iron out any of those issues before I ever set foot on an inter-galactic space vehicle. It'd take forever before I could lodge a complaint. And I wouldn't be happy waiting even longer to get a response.

There were Viz characters in my neighbor's garden today. On a fine day like today, they turned the air blue. I've got bairns in my garden, and they wouldn't hear that filth in a million years in my house. So why when they're in the garden should they suffer? I mean they wouldn't understand half of it anyway. But even worse I had to put radio 1s top 40 chart show on in order to muffle their drunken conversation. I definitely don't want them listening to that kind of toxic brain rotting music. Its effects are longer term than the swearing.

A 79-year-old German almost died after using a sink plunger as a bath plug and impaled himself after slipping. Nothing funny so far. *He couldn't find the bath plug so used the plunger instead, but as he stood up to soap himself, he slipped and fell heavily onto the plunger, wedging the wooden handle up his bum. He was screaming for his wife to pull him free. They called emergency services and it was an eight-hour operation to repair the internal damage.*

Jamie: What's the chances of that happening?

Christian: If you're using a plunger for a plug, I think the chances of that happening are quite high, don't you? You're standing up on a slippery surface, while messing about with soap. It's going to happen. Sods law isn't it.

Serbia men are swapping their prize cows to get bigger unmentionables. Roughly worth £400 each. The exchange was revealed by the country's top plastic surgeons. A urologist told the news agency that some farmers had unrealistic ideas of what they could get for their money. He said, 'Some of them want to add 10 centimeters. And that's just not possible. At least not for just one cow.' Did you see what the penis doctor done there? Cracked a gag on the expense of these modestly endowed farmers. Something we would never do.

Christian: This is the show that may never have been. Because we weren't sure whether we were gonna make it or not.

Jamie: Well, I was.

Christian: Oh, you were always sure?

Jamie: I'd do a show next week if I was sober enough to drive.

Christian: Christmas Day you'd come in? That's really, really sad.

I went to the dentist again. I got two injections in the gum. It was a bit jagged, and she said, 'Oh yeah, cause your filling has fallen out.' It was only one of those temporary things. And so she injected me then drilled the surrounding bits out, and then realised I had some more teeth that were fractured. So, she couldn't fit this strengthening thing. So, she patched it back up again.

And in the morning. I bit into some toast. It just dropped back out again. I thought, 'I had two injections for that.' You know, when you keep it, you've washed it a bit, rinsed it and then put it on the kitchen windowsill to show it to everybody. And then it dawned on me, 'put that under my pillowcase.' I could get some money here.

Jamie: But that's filling. It's just shrapnel, isn't it? That's fraud. You're ripping off the tooth fairies.

Christian: I should have known not to ask you. I should have
              just tried it. See what I get. I'll try it next year and
              tell you what happens.

Jamie: To Renegade Radio I say, 'Happy Christmas.'

Christian: They've got these attractive ladies posing with
              motorbikes in skimpy outfits. It's part internet
              magazine and radio station. May I add these are
              calendar girls Jamie. I thought what we could do, is
              we could send them a photo of you wearing
              something revealing for maybe December, as it
              gets cold outside. Maybe we can all see just how
              cold. Although we'll take the picture in summer
              with you wearing only a Santa hat. Big it up Jamie.

              Renegade Radio says, *'Hello. Love it. Thank you.
              This is amazing. We have a small coffee shop
              called 'Beans, Bikes and Books', and we play your
              radio show on the morning throughout the shop.
              The customers love listening. And I watched the
              look and grins on their faces. Thank you.'* It
              depends what books they're reading as well of
              course. I've seen Jamie grinning over a sly one.

              Anyway, speaking of grins. After I got my two
              injections my dentist told me off. She was trying to
              take an impression of my lower teeth by holding
              foam resin in my mouth and pressing firmly down
              so she could get a good mould. I've told you I
              suffer post Bell's palsy, and I get some really
              horrible feelings down my neck. So, while she's
              holding my mouth open wide pressing onto my
              teeth, my jaw begins to involuntarily wobble. And
              while it does, she's telling me off to stop it from
              happening, 'Stop this. Stop this.'

              I couldn't help it. So, she had to throw away one of
              the gum shield imprints and start all over again.

'I'm sorry.' She made me look quite bad. I felt bad.
I felt like I wasn't man enough to stop my jaw from
spasming. Then I remembered it was costing me
£214 for her troubles, so it was really in her best
interests to drop the attitude and try and support
my chin a little bit better. Obvious solution. Here's
another one. A guy at work bought a strip of five
white raffle tickets.

Jamie: What were the numbers?

Christian: 256 to 260. When the winner was announced they
                said, 'It's orange 146 to 150.' And I shouted over
                to him, 'Stop looking. They're white. You've only
                bought white. The moment they say the winning
                ticket is orange, you can stop looking. Throw all of
                them in the bin.' Instead, he's going through all of
                his numbered tickets seeing if he has any that
                match. Can you be colourblind and not know the
                difference between white and orange?

Jamie: Yeah, I suppose.

Christian: Just say you don't know. Sometimes it'd be so
                much easier if you just told the truth.

Jamie: I'm being diplomatic.

Christian: I would like you to try that in the new year.
                Honesty. I think that would go a long way with you
                Jamie instead of this complete 'winging it.' Yeah?
                We were discussing at work who's allowed into
                your lockers or drawers. Now, they're not
                technically yours - it's the property of the company
                you work for. You've had your mail opened here
                because it was addressed to the radio station.
                Technically, the management are able to open all
                the mail addressed here. We don't know the
                legalities. But at work, they're allowed to go

through your personal locker. Or at least have you
standing by while they perform a locker search.

Jamie: In my place you have to be there.

Christian: Why don't you just say, 'No' to them? I mean,
                that's a sign of guilt anyway - 'No.'

Jamie: If they have a key, then you don't even need to be
                told until after they've snooped.

Christian: And planted the evidence against you. I'd be happy
                doing that task, wielding a crowbar, 'This seems to
                open everything. What's in people's lockers today?'
                I would find it a complete breach of privacy. I
                could be hiding sexy Christmas gifts for the wife in
                there and the janitor and his skeleton key has
                already unboxed it and used it before my shifts
                even started.

Jamie: You might not know and complain to the shop that
                sent you it. Accusing them of soiling your goods.

Christian: I'd never keep kinky gear in my works locker. I
                need easy access. It's fifteen miles away. Perhaps a
                gun. Mark your territory with fear. I do like the
                idea of leaving a soiled item for any nosey
                manager who comes snooping around.

                There's a guy at work who got told, 'You look like
                Macaulay Culkin.' I think we'd been talking about
                Home Alone because it's Christmas. It was
                because of his ears. And he asked, 'As he is now?
                Like an addict?' But is he? I don't want to say that.
                I mean he could be addicted to love. Yeah, that's
                what he meant.

Jamie: Does love make you lose loads of weight?

Christian: Maybe the wrong kind of love. There were some
             nicknames going round, but they're not nicknames.
             You know where you just put a nasty word in front
             of someone's name, Fat Tony. 'That's not a
             nickname.'

Jamie: It's just adding a fact. Like, ignorant Christian.

Christian: Stupid fat stinking loser Jamie. See, it's a friendly
             nickname, isn't it? Now, that's the kind of love that
             can make you lose weight. The kind of love that
             keeps on bullying you.

             I went to the traditional Panto.

Jamie: Oh, no you didn't.

Christian: Oh, yes, I did. Sleeping Beauty is running until
             January the fifth at the Middlesbrough Theatre.
             Kim Hartman who played Helga in 'Allo 'Allo!
             and there was also Vicki Michelle who played
             Yvette the waitress. Oh, there were references to
             the classic sitcom, like 'I shall tell you this only
             once.' But there was nothing about René, you
             know, looking for rent boys.

Jamie: Had the jokes been about real life. So, what does
             Kim Hartman look like now?

Christian: They're both fit and very good looking. I think
             they could give Carol Vorderman a run for her
             money. At the time, the Gazette gave a good
             review and I thought the critic was sat behind us.
             There was a man in his Mac sat at the very back of
             the theatre. Because Joanne said, 'Who's the
             porv?' I said, 'I think it's a critic.'

Jamie: Did Joanne really say it exactly how you
             described?

Christian: No, I threw in a bit of theatre to help the listeners. I was there. But it turns out that the critic was a woman, so I don't know who he was. There was a lot of tracksuits and tattoos for my liking in the audience. This dragon came out. And I don't mean anyone from the audience. It was a big, huge windsock that had been blown out by a fan, designed to look like a dragon. And it goes out into the audience. I seen it, and thought, 'Wow, that's amazing.'

Even the critic in the review, didn't want to spoil it for anyone. She says, '*It's got one of the best finales that anyone has ever seen. And I don't want to spoil it for anyone, leaving everyone with an open mouth.*' So, I've just told you all, 'go see it because it's great.' Because if you're an adult and you're paying to take the kids, check out the dragon that comes out. And then look around at the kids in the audience. They're in fear of their lives. It's hilarious. I was looking around when the kids are screaming and getting hysterical. It's excellent.

When the fans are blowing, the dragon is going randomly everywhere. This big, huge head of a dragon with lit up eyes is excellent. Well, of course Prince Charming slays it, and it dies, and everyone goes 'Whoo!' and applauds.

Jamie: Who played the prince?

Christian: I don't know. You're getting me to find out. Simon Schofield and the songbird was Lucy Lavelle. None of these are people, but support your local theatre.

Jamie: None of these are people?

Christian: That's unfair. You knew what I meant. They're celebrities as low life as the paparazzi. Famous people need tabloid journalists as much for their career as anything else. They feed of each other, it's a circle of survival thing. Like parasitic hosts. It's funny when a celebrity complains they've had their privacy invaded by a newspaper.

If the papers actually lost interest in one of the celebrities, their media career would nosedive. They create interest and sell rags and gossip magazines. Have their lockers opened with a crowbar then they can complain about their privacy. Imagine what unboxed items they'd have found in René's lockable cupboard?

Anyway, they were on stage. And they were doing this audience participation. You're thinking what they do in Amsterdam. No, this was different. 'And she signed that with a pen, you say? It looks quite good considering she didn't use either hand. With a banana you say?' Anyway, he was getting the audience to sing along. You know, 'Just the left-hand side of the theatre', 'Now just the right-hand side of the theatre.' He done a song I hadn't heard before, which is more a reflection on my age. He said, 'What does the cow say? Moo! What does the dog say? Woof! What does the duck say? Quack! But what does the fox say?' Yeah, you know it.

Is he just swearing? I don't know if he's trying to get away with that. We done a jingle once when I presented a show with my friend James Fox and it was 'Frankie, who the Foxey.' We got told off for that. Prince Charming said he had to go into a dark room and rethink his career. I can't blame him. Probably a Christmas number one contender.

Went to see, not just the pantomime of Sleeping Beauty, but also Cinderella on ice. And the thing about pantomime on ice, is it's not really a panto, it's just a lot of people skating around each other. There were a couple of falls, but apparently, you're not to laugh at them. They're all under 18s and very talented. They make ice skating backwards look so easy. It's one of those things I wish I could do. And they do it to music. So, they bring in some charts songs that I'd never heard of, 'Down with the trumpets.' That goes to show just how down with the wicked I am these days.

Jamie: I know its Rizzle Kicks, 'Down with the trumpets.'

Christian: Oh, 'Mama do the hump'? But they came out doing the most uninspired connections between song and story I've ever seen. Cinderella skates out saying, 'You're so toxic,' before launching into Britney Spears, 'Toxic.' I thought, 'That's not even part of the plot. You simply said the word 'toxic' and then went into a dance. Prince John says, 'Do you think I'm sexy?' And then proceeded to dance to 'Do you think I'm sexy?'

There were no men at all skating, very underrepresented. There were maybe about four little boys that were doing skating, but the rest of them were all women, but all the male roles were played by women, but that's panto anyway, isn't it? There's a lot of clapping going on. My hands were tingling at the end of it all. Last year you may recall I had someone's boots pressing into the back of my seat. Well, this year I was spared the cultural treat of locals lacking consideration.

Joanne identified the woman that had done it, and she was sat at an end seat this year, and just from looking at her, I knew why my back had been crushed. Her bum was huge. If you go to ice skating rinks, the spectator's chairs are arranged so close together they create deep vein thrombosis. They're not designed to accommodate such a massive backside. It explained why her legs were pushed onto my back. She needed more than leg room. I felt slightly guilty that I'd had a go at her from last year. But equally, I thought, 'You've had 365 days to have lost some of that size.'

She was so big her legs were literally forced up against me that she probably couldn't help it. Her legs just popped out from underneath that morbidly obese frame and landed on me. So really what she should have said was, 'Sorry, but I've got a massive ass haven't I?' And I'd have went. 'Alreet pet.'

In front of us, I don't want to sound like a snob, but I'm going to, there was some kind of council estate youth club on their annual trip out. I could smell poor. Do you know the chilly ice blast that comes from the ice rink below? It was wafting up and I could whiff them. And they were really common. There was an element of tracksuits and trainers I'll be honest. When the kids were being a bit interactive with the panto, and shouting, 'Oh, no you didn't', one lass kept turning round unsure what all the people were doing behind her and quacking like a chav at her annoyance. It's a panto, deal with it. Then one of her boyfriend's threw something at her and she turned around looking at me as if I had thrown it at her scrunchie covered head. Jeremy Kyle on ice.

I didn't want to mention this because the Clarences have been flooded. And there's a lot of people collecting money towards the damage the water has caused. I know that our local churches have been chipping in too. I haven't. And I'll tell you why I haven't. I'm allowed not to. There's plenty of good people who live there and need help. But my car got stolen by someone who lived down there. I know it's wrong but that's how I feel.

I don't want to give away any names, but a relative said to me, 'A lot of the people blame the Council for the tidal surge that flooded the houses.' He also said, 'They didn't have home insurance and contents insurance because these houses are owned by housing associations.' So, they're the ones that have to repair and fix it. Some residents didn't lift a finger to help salvage their own property by moving it upstairs. They literally watched workers from the housing association moving all these items for them. That's what entitlement looks like.

Also, he was speaking to someone evacuated to the Billingham Forum, I think they were in front of me at the ice rink, and while they were there, three of their homes got burgled. Real community spirit there. And one of them said, 'I've got to go back home for my medicine.' And he was asked, 'What medicine do you need? Because we've got a doctor on site. We'll write out your prescriptions for you now.' 'Awww! Mega! Mint! Methadone.' So, they went back to get their meds from their dealer.

Now I don't want to paint a picture of everyone like that, because it's simply not true. There are some really unfortunate people who are stuck in a situation. And their situation gets made worse sometimes by minorities. It's terrible, isn't it? And so, I said, 'Should I even tell that story?' It's factual. So, I've told it. I think donating money to any charitable cause should be an informed choice and never coerced with emotional guilt.

Jamie: You're creating a public service.

Christian: Hey, Jamie, what kind of festive tattoo could you
                get that would last all year through?

Jamie: I would have Father Christmas, our good friend
                Santa with Rudolph with his broken nose on a
                beach vegged out sunbathing, but still in his suit,
                and not tackle out as it were. Fully clothed as if
                he's dressed to go Christmas shopping, probably
                for some beach towels.

Christian: They're almost gang colours. Are we going to have
                to get the same tat just to fit in? I guess it's sexy.
                But it says, 'Morgan.' The Morgan gang.

                Do you have Yorkshire puddings on your
                Christmas meal? I had parsnips for the first time in
                a while. Our works Christmas meal apparently cost
                us £6.60 a head. We didn't pay for it, the company
                I work for did. After I ate it, I thought, 'That was
                more like 60p per head.' We were promised a
                bonus. And so when the boss phoned me up and
                said, 'What type of sauce did you have on your
                bonus?' Good job he can joke about it. I guess he
                can afford to laugh at it. I can't. You know the
                small gravy boat the restaurant serves you with the
                brandy sauce in? It's never enough to cover the
                small bit of pudding you get for your dessert. You
                end up eating the last bit dry. There wasn't enough
                sauce.

                You know when you go to get a quarter of sweets,
                and you get served by the shopkeeper who's really
                stingy. And they're looking at the arrow on the
                weighing scales with precision and they're not
                going to give you a fraction of a gram more than
                you paid for. Well, it was a bit like that with the
                turkey. It was wafer thin slices of turkey and bits

were breaking off it and the guy carving wasn't doing anything about it. He kept taking the off-cuts and scraping them to one side. Probably gather up enough and have himself a feast. I felt like throwing the plate at him saying, 'Look, if you don't want to give me anything, don't give me anything. At least don't pretend that you're giving me something substantial to eat here, when you're not.' I was thinking all this while wearing my paper crown, which is Roman in tradition. And I got a novelty little plastic yellow lobster in my cracker, which is rubbish in tradition.

Jamie: What was the joke?

Christian: What's green and unhappy? Apple grumble.

By the way, in the middle of the panto, Cinderella on ice, they done the raffle. Not a meat draw, because I'd probably have put my money in for that. You can't go wrong with winning a meat tray for Christmas. Meat trays are normally raffled in pubs and social clubs. The organizer knows there's nothing better to get a drunk customer returning home off the hook from their annoyed spouse, then having a tray of meat under your arm. It completely disarms them. 'What time do you call this then?' 'Hic, wait till you see the meat I'm packing.' They'll be so happy they'll go to the fridge and get you a beer as a thank-you. All the holiday food is sorted just by you going out to get drunk. It really is a Christmas miracle.

My wife's doing a college course at your place, and she doesn't seem to be there ever. They're always off, and I pay good money. My children go dancing once a week as well. And their clubs have all broke up. They've missed loads of weeks and

yet they're still asking for the same amount of
money for each term. I want my money back.

Jamie: Your better half is doing a course which is still
ongoing. The college is still open. But her course is
off for this week. The whole of that particular
course has got an extra week off.

Christian: Well yeah, that's my beef. I'm being swizzed.

Jamie: What Joanne doesn't realise, is that all this missed
work has been bolted on at the end of the year.
She's not gotten away with anything. It'll be a
crippling amount with tight deadlines, don't you
worry.

Christian: Oh, good. I demand value for my money. What is
it you're wanting for Christmas?

Jamie: I've asked for money to pay for the wedding.

Christian: That's rude. I think asking for money is just rude at
your age. A bit wrong.

Jamie: They're happy with that. So, I don't know. But
that's not what we're getting. Apparently, there's
stuff wrapped up under the tree. So, I haven't a clue

Christian: It'll be a selection box. Hopefully an assortment of
coal lumps. I also think it's a bit rude to have a
wedding list for things that you've already got. 'But
it's rubbish, I want better stuff. I want Egyptian
cotton.' No, you can have the towel you took from
the hotel. People who have lived together, co-
habiting couples, over the years have pretty much
everything they need. Surely that used to be a
tradition when they left their parents' home and
began married life together in a new house.

Women used to spend all their money before they got married on having a linen draw. You don't know about this, but women years ago, before they got married, used to spend all their savings on things like new sheets. They used to keep them in a bottom drawer in their bedroom. I got that information from museums and such like. York castle museum was actually where I read about it.

I talked about seeing Chris Rea a few Christmases ago in a restaurant in Whitby. Well, I was in that same restaurant the other weekend. This owner had donated several hundred pounds to charity. And because he'd gave so much, they'd wrote him thank-you replies for the generous donations. And he'd put them up on his window. Now I thought, 'First of all it's not truly selfless', but I still thought, 'good on him.' They were all amazingly worthy causes. And if I was gonna think about which restaurant I was gonna visit, I know that if I should dine at his, some of my money, some of that profit is going to go to some very good causes. I think more little businesses should do that. Put the letters you get back from charities up for all to see. Put them in your window. I'm telling you it'll attract people to come in. What would you be able to put on your business window Jamie? When you gave blood?

Jamie: I can't give blood because of my medication for epilepsy. They could extract the medication out, but it would cost more money to do that. They could filter my blood, but the process is costly.

Christian: What happens if I was the same blood type as you, I needed a blood transfusion and I also needed brain medicine? Couldn't I just have your blood straight away?

Jamie: You wouldn't have any fits for a while.

Christian: I need to ask you a personal question. Can you wrap presents with your hand, as it is? Are you physically able or do you get out of it? I would love that excuse.

Jamie: Well, it's not really an excuse. I tried it once and it just went belly up. So, no, I can't physically wrap presents.

Christian: But I try wrapping and I can't physically do it either, with or without disability excuses.

Jamie: It's a man thing apparently. I can't, but my Dad does it very easy. So, he lets the side down.

Christian: I thought you were gonna insinuate something there. I thought, 'Jamie, he's your Dad.'

Jamie: I don't care. Probably kept a linen drawer as well.

Christian: What's that about?

Jamie: Yeah. Packed with meat. Loads of winning meat trays, all beautifully wrapped.

Christian: That would turn any fair maiden's head. I haven't even started my cup of tea, and we've got some mince pies. They're 'No Frills' mince pies. Everyday value, 'contains real mince.' I'll play some Christmas music, and we're back with something after this.

                I had a chocolate, what was it? Came out of a 'Roses' tin? It was a strawberry one, but it was actually just solid chocolate. And I thought I should have sent that back because normally they get sold in a factory outlet store as 'Mis-shapes.'

You know, the ones that came out a bit wonky, a bit dodgy and you buy them cheaper. So, I should have sent that one back. It would have been half bitten though. But maybe they'd have sent me back a full bag of 'Mis-shapes.' In fact, I would have said, 'Look I'm suing unless you give me a one-pound bag of 'Mis-shapes.' I'll take this to court unless we can reach some chocolatey agreement.'

We're outside the supermarket in Guisborough and there's a memory tree there. Obviously, it's got people's prayers and thoughts for loved ones, like Nanna and Granddad or Mam and Dad no longer able to celebrate the season with handwritten messages, 'Hope you're in Heaven,' and things like that. And it's been placed right next to the public toilets. Yeah, same toilets that sell the 'Stay Hard' tablets in the vending machine. And I just thought, 'How inappropriate is that memory tree located.' With all these outpouring of emotions onto these baubles, and it's stashed there, probably doubling as a cheap pine freshener, it just seems wrong.

And it came to me that even if you're not religious, surely that tree, even if it was in a church would be moved somewhere better than outside the toilet as a mark of respect. Jamie wants to know where these 'Stay Hard' tablets are - it's Guisborough Sainsbury's. All right, okay, now we can move on. Christmas is coming early at the Morgan's.

Jamie: Not anymore. Three one-pound coins you say.

Christian: There's a guy at work who had to judge, a decorated pod. It's in a call centre. So, picture the open plan floor space with these circular pod desks with different departments working at each one. He said he couldn't think of a worse task to be roped into, and he's totally indecisive with everything like, 'Well, I mean, that pod could win, depends on the other pods really. Maybe that pod could win, I mean, I don't mind. Some of the costumes I've seen are okay I suppose but you know, the ones that they had on that pod over there were just as good, maybe a bit better, I don't know.' He's one of the most anal-retentive boring people you could ever meet. So, you can imagine that simple task becomes a full day's work. I said to him, 'In my head, I would have already known who was going to win before I even seen them.' Now, that sounds a little bit wrong. But it's fair, isn't it? I've not seen them, so what's it matter? I've just decided right then and there.

Sometimes I have the kids arguing over which game they're going to play on the PlayStation. So, I'll say pick a corner in the room and go stand in it. And I'll be in the other room and go, 'The corner with the window near the computer.' And it'll be Emmaus, and I'll say, 'Right, go play his game.' Yeah, I don't care. Don't get me involved in it. And I think people have invested so much time and effort into these competitions. You know, doing up their pod and making it look pretty and presentable. And I come in and go, 'Well, I've decided that it's going to be the pod over there. The corner with the shredder.' I decided before I even opened the door to see them.

So, I told him to just choose the winning pod before going out onto the shop floor, and he didn't get it. He thought, 'Well surely I've got to award the one who's made the most effort.' 'Pah!' Surely the person who has done the most effort doesn't deserve to win, because they're taking it too seriously. Give it to the person that's having a laugh, that's just left it as it is. A bit like this studio here. It couldn't be any less festive. Is there even the slightest bit of tinsel hanging up? Why is this chair full of glitter?

Jamie:

The previous presenter was wrapping presents during the show.

Christian:

My other question of the night was, and I couldn't get the Daily Mail on, but their readers want to bring back capital punishment for the lead singer of the Lost Prophets. He was sentenced to 35 years. Good, but he won't serve that. I'm all up for hanging him because some of these crimes that sick individuals do, frankly, I can't imagine even the most liberal person going out there to say, 'Oh, don't put that piece of filth out of its misery.' So, if the law changed, and it was a capital offence for doing what he did, then that would be it. Now what I wanted to know, because some people aren't happy enough with executions, they want public executions. So, this is my question to you. You get two tickets, technically one is spare, are you gonna take me? Because you know for a fact I'm just itching to go. We're off to London to see the gibbet.

Is it going to be just one execution or is going to be like a full 24 of them or whatever like they used to do in the old days at Tyburn? We might get grabbed though, because it's a small slippery slope isn't it, to bringing back capital punishment. All of a sudden you go back far enough, and they'll make homosexuality a capital offence, and then we'll get lynched as we're together. It's not like they needed evidence. Just someone's word against yours. I'll be sat with you, a blanket over my legs, and you with your flask of Horlicks waiting to be entertained by the hangman, and we'll be the ones getting lynched. 'Oh, Jamie it's a sting operation.' We'll be getting flogged even before our trial. I don't like that. People will judge us. And they'll find those tablets that you've just bought from Sainsbury's.

Jamie: I'll quickly hide them into my Horlicks.

Christian: You've still not answered my question.

Jamie: Yes, I suppose if it's something you really want to go and see. And if I had two tickets, like the golden ticket in Charlie and the Chocolate Factory, yeah why not? It could be your Christmas present.

Christian: There's so many crumbs here. Is most of that pastry that's fallen off? You know, I was telling you about Joanne using my onesie, and her skin, she scratches, she scratches a lot. Well, the other day I thought she'd been eating biscuits in bed. Because I started dusting the sheet, I said, 'You mucky bugger, look at all the crumbs.' But it was her skin. And then I said to her, 'Merry Eczema.'

Jamie: I saw what you did there, and it was an amusing pun on 'Merry X-mas.'

Christian: I wanted to tell you about her sister who cut her finger while making lasagna. And she sliced off a chunk. You don't realise or appreciate just how bad that is? But to slice off a part of your finger while you're in the kitchen preparing a meal is quite traumatic. It's also hunger inducing, because they still ate the lasagna. It would have been a shame to waste it really after that nasty accident. You want it to have been worth it I suppose.

Clearly one of them, they don't know who, ate a bit of her finger. It's like Russian finger roulette. If I said, 'Part of my finger's fallen off into that chicken pie, I mean, you would, you're greedy. I really need to ask somebody who's a bit more choosey about what they'd shove in their mouth. It's not even a question for Jamie.

Jamie:	I'm a carnivore. I don't mind where the flesh comes from.

Christian: I'm watching Monk again because Joanne's got the boxset on DVD. I said, 'We've watched this. He's a detective. I know what happens. He gets killed. He's the murderer.' And Joanne said, 'Don't spoil it for me.' I said, 'You've watched it five times. How could you not know?' And Joanne says, 'I've forgotten. Let me just watch it again.' How can you not know who the murderer is? It is a great series with a fantastic final episode. Ten out of ten.

I watched the last episode of House by the way with Hugh Laurie. I gave it a nine out of ten. House is a good medical drama. And sometimes we put a lot of eggs into the basket for a final episode to a TV series we love. It was outstanding throughout, and it provided a good climactic episode at the end. And I thought, 'Yes, this is how it should end.' People who've watched it know what I'm saying. It ends how it should.

There was something rather un-Christmassy I saw in Whitby. You know when you cross over that little bridge that goes over the river Esk? It's the one that cuts off the traffic when a boat sails underneath. Well, it was busy with people and cars and there were grownups basically pushing my children onto the road. Not physically but barging into their space forcing them onto the road. As an adult, if you see a kid on the edge of any pavement, you walk so you're closer to the road. You're not taking any extra risk, but you're ensuring the small child is a good distance away from a silly step into oncoming traffic.

But they didn't. They actually held on to the railing and pushed past my children. So, my kids were closer to the busy road. What is wrong with some people? Well, anyway for anyone listening who may do what I've just described, if you see a kid next to a busy road, move them inward to a safer position by taking the outer lane. You're sturdier than a youngster. You've got your senses alerted. You know you're statistically less likely to get knocked over then a child teetering on the kerb. Why do you think they have warning signs to cars painted all over ice-cream vans? Children don't think about dangerous situations and deadly consequences. That's the job for us adults.

Jamie: That was a better message than the Queens speech.

Christian: I can't say any more sincerely than to have the best Christmas you possibly can. If you're stuck in hospital over the Christmas, please try to enjoy something from the season. And I do pray that you get yourself better very soon. Until we meet again, take care. God bless.

Christian: Middlesbrough's Newport bridge has been closed for 16 weeks. And have you seen how much work they've done on it?

Jamie: Nothing.

Christian: Nothing. You've been given 16 weeks and it's still just patches of rust. Do they give the contracts to the company who gives the cheapest quote? 'We can do that in five months, and it'll cost you 50 grand.' 'Oh, well, that's a lot more expensive than our current quote that said they'll do it within thirteen years, but was only charging, 40,000. We're happy with the current guy.' They normally always are, its usually a mate or a relative. And it always goes over budget and takes longer than they first realized. 'Sorry we didn't fully understand what you were asking us when you said, 'Can you build a Cathedral? We thought you meant 'broken paving slab.' My mistake, but it'll cost ya.' And when he says 'ya', he actually means the taxpayer.

Jamie: I would have thought by now they would have made something that resembles some kind of improvement.

Christian: These structural engineering projects have a habit of going over their deadlines. You don't realise it but it's a scientifically proven fact that God snuck into the Bible just the six days of creation, but we know it was a lot longer. We know that now. The Holy Spirit breathed through man to transcribe this important document to capture the relationship between man and our creator. God went, 'It was good. Put me down for six days. It was all good.'

'But the world is 4.5 billion years old.' 'Shhhhh!'
That's God.

Speaking of religion, it's a religious exercise going
on outside on Guy Fawkes Night. Burning effigies
of the Pope. I assume he was still reeling from the
Reformation. Anyway, one of the conspirators to
blow up parliament foolishly warned the speaker,
who quite rightly went and told the king and on the
fourth of November Guy Fawkes was caught with
36 barrels of gun powder under parliament ready to
detonate the load. It would have killed thousands
of innocent people, and a few politicians. 'What do
you want all this gunpowder for Mr Fawkes?' 'For
me night. For me night.'

We seem to forget it was November the fourth that
the plot was foiled. Historians have calculated they
stocked far too much gunpowder already. The
others must have been out still buying more. It's
greed what got them caught. Or no appreciation of
what damage their explosives could do. If I was an
MP, I'd have suspected the strange, bearded staff
coming and going through the corridors of
Westminster with their prayer beads and
wheelbarrows full of mysterious powders, who
kept shaking their fists at any portrait of James the
first.

Historians guess at which member of the group
betrayed them. I'm guessing like most religious
terrorist nut jobs you only have to look at them to
know they're not a full shilling. Why should it
have been any different four hundred years ago?
Same mental illness. I suppose celebrating the
execution of a deluded whack job with fireworks
doesn't sound right in these progressive times. In
truth, it's just an excuse to have a big fire, set off a
few rockets and scare the neighbour's cat that

keeps cacking on your front lawn all year. Can you do a firework noise?

Jamie: Whizz Bang!

Christian: That's brilliant. I know mine sound like Bruce Forsyth 'A-th-th-th-th-th!' We have a listener who confessed he bought his fireworks from the back of a carpet shop. They've got to be rockets straight from China. Military grade. I don't think I could even shout the sound effects to those explosions.

Jamie: Did you hear about that stupid boy who lives not far from me, lit a firework in his bedroom to impress his girlfriend? He started to panic but he had nowhere to put it, so he placed it in his mouth. Probably thinking it'll be wet with saliva under his tongue. Then to be double sure of controlling the explosion, he puts both hands over it to soften the blow. He lost a couple of fingers.

Christian: Dial 999. 'What's your emergency?' 'Police.' You don't want to get them medical help, we want to get them arrested. 'Will you also be needing an ambulance?' 'No. No ambulance. Don't bring that. Just bring the police with hand cuffs. Actually, you'll only need to send for one cuff, he seems to have lost the other hand.'

                I remember as a kid buying a banger that didn't blow up, so I cracked it open, poured the contents onto the pavement and lit it. They called it a 'genie' you know, you singe your eyebrows. Whoa! You just see a big flash before your eyes and you can't adjust to the actual darkness for a while because you've been temporarily blinded. I think that when they have these organised firework displays by the council or rugby clubs, or the cricket grounds, what they should do is just have a big pile of discarded contents. Everyone standing there. And in just one second, light the powder with a single match. An almighty white phosphorous flash later, and everyone has to make their way back home without any vision. The streets littered with blind idiots feeling their way to their front doors. Or to their parked cars. That would be an interesting road trip back home.

Jamie: And anyone caught can be hung drawn and quartered.

Christian: Guy Fawkes wasn't executcd that way. He was going to be, but jumped off the scaffold and broke his neck before they could carry out the punishment.

Jamie: Do you think that was deliberate?

Christian: No, no, he was wanting to do it for another reason. Of course it was. He knew fine well what was going to happen. He'd been tortured almost to death. You see, there's two famous signatures of Guy Fawkes. Yeah, check out the autograph he signed without being under duress, where he hasn't been beaten and tortured for days. And the other one, where the man is broken, and they've got him to sign his confession. These days, not a jury in the land would accept that as evidence. Well, I mean, he did confess, he was caught red handed.

He wouldn't have been able to have his pipe either. I imagine a lot of people in those days had pipes. If he's down in the chambers of Parliament with all that gunpowder, he hasn't got his pipe on has he? I'm sure they knew the dangers of smoking next to high explosives. 'I'll have one final smoke of me pipe.' Ker-boom! He didn't even get to do that. Surely, he was suicidal. He wouldn't have had

chance to get out of there before it ignited. How
long was the touch wire? We don't know these
things. But he was definitely like a modern-day
suicide bomber. So, I doubt having a final drag on
his clay tobacco pipe would have been his biggest
concern. Might have helped him calm his nerves.
It's a good job he was lynched when the early
evenings are dark. Otherwise, if he'd have done
this in the middle of summer, you'd see nothing at
the displays. Yeah, rubbish.

Jamie: He was born in York.

Christian: Hold that thought. wanted to start the show
                    already. All we've managed to do is keep gassing
                    about Guido Fawkes. So, are we finally finished
                    talking about him now? Somebody asked me,
                    'What's the least amount of songs you've ever
                    played on your two hour show?'

Jamie: Three wasn't it? One to open the show. The second
                    was after 45 minutes for the simple reason that the
                    tape had stopped recording. So, while you turned
                    the cassette over you played a song. And the third
                    track was played after we said goodbye.

Christian: We could have whittled it down to two tracks if
                    you could have managed to talk while I turned the
                    tape over.

Jamie: I did talk. I said, 'I don't think it's too much to ask
                    for a song to be played every 45 minutes.' It's
                    professional.

Christian: There's a show on TV called 'Human Universe',
                    and they had a bowling ball and a feather dropped
                    together in this huge, vacuumed silo owned by
                    NASA. And in order to get it to become a vacuum,
                    they have to pump air out for over three hours. You

can do it for longer to be honest. But because
there's no air resistance they both land at the same
time. You'd still want to get hit by the feather
rather than the bowling ball. Air resistance or not,
it would crack your head.

Jamie: It depends on how high they're dropping it.

Christian: I assume you probably don't have to drop a
bowling ball too high for it to crack your head.

Jamie: And Isaac Newton decided this.

Christian: We call it 'discovered', not decided. There's an
underwater laboratory, which is about 15 metres
deep, and they can't stay in there too long as they
can get the bends. And you might think 15 metres
isn't too deep, yet two metres under the pool makes
your ears pop. I guess it is. They obviously know.
And the biggest recorded deep-sea dive was 145
metres. Do you know during some of them, and I
don't know if it's cheating, but in order to get to
those depths, they jump in with a heavy sled to
take them under the water as quickly as possible.

Jamie: I had a watch that could go down to 50 metres. I
never knew if that watch really worked at that
depth. To be honest it could have claimed 200
metres or even 1000. It could work on the ocean
floor for all I know. Someone saw my 50-meter
resistant watch and said, 'Mine can go down to 100
metres.' I said, 'Yeah, but will you?'

Christian: I don't think that's how water-resistant watch
numbers work. Unless this free diver could test
your watch for you. And they also use a rope to
pull themselves back up really quickly. Is that
cheating as well? I think they should have to go
down on their own accord and get back up as

quickly as they can. It's entirely dependent on their lung capacity, I imagine that they're adapted to it.

Now if evolution is what it is, surely, if you get someone who could deep sea dive, like a couple of pearl divers. Get them to breed. They'll have a little pearl diving baby that can get even further under the water. It's all to do with mutations. Actually, that's one of the evolution myths, that a mutation leads to another species. It doesn't. It just makes some member of the species mutated. I think that's the difference.

When I went onto Wikipedia to find this information out, there's a guy there. Standing next to the sea, you can see the ocean. He's got his swimsuit on. Jamie, you're in the record books and someone has taken your photo and uploaded it. My question to you is, if you had broken that world record, would you really want your photo to be so on the nose, like standing on the ship that you're going to dive from with all your snorkeling gear on? What about dressed like Guido and his pipe? Maybe, leaning on a mantelpiece with Christmas decorations up. And people will say, 'Who is he?' 'Isn't that the world record holder for deep sea diving.'.

I think you should give them what they're not expecting. If you broke the record for eating loads of boiled eggs in a minute, and I said, 'Can you put this bib on and stand holding your cutlery over an egg cup.' You'd say, 'Actually, you know what, no. How about you get a picture of me dressed as a deep-sea diver.'

I was watching 'Call the Midwife', it's a woman thing, but I watch it anyway. It's okay. And on it this guy lost his leg, lost his foot. So, this is how I think I've mentally switched off watching the programme, instead I'm deep in thought thinking about if I had one foot, and I'm forced to buy a pair of shoes, having to throw away the one I won't need anymore. It's a bit of a waste, isn't it? Because technically, if you've got one leg and you're hobbling around on crutches anyway, is it really that inconvenient to wear the wrong shoe, on the foot that it isn't designed for? I mean, really, it's not the end of the world is it? Kids do it all the time, putting on the wrong shoes.

Jamie: Well, they're thick.

Christian: True, but they barely notice it though. I'm thinking you probably wouldn't notice the difference between wearing your left and right shoes on the wrong feet.

I think there should be a buddy system in place. At the hospital, if you lose a leg, the nurse will say, 'There's another guy who's lost his opposite leg called Jamie. Christian why don't you get in touch with him, and you can both swap the shoes you'll no longer be using.'

Jamie: But I don't like your shoes.

Christian: Oh, yeah, you'd have to have a coming together of ideas. Negotiating which shoes we both like based on comfort and cost. I suppose we can't go too far wrong with plimsolls and Wellington boots. If you don't get informed of a buddy system, is there a website for amputees where they can go and meet?

Jamie: Let me just jot that down, 'dot com.'

Christian: There's money to be made for the shoe manufacturer, and if you're determined not to let them make a profit on you because of your circumstances then host your own shoe swapping party with fellow amputees. In fact, I am going to ask Jamie when we play the next song to swap shoes with me. And you have to hop because it's not gonna be like walking. I need you to hop around the studio, then come back once the song's ended and tell us if you can actually get away with having shoes on the wrong feet? Will you do that?

Jamie: Okay, in the interests of science, which is exactly what we're doing here. Yeah, I'll move around a bit and see how it feels. And if it's noticeable I can report back for anyone listening with one foot.

Christian: My other question is, would you go for a peg leg? Pirates are way cooler than wearing some random shoe stolen out of the supermarket carpark recycling bank. Or get a Pistorius blade? What else can you get? Oh, Robotic. Yeah, a robot leg like Robocop. I don't know, what would the robot leg do? It would be programmed to look normal I suppose. But would you programme it if you went to the doctors and he was checking your reflexes? Would your robot leg jerk upwards WHIRL! BEEP! when he hits the knee? TSCHZZ-CHK! Just so it knows. And it also gives you cramp when you're in bed, 'Argh! Damn you robot leg. Who's put it into cramp mode?' Just when you get romantic.

Jamie: That would be awesome. You could pick up the internet and have all your exam questions answered if you're in school.

Christian: No, you cross the line when you allow disabled people to have an unfair advantage. You're not allowed to cheat. They'd have to take it off before going into the exam hall. Confiscate it and put it with the other school contraband like sweets, stink bombs and vape pens. People lose false legs all the time on the London underground. Their lost property box is full of them. That is carelessness. However, that's probably why they ended up losing their limb in the first place. Let's be honest, if they ended up playing on railway lines as a teenager and they lost their actual leg that way, then they're hardly gonna be the most careful and responsible owners of their fake leg.

Jamie: I imagine these robotic legs are going to be pricey, so you'd be stupid to take it off or leave it just lying around. Maybe it's one that realises it's not on its owner and then starts hopping to where you are. 'Stupid owner' mode.

Christian: Jamie did not do the experiment. He said, 'I'll go on air and lie to the listener.'

Jamie: I've got cataracts. I might fall over and not see anything.

Christian: Well, I swapped my shoes over. When you said, 'you wouldn't notice,' you can notice. You would notice immediately. It's uncomfortable. It's actually quite uncomfortable to the point that you'd probably start twisting your ankle.

Jamie: I put my shoes on the wrong feet at home because I'm stupid. And you can feel it doesn't fit right.

Christian: As soon as my foot went into there, I could feel it straightaway it was wrong. Can you smell feet now?

Jamie: Yeah, you've got left foot pong and right foot pong. Completely different flavours.

Christian:	I think if we start wearing our shoes like that though, Darwin says we will evolve to have feet that look stupid. Or the wearing of a restricted opposite curve will cancel itself out, and we'll all grow straight plates of meat. Then anyone losing a foot wouldn't need a buddy system. It's the future of the future.
Jamie:	I think your shoes have restricted the blood flowing to your brain.
Christian:	Jamie, how manly would you rate your handshake between one and ten?
Jamie:	A four. I don't like shaking people's hands with my arm having a palsy.
Christian:	So, first impressions are usually formed they say when you shake hands. See, I like that idea, that if I shake your hand, and I've made my impressions on your weak handshake, that's good enough to distrust you. Actually, I've got many reasons to do that, but the handshake seems the ideal excuse.
Jamie:	It's when people see my hand to shake it, and then they kind of grimace. I said, 'It's not broken. It won't fall off.' I've heard that before.
Christian:	I've never done it to you have I?
Jamie:	No, not yet.
Christian:	That's awful, people actually done that. It's alright. We joke a lot about everything. Well, we just joke, that's all we do. We could get very serious about it. That's disgusting that someone would do that. And I don't mean the way that they could be shocked. I think you're adult enough to know that some

people might be a little bit taken aback in surprise, but to not shake your hand is terrible.

Jamie: Oh, they shake my hand, but you know it's under duress. Yeah, I've heard that.

Christian: What you want to do is not wash your hand after wiping your bum. And then when you do go to greet them with a handshake and they recoil, just slap your hand in theirs and go, 'Pleased to meet you.' They'll sniff and think, 'Is that his left foot I can smell?' You wish. Next week Jamie will be swapping gloves.

I am quite conscious that when I shake someone's hand, I try not to crush their hand. You know, the manly grip, because I don't have time for that machismo when idiots try to impress, but you also want to have a firm grip. You know shaking a wet fish is definitely going to make people distrust you. So, would it not be in your best interests to only offer them your good hand?

Jamie: I've done that before. One of the things that's wrong with me apart from all the other things, is my palsy hand sweats a fair bit as well, because of the heat.

Christian: I get sweaty hands, that's not an excuse. I get sweaty palms too. Don't you just rub your hands on your pants?

Jamie: Like a chav? Down my trousers?

Christian: No, that's hands inside your pants. I still mean keep them visible. I always think it's unpleasant though, where the person about to shake your hand sees you, and it looks like you're trying to buff up a corky ball before bowling it in cricket. 'Quickly

shake my hand now before I start sweating again.'
SWEAT! SWEAT!

I'm going to outrank you on the manly handshake
and give myself a six. So, collectively, we've got
ourselves a 10. To be honest, if you do shake our
hands, a four and a six, those impressions you'll
form about us are probably right. That's nature
there going back to natural selection. Jamie did you
blame God for your hand? Did you ever think why
has He given me a bad hand? Is it because he
wanted the people who do shake your hand to
know just what an insipid wet fish you are? A
divine tipping off.

Jamie: I was born with a paralysis down my right side. It's
                  just something that's happened. I've had to accept it
                  as part of my life. It's part of me.

Christian: I guess I've had to accept it as well, don't I? I
                  suppose I better come to terms with it. It's great
                  that we can actually joke about it because I told
                  you when I had Bells palsy, and it was only for two
                  weeks, I could hardly deal with it at all. I got some
                  right grief from people, that to this day, I'm still
                  disgusted at humanity for. It was like wearing
                  someone else's shoes correctly, of course, and the
                  way that people perceived me because I couldn't
                  speak properly.

Jamie: No, it's because you laughed like Popeye.

Christian: My eyes have never fully recovered. I still cry
                  when I eat. My facial nerves have re-wired
                  themselves in the wrong order. But when I went
                  into the fish and chip shop at Whitby and asked for
                  mushy peas, and they couldn't, or rather wouldn't
                  understand me, and they treated and spoke to me as
                  if I wasn't worth knowing. That's what I mostly

remember. And so joking aside, it's a terrible thing for people to be unwilling to accept imperfections that frankly make us who we are.

Do you give feedback to whoever has made you your meal? You've just had chicken for tea, right? When you go home will she ask, 'Was it nice? Did you enjoy it?' Are you enthusiastic about your reply?

Jamie: She's more enthused about her food than anybody else. 'You've got to admit Jamie, you really are bloody lucky having me make you all your food.' There's being confident about being a cook, but there's also being conceited.

Christian: Is it more to do with the fact she's sweated over the stove for a few hours for you and you've not even said, 'Thank you'? Now Joanne is a very good cook and I do compliment her. She'll say to me, 'Did you enjoy your tea?' And I'll say, 'It was all right.' You know, she's made something. It's like she expects a few more words. I mean, I really enjoyed it, but I'm not going to struggle with a thesaurus to describe the tastes and textures. 'It was alright.' 'It wasn't bad.'

Jamie: 'I'm not gonna die of poison tonight.' Or 'I'll have some more.' I dumb it down regardless of how much I enjoyed it.

Christian: There's a slight chance you say, 'It wasn't bad,' and you run the risk of her saying, 'Good, because you've got it for the next five days.' When really it was horrible.

Jamie: I've got money in my pocket, and there's a bin at work. A small price to pay to protect people's feelings. TIP!

Christian: I always think just licking the plate clean should be
                  evidence enough you've enjoyed their cooking.
                  'I've got very little to scrape into the bin, take that
                  as a compliment on your meal.' Did you say you
                  had a dishwasher? Which I find incredible. I don't
                  have that kind of space in our kitchen.

Jamie: You haven't been to my house.

Christian: Well, I haven't been invited.

Jamie: It's an open invitation to visit, you numpty.

Christian: There's just no address been given.

Jamie: You've got my email.

Christian: What put me off the dishwasher is you've got to
                  scrape the plate and give it a rinse before switching
                  on the machine. And I just think, if I'm doing that,
                  I may as well wash it already. A quick swish with
                  the sponge. Some items aren't dishwasher friendly,
                  because it gets very hot, labels can fall off jam jars
                  and everything.

Jamie: You can stick most things in straight away, but you
                  just need to clean the filter more frequently. See
                  that's the thing. You remove the caked-in stuff off
                  to save on the filter.

Christian: There must be certain items of food that are more
                  difficult to shift than others Once it's finished it's
                  wash cycle, you bring it out and most of the plates,
                  say 90% of all the plates, are very clean, crystal
                  and sparkling, but yet one will still have cornflakes
                  stuck to the bowl. And yet it's been through this
                  huge process of cleaning and steaming at 70

degrees, and yet there's still some grub there. What type of foods do you notice?

Jamie:

You're right, it's cereals. Cornflakes are the worst.

Christian:

You're forced to soak a breakfast bowl immediately, otherwise the cereals dry onto the surface within minutes. It's terrible. If you don't wash it the cornflakes glue themselves with the milk onto the ceramic bowl and that's it. There's no getting off. It has remnants for a few more washes after that.

One of the biggest football clubs in Brazil is set to open a cemetery for fans who want to be buried close to their favourite players. That sounds weird, but I guess if you can make money. Is there maybe something that you're interested in, say radio? Isn't there a dead Radio One DJ that's missing a headstone these days who you'd like to be buried next to? A former hero of yours, buried at a disgraced 45-degree angle in Scarborough? I'm gonna get you there. I can edit the show and make it sound like you're saying, 'Yes, please.'

Let's say you did like Radio One DJ's, and all those DJs have to sign a contract to say they'll all be buried in the same cemetery, because these footballers must be. The entire history of that football club must have had their players or star performers buried in the same plot so they can raise money by having fans buried with them. So surely, if you become a BBC DJ, they could say, 'You do realise you have to be buried in the radio one cemetery.' 'I'm not sure about that.' 'Well, you have to because some of the weird fans want to be buried with you.' 'But I want to be buried next to my wife.' 'Oh, no, she'll get buried in the World Service vault, you're in with John Peel.'

A tightrope walker has smashed two world records after completing back-to-back skyscraper crossings above Chicago, the windy city, without a safety net or a harness whilst blindfolded. Now, if you done that, how would you want your photo taken? Would you want to be in a pub playing dominoes just so no one has any clue as to what record you've set? It's like, 'Who is this guy? What did he do? Did he win at a pub game?' 'No, no, he's a tightrope walker across Chicago.' Chicago. Yeah, you're not even in an American pub, you're down the Red Line in Norton.

Jamie, do you recycle everything? Because I was talking about my peanut butter jar that I don't recycle, because it takes too long to wash. If I had a washing machine like you do, maybe I'd pop it in and get it cleaned. If you get really cheap peanut butter, there's an oil on the surface that I tip out. Do you mix the oil back in again?

Jamie:	No, I don't. But normally people don't buy the cheap peanut butter.

Christian:	You can take it and shake it. It sloshes in the jar when you pick it up from the supermarket 'Whoops!' shelf. If you can hear the grease churn, put it back down, it's not worth it. It's probably bad for you as well all that nut oil. It is nice though. Oh, I love it. Crunchy or smooth? I like a bit of both. These are the burning questions of the day. We'll come back to recycling envelopes with windows in them and yoghurt pots. It seems like it's a big, big, subject just waiting to be attacked by another radio show.

We watched Maleficent on Halloween night. And I've got to tell you this, for somebody who doesn't rate Angela Jolie as an actress, she's done a really top job. I won't obviously say it was just her that made it a good movie, but she does the role very well. We've been here before, we know there's a dark side of Disney and how it's a corporate thing, and its capitalist and blah, blah, blah. But they know how to make a bloody great film, don't they? Walt Disney could almost offer a money back guarantee. I mean, they would rarely give money back out. Wreck It Ralph was awesome, wasn't it?

Anyway, I was completely in awe of everything that went into that movie. I thought it was fascinating. I thought it was brilliant. I thought it was so well done. I thought there was a big piece of me in there as well. I just thought everything that I like was on that screen. The story that it was trying to tell would be a story I would wish to tell as well. It's just such a nice story, that you don't have to be good or bad. You just have to be yourself. And that's it. I'm not spoiling the plot for anyone. It's just a really nice movie. And I can't recommend it any more than that. I'll give it a nine out of ten.

Can we get behind and spearhead a campaign to bring back 90-minute movies? You know where you've got 90 minutes to watch an entire movie, and then we can go to bed. Because at the moment Batman, dark knight rises, was 160 minutes. And as much as it was enjoyable, seven out of ten, I think it lost its three points because it just kept going on. It didn't know when to wrap itself up. It didn't need to be that long. The perfect length film is 90 minutes.

We grew up with 90-minute movies. And then, all of a sudden, it just got out of control. I blame Lord of the Rings, and it kind of printed its own money.

'Oh, we'll make the Hobbit into two movies now. Oh, no, hang on we can turn it into a trilogy, if you have all the dwarves washing dishes for 40 minutes.' That's what they're paid for in Hollywood to make movies shorter and sharper, movie size and digestible. Don't make it as long as it would take me to read the entire novel. If you can't do that in 90 minutes with your audio-visual medium, it's time to shut up shop.

Just so that everyone knows when we're off air and a song is playing Jamie goes on to the internet and amuses himself. Jamie gets lost in a world of his own, happy to listen, unwind and relax and go on the computer completely forgetting we're doing a live radio show. I went on Facebook the other day and it had suggested people you may know, and it was my Dad, because I'm not friends with my Dad. I don't go around asking to be anyone's friend, that's the thing. I only use it as a news feed.

Jamie: And you're not popular.

Christian: It's your 39th birthday next week Jamie and who's invited to that sad little get together? Just me. And of course, the listener, if you're still in hospital and you've been here a full week already, you may as well stick with Jamie for company. We could use that as a strap line to the show, 'If you've been stuck in hospital for a week you might as well listen to this. It seriously can't get any worse than it is already.'

(L-R) Calvary, Nicea, Trinity, Emmaus, Cana

Jamie in pensive mood   Me in pensive moods

In-laws (Joanne centre)   Emmaus   Me and Joanne
The Anderson clan

The Frank, Anderson & Stephenson family on a day out to Shildon

Nicea & Emmaus   On the doorstep   Trinity

The Easter Egg hunt at Ormesby Hall, Middlesbrough

Christian: The lady in that advert who pronounces her V's like W's offering legal **adwice**. But an accent that beats that hands down is Arnold Schwarzenegger as Mr. Freeze in Batman and Robin when he says, 'I must find a **ky-oo-er**.' His wife has died from some disease and has been cryogenically frozen until he can obviously find a cure because he's some mad scientist, 'I will find a **ky-oo-er**,' whose spoken English is the equivalent to a doctor's prescription note.

Easter weekend? How many chocolate eggs did you get? And don't count cream eggs, they're not really officially big enough to count.

Jamie: I don't like them anyway.

Christian: I know this might sound blasphemous, Christ in the desert for forty days and nights tempted by the devil. But if satan had offered Him a cream egg though, Christianity would be so different today. Or we'd have much larger numbers in church if the disciples had eaten them at the last supper instead of sharing a loaf of bread.

Jamie: I didn't get any eggs. I got a new pair of jeans from Next which I was needing.

Christian: Can I tell you a little bit about Jamie. I think there's been quite a few years I've known you now. And you're a little bit spoilt. A little bit snobby. If I had to put all my friends 'snobbiest to scruffiest' in a row, there'd be a massive gap between you and my next mate, Lord Snot.

Jamie: No, I've just got standards. You're talking as if I was the one who went out and bought them. I wouldn't spend that on a pair of jeans. Tesco is fine. I could have had eight pairs from Tesco for the pair I did get.

Christian: I suppose the crotch will last longer and keep your testicles from rudely announcing themselves at an earlier opportunity.

Jamie: Regardless of the denim's quality, some underwear wouldn't go amiss with you. Or am I sounding like a snob?

Christian: Does anyone get given socks for Easter?

Jamie: I purchased my own socks. A couple of quid from Tesco. And I keep them even when they get holey. It's not snobby, it's frugal.

Christian: Scruffy is what it is. The smell of the newsagents as we came in. Jamie doesn't like the smell of newsagents. Harrods is what he likes. What's wrong with the newsagent smell?

Jamie: As a kid I don't like the smell of paper. Like I love the smell of freshly made paper but not newspaper. I don't like that printed ink smell.

Christian: I don't understand. What about magazines? The smell of top shelf magazines?

Jamie: Magazines are different. And the smell when you open up a ream of paper, fresh paper, is a lovely smell.

Christian: What about paper money? A fiver that's been in a sweaty thong somewhere in Soho?

Jamie:

That's a good point. In case you think it's a bit dodgy looking, try and smell it, because that smell's put on when it gets minted.

Christian:

Or is it from the dodgy looking guy holding the money… in his thong? Yeah. I think that's dodgy. Is he paying you the money for sniffing him?

This was one of the earliest Easter's you can ever have. The earliest is on the 22nd of March and this year it was on the 23rd. If you're waiting to see Easter happen on the 22nd, it'll be 2285, you're waiting a while for that. You should have just enjoyed the one we've had. Although it snowed, didn't it? What are we paying the Met Office for? They haven't got a prediction right once. Or it can only show me the morning if it's going to rain at about 11 o'clock. It could be sunny again. Did an entire cloud disappear off your radar? A cloud the size of Northern England wasn't there. They make it up.

You know, when people say this country is flooded with people, it's just a small island nation. Well, there's none more so obvious to back up that argument then on a bank holiday Monday at a McDonald's. Where did all these people crawl out from the woodwork? It's heaving. And the Metro Centre on a bank holiday, it's hell. It's just awful. That's why I think the Sunday trading hours should be revoked, you know, where people don't work on a Sunday and people have to spend the day outdoors or in church instead. I think we've got to the point where there are just too many people. I don't enjoy it. And if I don't enjoy it, why should they? Everyone should stay in.

Went to see the Angel of the North. It's big. You can get up close to it and walk around its feet.

Jamie: I've waved to it from the car, but I've not stopped to pay an actual visit.

Christian: You can walk all the way around it and see the full panoramic views of Gateshead. And it's fascinating. I think they deliberately made it look rusty so that when it does go rusty it isn't gonna be noticed. Doesn't rust weaken the structure?

Jamie: Oh yeah, it's gonna fall onto the road eventually. Straight across the A1, stops everything. A big tail back all the way to Darlington.

Christian: Did you see that pile-up on the Autobahn in Austria? 100 cars it said on the news, but it must have been a ballpoint lie from the Met Office that gave the figure. CNN reported today it was 60. I mean, there was loads of people injured but really, they're lucky the death toll wasn't higher.

Apparently across Britain, the worst bullied word in school is calling someone 'gay.' However, when they did a study and asked the children, it actually means 'uncool'. Like that pink top you're wearing Jamie, it makes you look gay. Now Jamie's sat there thinking he looks uncool. Do you think kids are saying that to get away with the homosexual slur if they get caught? 'I meant Jamie was uncool Miss.' Of course you did.

Jamie: 'You're gay Miss.'

Christian: Yeah, she's the PE teacher. They're so uncool.

Jamie: They say it at my place. They say, 'The computers are being gay.' And I said, 'Well, it's in good company then.' Always gets a laugh, except from the person I say it to. I assume because they're uncool. 'Interchangeable word', balls it is.

Christian: I'm thinking about throwing this in over the show, see how it goes. See if we can identify its true meaning. Now my record collection is quite old. So, in the 50's 'a gay old time' meant 'happy'. Then in the 80's it come to mean 'homosexual' and now it stands for 'uncool'. So, we'll start off with Cyndi Lauper doing a duet called 'Early bird' with Andy Bell from Erasure. This is so 'gay.'

I went and done the Lent thing. How did your Mam do with giving up swearing for Lent? Oh, that's right she swore before it even started, which is a shame. Well, you're her son, you'd press the nerves of any saint. Anyway, I managed to give up chocolate this year. Apparently, I could have had chocolates on Maundy Thursday, just before Christ's last meal. However, lots of people consider Lent to continue until Easter morning. Which I managed to do.

Now when I was around 13, this is the story before the story, which I've told you many times before, I went to the doctors because I used to get searing sharp pains. As if someone stuck a screwdriver through my temple, and I'd be in absolute agony. I couldn't open my eyes and I thought I was dying. The doctor said I suffered from acute migraines. It hurt so much that even after it disappeared, you're left with a mild headache. I rarely get them, but when I do get them, I know about it.

So, I must have eaten about three cream eggs, half an Easter egg, a bag of those mini eggs, and some small Smartie eggs, now they're allowed to make the blue ones again. They use some kind of seaweed for colouring. And within about half an hour of eating all that chocolate, the shooting pain in my head began.

I was talking on the phone to my Mam in Australia
when I explained to her how I was suffering. Then
she said, 'Ah, your Nanna had that with chocolate.'
So, when I was 13, she took me to go and see the
doctor about my migraines, and I now know my
mother was aware of her own mothers crippling
headaches caused by chocolate. But decided that
little bit of information wasn't of any interest to me
or the doctor. And the doctor says, 'Here, there's
some paracetamol. Nothing else we can do.'

20 years later, I mention the fact I may know
what's been causing these migraines. 'Hey, that's
interesting. Because your Nanna used to get the
same problems.' 'Could you not have mentioned
this possibly way back then when the doctor was
looking in my ears with a torch?' 'But I wouldn't
have thought it could be related.' Yeah, because
genetics are never related to health. It saddens me
that we don't live in the future, when slapping
someone virtually down the phone is an actual
punishment for past poor parental performance.

My Mam said it could be caused by coffee,
caffeine related migraines. I don't think to any
degree it's caused by coffee. I don't drink the stuff.
But fizzy pop could be an issue. I do like fizzy pop.
Shouldn't we have a fizzy pop day? Because Easter
day is dedicated to chocolate. Can I say that in a
survey on GMTV not one person asked on the
street knew that Easter was about our risen Lord
Jesus. They all said it was about eggs and stuff, the
commercial side of things. That's pretty sad. Even
people who don't go to church should at least know
it's based upon the Christian faith. I mean, they are
right in a way though. Even if I was to do the
interview, I wouldn't say they're completely wrong.
It is a bit about the chocolate. It wouldn't be the

same without it. So, I do agree, Easter Sunday is about chocolate, with a little bit of a religious side dish.

It's coming up to roughly half an hour into the show. By the way, the countdown reminded me of putting a bid in on e-Bay. Have you ever put a bid on e-Bay where you've taken it to the last minute? Because if you put it in any earlier, someone might outbid you. So, you're gonna wait to the end. That's when bids really start to go up. I was gonna go up to 17 pounds from 13. And then I typed in 173 pounds by mistake, I was never so relieved to have missed out on the deal, the countdown got there before my typo. I mean, don't get me wrong, I would've never paid it anyway but at least I don't incur a negative mark on my feedback.

The person who bought my Jive Bunny 12 inch single still hasn't paid me yet.

Jamie:

Has he not?

Christian:

Well of course he wouldn't, it's Jive Bunny. I can't blame him. I'm not leaving him any bad feedback, he's got sense. He's messing me about though, because I could have flung it by now. Someone's bought my Kylie's, and someone's bought my picture discs. But no one's bought my gay camp cheesy 12 inches yet. 'Do I mean uncool?' No. Damian, the time warp, Marc Almond and Jacky very cool tracks indeed.

Oh, and the question of the week is, 'How fat do you have to be to burst your partner's bladder?' Jamie nearly spilled his tea there. We were talking about Fatty Arbuckle and the kind of shenanigans he got up to at his party. And a lady at the shindig died from a urine infection which set in after her bladder burst. It kind of begged the question about Fatty Arbuckle, yes, he was fat, but how fat is the question? I kind of thought to myself, that's got to be fat by anyone's standards. I must add he was acquitted for causing anyone's death. There's a little bit of celebrity news from the early 1920s. I think about 20 stonne. Do you think he heard a Pop! and a Whooshing! noise? 'Hey, what was that?' Jamie, do your burst bladder noise.

Jamie: Ssss-sh!

Christian: That's the sound of leaking or sucking up spaghetti.

Jamie: Sh-Bha!

Christian: That was it, bless her.

I used to have a Pet Shop Boys, Behaviour poster on my bedroom wall. I think my Dad thought I was very uncool.

We went to do an Easter egg hunt and there were letters attached like B for bench and G for gate. Okay, so if I give you the letters, you can try to work out the secret word. Get a pencil and pen Jamie, I'll give you the letters in a second. And so, we're doing that, you can now get Easter eggs without boxes. They're still wrapped in tin foil, brilliant, isn't it? We'll start saving the planet.

I missed taking out the recycle bin, and it's now another two weeks before it comes again. I'm not driving to the tip and using up my petrol, that's hardly any good for the environment. By the way, can you also mention the bin men cause more trouble than good. When they go around the streets and empty the bins, when litter falls out, they don't pick it up, they let the wind blow it. So, you end up with the street littered with bits of tin cans and paper. They just don't care. They should have one of them patrolling for the debris that falls off the truck.

Now listen, we sit in here, and do a long show, how do you go about stretching your back? Have you seen those 'Innovation magazines'; were they have an old person looking really uncomfortable on a chair? It looks like it's tipping them backwards but is ergonomically designed to alleviate back pain. They're sat watching Countdown, sucking on an Everton mint.

Imagine you've been sat leaning forward all day. Then you sit back like this, it actually feels good. It's not me getting old, because years ago, I'd have thought that position to be painful. I sit down a lot at work and have to complete workstation assessment forms. You know, it's to make sure your knees are positioned in relation to your elbows and your shoulders shouldn't be hunched. And something to do with right angles to your arms or something. But there's no mention of pushing yourself all the way back in your chair, it feels good. You have to give yourself a twist. It's especially satisfying to hear a few clicks here and there.

Have you ever cracked your knuckles or only when you're about to fight someone? I've never done it. The audible clicks sound like it really hurts. There was a character who pressed all his fingers back like that in Bugsy Malone, he was called Knuckles. I hear it causes arthritis. And swallowing chewing gum sticks to your lungs. Either way it doesn't sound healthy. It certainly can't help fixing joint problems. But then does wearing a copper bracelet really relieve rheumatic pain? We need medical research into these things rather than old wives and radio presenters making these things up.

Did you see those Tibet protests? Let's hope their placards are bulletproof. Well, Tibet's part of China isn't it? I've looked at it on a map. I've got a world map in the bathroom. So, while you're laying cable you can educate yourself at the same time. My in-laws used to have a chart of the kings and queens of England. So, while you're straining you can focus on the Tudors line of ascension. You feel like after you've finished and flushed you've learned a little bit of extra knowledge, you know, you're thinking, 'Where was King Arthur? Oh, there's Richard the third.' See what I done there? Cockney Rhyming. Do you have anything in your bathroom to learn from? Is there a book you can browse and try and better yourself?

Jamie: The Viz.

Christian: I'm thinking more along the lines of a times table chart. Something you can learn your three times tables with. You're the guy who actually thought Adam Hart-Davies was dead because you read it in The Viz. How very bizarre. Well, if you think it boosts your IQ, why not?

Easter is calculated using the full moon after spring equinox. It's called the Paschal full moon. Anyway, this is a rule of thumb, and I don't believe it. You get a pencil and point it at the Moon. Sometimes the moon appears bigger. It's an optical illusion, it just depends on whether the moon rises low in the sky and looks bigger than it actually is. When you get a pencil at arm's length. Not like Mr. Tickle, just a normal arm's length away. You have to close one of your eyes, like aiming down the pencil. It should block out the moon. A pencil should block out the moon in the sky.

Jamie: I've never done it. But the moon must be pretty tiny to fit behind a small pink rubber.

Christian: With the bank holiday thing, and the overcrowding of Britain. I was in McDonald's at the Metro Centre and I seen this European guy. He was a spotty 18-year-old, possibly an exchange student. He came over and asked if our seats were taken. Which they were. So, he turned around and didn't ask this woman with two kids, he must have been sick of asking people and was desperate to eat his food, he just sat next to her. The restaurant was full. There was lots of people eating outdoors, along the corridor near the benches.

Anyway, he just physically sat next to this woman. And this woman looked at him in complete surprise. 'What's this about?' And then her husband came back from the counter being served with the food. And instead of having the cojones to say, 'Look, that seat was already taken. Get out of it.' And he was a lot older than this lad anyway. I'm guessing he could have taken him out no problem. But instead, he just stood there eating his chips standing next to his wife and kids while this spotty lad was sat on their table.

I'm glad he didn't rudely sit down at my table.

Jamie: Because you'd have said something?

Christian: Well, I wouldn't be happy. Physically we were there before he got there anyway, so yeah, I had every right to say, 'Get lost.' Much like that woman did. But then if you say anything, he could play the racist card. Unless you're burning Danish flags. It should be illegal to burn anyone's flag, anywhere. That's racist. There's only one reason to burn a flag and that's to provoke. Which gives me an idea.

Did you watch Horizon last night? How your memory works? There is a part called the 'Hippo-something' or other. I forget what it said. There was this guy who was born premature and hadn't developed this part of the brain that gives him memories. Have you seen Memento? He has to take photos to solve a crime that left him without any recollection. He's got such a short memory. I don't rate it because I didn't really understand it. It's critically acclaimed tosh. You might enjoy it. I can't stand pretentious films like that, '12 Monkeys.' I like to know exactly what's happening in the movie. Don't be given me 'Brazil.'

So, anyway, every day he has to sit with his mam and dad and go through the photo album and they say, 'That's your sister. That's you.' But when he speaks, this is the really bizarre thing, when you get smacked on the head like Mr. Bump did when he fell out the window, he ends up banging into an apple tree later on, and he gets his memory back just towards the end, like when Harold Bishop fell into a pond in 'Neighbours.' Oh, by the way, Tom Fletcher is dead in 'Home and Away', but Sally spoke to him because she's having a near death experience but it's really Tom, who was with Pippa in the original days. He's back just for a one-off episode.

So, this guy loses his memory. When you have amnesia. How do you not forget words? How can you still know all the full English language? 'I don't know who my mam is. But I remember how to say, 'I don't know who my mam is.'' Why did they retain all that? Some end up speaking a different language. Have you heard about that? People have even started speaking Czechoslovakian. How does that work? It's only a temporary thing. Would you remember your racist enough not to have any desire to speak their uncivilized language? I'm happier to believe that can happen, then I am about the pencil and the moon.

This is the thing, you bang your head and you remember how to speak in English though. Because this guy who had a problem with his memory spoke, to be honest, quite eloquently. His intelligence wasn't affected by it, and yet I know someone from work very similar who has to jot down everything he has to do because he forgets basic things like that. I also know someone, totally different story, because I was thinking about it while watching the programme, 'Isn't that a bit like such and such?' He used to get a bus to work, and one day got off at the wrong bus stop. It took him hours to get back home. They'd changed the poster at the bus stop he normally got off at. His logic was, 'It couldn't be my bus stop, because it was advertising a new movie.' And the bus just drove off with him still on it.

I guess there's a big difference between memory and being a little bit slow. His friends came over years ago and said, 'He's collapsed. He's having a bit of an episode in the graveyard.' My brothers went out to find him. He was just drunk. Obviously, you know, you take them back to make sure his parents know about it. Because otherwise he wouldn't have gotten into trouble. You don't want them to just get away with it scot free.

Did you know St Patrick's Day this year didn't fall
on the Monday following the Saturday, because
apparently the church worked out that it fell in holy
week. Therefore, it got a lower priority even
though it actually falls on the 15th. So, whoever
celebrated St. Patrick's Day on Monday was
actually celebrating on the wrong day.

Speaking of holy week, did you watch 'The
Passion', the BBC series? I watched it with my
children. I thought I'll let them watch it, rather than
the Mel Gibson movie. But I think this version
scarred them for life anyway. Calvary, who's
obviously named after the hill where Christ
Himself was killed, said, after watching the
crucifixion scene, and I don't know how it works in
his head, but he said to me, 'Don't let that happen
to you Dad.' As if people are still grabbed for
doing nothing wrong and crucifying them. He must
see me as a bit of a do-gooder and likely to be
arrested for my kind charitable works.

But he did say, 'Don't die', as if he really meant it.
I assured him I'm not going anywhere for a long
time. All my kids were asking, 'Why is He getting
nailed up? He hasn't done anything wrong.' I said,
'They're nasty. They're evil.' I suppose childhood
logic is that evil doesn't need a reason to nail a
good person up. Which I guess is profound and
truthful. I like the idea that they wanted to protect
me because my nice charms have put me in the
same league as Jesus. Well, we all wear masks.
Some obviously better than others.

Jamie: What went wrong?

Christian: Oh, you don't want to think about things you've
                done wrong in your life. One of these stories
                entered my head, you know, I'm not as nice as my

children believe. Not even slightly in Christ's
league at all. No harm in trying though. It's a story
about one of my best friends at secondary school.
My Dad read in the local newspaper, you know
what parents are like if they read someone's name,
'Do you know so-and-so?', or 'Is this a relation to
your friend? blah blah blah.'

Anyway, it transpired the name in the paper was
my mates Dad. 'Well, by the looks of it, he was out
with his friends drinking and he got thrown on his
head by a bouncer, outside a nightclub.' And I was
about 13 or 14. Obviously, when you're that age
your parents are usually close to around 40. Yeah,
40 moving upwards. And I just thought, 'That's a
bit sad.' Imagine if your own dad had been in
bother at a nightclub, getting thrown out for
causing trouble. And what does he do? My Dad
rips out the newspaper article and gives it to me.
So, I take it in to school and ask my friend if the
story is true.

So obviously, I was like, 'Oh, yeah, I'll go show
him in case he doesn't already know.' In case he
doesn't know his Dad's been beaten up by some
door staff thug. I actually remember doing it. You
know, sometimes you put certain events to the
back of your mind. And that's where I recalled this
story. I took that torn news article into school and
showed it to everybody in my class. And the worst
part about it, was my friend, as soon as he seen it,
grabbed it and ripped it up and didn't want to talk
about it, claiming it was a load of lies. 'Oh, you
probably won't be interested to know that
everybody in the class has already read it.'

Because of my youth, I'm going to blame my Dad.
My Dad must have known what he was doing
when he said, 'Here, let me tear out this news

clipping. You'll want this so you can go and show your friend it.' I admit he didn't say I should show the entire class, just ask your friend if it's definitely his Dad. Actually, now I'm older I should perhaps reflect more on his Dad's behaviour rather than my Dads. Getting hoyed out of a nightclub for being a middle-aged drunk, what a loser.

Speaking of childhood bullying, 'Minnie the Minx' in this week's Beano pretends to be a good girl. She takes a pram out with a doll and drives it over this lad, and he actually says, 'I've been sick in my mouth a bit.' It's all in the speech bubble. Minnie has basically bullied him to such a point, she's made him vomit. And I think that's beyond bullying.

They no longer want to show the reader Minnie getting hit with a slipper anymore for being naughty, because corporal punishment is wrong and all that. But it's happy to show a female thug bullying a boy to the point he's very actually become physically sick. That's fine. I mean, I must say, I did have a bit of a chuckle.

Jamie how did you get along with the egg hunt? Now remember this is for kids. The letters I'll give to the listeners in case that they might have a better idea, A Z G O E B.

Jamie: I need another 'A.' Hang on. Oboe Gaze?

Christian: Close, the Easter bunny was hiding in the Gazebo.

There's a lot of different types of super glue out there. Years ago, there was the traditional strong adhesive super glue, but now there's different glues for different fabrics and textiles. If you put a bit on one side of a finger and leave it for about five

minutes and then stick them together, you'll soon
have a mild panic. I got all my old He-man figures
out from the attic, and I don't know if you
remember He-man dolls, but their arms would
come off after years of playing with them. They'd
pop off, but now I can put some glue on them and
stick them back on forever. It means they're no
longer posable figures anymore. I mean the arms
will pretty much stay as they are.

I went onto eBay to see if I could buy Prince
Adam, and I saw a He-man character, still in its
box, Scare Glow, on offer for £820. What's going
on there? If you kept them boxed, they're worth a
fortune. I mean a real fortune. But that spoils the
fact it's a toy for kids. My childhood would have
been miserable keeping all my toys in their original
boxes. They're called collectors. I think we know
what they're called. There's no way on this planet
you would be spending that kind of money on toys.
Not to open it either.

Jamie: You said superglue, if you roll your fingers away
                from each other they can be separated.

Christian: I'm talking about just letting it set around an iron
                bar, like a railing in a park. Then the firemen will
                come down to remove the top layer of skin to free
                you. To make you feel better for having no palm,
                they might let you ride in the fire engine.

Jamie: Could I press the siren?

Christian: No, your hands are in a bandage for the next
                couple of weeks. So, there'll be no playing with
                your He-man. Remember it's worth more in a box.

                I took a wet wipe to the TV because it was looking
                grubby. So, I started to wipe the screen and I could

hear the static getting wiped off it. I could actually
hear it. And as I removed the static electricity my
bottom touched the metal fire guard, and even
though I was wearing jeans, I kid you not, it was
like a little thunderbolt went up my anus. I couldn't
believe it. It was like a Whoo-Hoo! Not entirely
unpleasant. I didn't want to touch anything in case
I still got a bit of a charge. It was a different hair-
raising experience.

Jamie: And different hair.

Christian:

When we first started doing radio shows together, we probably used to talk about burping and bottoms and that kind of thing. And now we get into the car and Jamie tells me about his job. He starts talking about car trouble, and look we're still chatting about which USB stick is best for pod slurping. We're becoming grumpy middle-aged men.

My battery was dead last week. As a matter of fact, the bracket had rusted, and we needed a certain type of spanner to get down there. So, needless to say after a couple of blasts from the hose pipe, to help us clear away the rust and see the scale of damage, it wasn't as rotten as we thought - it was just a bit of muck that had built up over the years. Top tip people, wash your car at least once during ownership.

It was a £45 battery, but because it had a bit of damage, they sold it to me for 30 quid. You might say to yourself, 'Yeah, but is it one of those things worth taking a risk on by taking a cheap shortcut? It's a false economy?' Yeah, well, the car starts, and I saved 15 quid.

It was the 40th anniversary of decimalization on the 15th February 1971. I listened to 'Pick of the Pops' with Tony Blackburn and he done the charts from 40 years ago and he announced the first number one record that was bought with decimalized coinage was 'Love grows (where my Rosemary goes) by Edison Lighthouse but that was a year earlier in1970. It was actually George Harrison with 'My Sweet Lord.' The BBC need a good cleaning at least once during our ownership.

On BBC Radio One, Reggie Yates normally has a guest on, and that guest usually is there because they're going to be revealed as the nation's number one. Always. It's about ten to seven each week, 'We've got McFly in the studio, and I've got only two records left to play. I can tell you that last week's number one, is this week's number two. Congratulations McFly. How does it feel to be number one?' It's that kind of thing.

Well, last week, Chipmunk was number one on the mid-week charts. They're published on a Wednesday and indicate how the chart is shaping up for Sunday. So, all of a sudden, the BBC are phoning him, 'Can you come in for the live top 40 show? It'd be good to have you there in the studio when they unveil your new number one.' It turns out that didn't quite happen, did it?

Reggie Yates	*"We have got two of your contenders left. And one of them is this week's number one. Who is it going to be? Chipmunk is still live in the studio. He's not saying anything.*
Jamie:	Come on Chipmunk! You've got this.
Reggie Yates	*"There's only two contenders remaining and one of them is standing in front of me right now."*
Christian:	'I can see your face. I'm actually looking at the chart as I speak. You should have taken a cheeky look; things have changed a lot since Wednesday. You know the producer asked me to delay this moment. So, I'll read out some positive text messages first to hopefully sugar coat the inevitable.'

Christian: Yeah, but not enough to get to number one. 'I'm ecstatic you brought me up to tell me I'm not number one. Can you at least pay my bus fare back home?' It's very rare that that happens. I thought, 'that's nice.' I wouldn't have had the mettle to build it up like that. It was beautifully set up by Reggie. So, kudos to him for adding to the drama, reading out all those congratulation texts, 'They all think your number one.' But it turns out you're a number two.

A bit cruel. I haven't heard his song, so I'll not review it unfairly. Did you know Edison Lighthouse stopped 'Leaving on a jet plane' making number one? It goes to show even more than 40 years ago people never had taste when it comes to crowning the number one in our pop charts.

Speaking of career peaks, Jamie, tell the listeners briefly what 'ring fenced' means?

Jamie: 'Ring fenced,' it means your jobs terminated and you're being put into a new role that hasn't yet been created. And say there's seven of you going for this 'new' job, they now only want five. So, you're basically interviewing for your old job, that's had a name change, but still requires the same roles and responsibilities. But you're fighting against your colleagues to be kept on. You have to compile a great cover letter and an updated CV and justify your existence. Basically, I don't know what 'ring fenced' means. I'm gonna find out tomorrow.

Christian:	So, you feel a bit of a Chipmunk at the moment? Not feeling like a number one, Champion?
Jamie:	I wasn't yesterday. I'm all right now. It happens in April.
Christian:	Don't you ever find, and this is me sounding full of wise lived experience, because my job's been on the line so many times over the years, that the threat of redundancy eventually loses its sting? You hear it so many times, 'Look, do what you want. I don't care anymore.' And that's true. It's not me trying to comfort you with hot air. It does get to a point where you can see a positive in them actually making a decision on your behalf, just so you can plan and get on with your own life. I think it's called 'past caring.' It also denies these awful individuals who get kicks out of mismanaging people like this, no satisfaction. I think that's when you deliver them your rather blunt farewell speech.

With my job I have the perk of printing the show before I arrive at the studio. I said to the IT lad I work with, 'I need a different printer because I'm printing it off, say printer 19, and when I go there nothing has dispatched.' He said, 'Try again because I'm going to the printer anyway to collect my own stuff.' So, he printed his thing, I printed my thing, and he got there and said, 'It's all printed out. In fact, it had printed out before I even got there.' I said, 'This is interesting.'

By the way the same printer is used to print letters to customers regards their bank accounts. So somewhere someone will receive a bank statement with an extra page containing the contents to this show and start to read, 'Chipmunk's a number two? Decimalization? A list of tracks to pod slurp.'

Luckily there's nothing rude. I probably should have checked the bin nearest the printer first. It'll more than likely be in there.

Talking about computers, particularly that we're living in 2011. When I save a file or copy over a file on my computer, it will display to me exactly how long I've got to wait for that particular action to complete. So, when I'm saving something, it'll say a minute left, approximately is fine. I'll give it that. Then it goes to 20 seconds remaining. All right. Then 10 seconds or 5 seconds. Then it gets to nothing. It's gone to zero. The egg timer is still up on the screen. I know the file is still saving.

Now I appreciate there's an approximate, but if you're saying it's zero seconds, then it's done. There's no approximate to no time remaining, it's done. Yet it's not. I'm waiting and now impatiently because I have no reference of when I can expect it to be complete. At least tell me it'll take 5 minutes so I can go put the kettle on. Microsoft's 20 seconds is a lot longer than my 20 seconds. And their zero seconds is a lot longer too. Maybe Bill Gates was being a bit liberal in his estimates. Try dipping a soldier into one of his soft-boiled eggs. I dare you.

Also, passwords that expire. There's a big drive at the moment across the company to stop hackers. There are websites where you can type a password in and it tells you how safe the password is. If you use an uppercase letter on a six-digit password, it takes 10 minutes extra for a computer to crack that than it would if it were lowercase. The push is to make the word as strong as possible. Now, if you're like me and you work with lots of different applications, I end up seriously, no doubt about it, with at least 10 passwords I've got to remember.

I've got to remember 10 passwords at any given time. Yet those passwords expire, usually once a month.

I can try and give it an extra number at the end, you know increment it by an extra digit. Eventually you start getting bits of paper lying around your desk with words like Saturncat5 with a numerical 5 for the capital 'S'. And like our show, we have to contain a special character as well. Bring back the good old days when you had a password set to never expire, and it could be all lowercase 'password1'.

I don't know if I've told you this story. But as I say, there's too many passwords to learn. So, I used to use work colleagues' names as part of my secret codes. I went through the people I know. It would be MorganJ for a month. It just so happened that I was working with a lady called Vicki. And she couldn't get onto an application during the weekend and was told to phone me. She said, 'Sorry about this, but I'm desperate. I can't get into my computer. I need to log on as you.' And of course, when I told her what my password was, which was her name followed by a number, it was a little bit awkward. It was sods law that she called me when she did, an uninspired code change but creepy, nonetheless.

We watched TV recently, when we were at Whitby for the weekend. We ended up watching children's channels. I can't believe it, and you can vouch for me because you still have a TV license Jamie, but the sheer amount of adverts is insane. When you watch an American show on DVD it's 40 minutes, but on TV with all the adverts, it takes it to an hour. How many adverts do they want to put on in-between a cartoon? And I'm not against advertising revenue generated during these shows, but these satellite channels you've already paid for. And the amount of adverts added is borderline criminal.

Jamie:

I hate the idea that no one watches movies anymore because they throw too many adverts in.

Christian:

If you're watching a suspense thriller, and it's really building up the tension, just throw the adverts in. It robs the viewer of the immersed visual story experience. You can't keep getting brought out of the story every ten minutes to watch a bingo advert, it completely spoils the mood. So, why watch it to begin with?

This is the best example ever, the sci-fi thriller 'Species'. It's a great horror. And the bit that is scary is when the team of researchers go outside following the alien from the nightclub, and they're trying to find this woman that's about to turn into a flesh-eating predator. And they follow each other into the back of this alleyway and there's a tramp sleeping behind a bin, and that's the scary bit. You don't realise it, but the director moves in towards it. And they're all huddled together in the dark, unsure of where this alien has gone, and then the bin gets knocked over, 'What are you doing boy?' The tramp has woken and shouted out breaking the silence, and that's the adrenalin rushing moment. And the audience can finally catch their breath.

On New Zealand TV we were watching Species, and they're all in the alley, and the bin gets knocked and the advert came on. I just thought, 'What have they done?' And the advert break ended, and it carried on, 'What are you doing boy?' The timing ruined everything. There's nothing at all slightly scary about a horror that has adverts so badly inserted. It was clear the broadcasters had never watched it before either. 'Just put it in here. Yeah, there's nothing happening in this scene, just a bin getting knocked over.'

Somebody at work has put an advert on the intranet, asking if anyone wants to be an extra in their zombie movies. A guy in the department told me, 'They've already made some and they're uploaded onto YouTube.' So, of course, from morbid curiosity I watched one. The overriding factor is I'm watching these grown men, adults, pretending to be zombies covered in tomato sauce running around. You know, I always thought Billy Elliot was the worst movie to be filmed in Easington. Turns out it's 'Dead not responsive' by Stuart in Finance.

Jamie: Zombies don't run.

Christian: Oh, don't worry about minor detail. There's no script whatsoever. They're shooting guns out of the window and the zombies are roaring. There's a comment, 'Oh, cool. Where'd you get that sound from?' It's probably an 11-year-old. And it's been ripped of a computer game. Tragic. All the people who've seen the final product to their rather pathetic hobby have deep down, felt some kind of pity. What goes on in someone's life to make them turn to making zombie movies? There's even a girl involved in one of their films. It's innocent lives that get caught up in these things. It should be made illegal. Keep it off our streets. Harsher punishments are needed to deter any further output.

I want to show you my grey beard and also play you track five, Zombies with 'Time of the season.' It's one of those amazing coincidences. This is so groovy. Check out the organ playing at the end. The idea that if you couldn't play an instrument, you couldn't be in a band. Not true. If you played one of those cheesy 60s organs, yeah, turns out you didn't need to play them at all. Check it out.

If you missed last week show I've got it here. Unfortunately, you wouldn't have heard it because the computer was playing in the background. Not sure you missed a lot. We were talking about being rushed on the toilet, squally weather, the medical term 'bariatric' to describe all things obese. The plastic egg inside Kinder surprises is orange if they contain a limited-edition item. The attendant who works in the Whitby 'pay-as-you-enter' toilets, that must be pretty bad on a Sunday shift. Deep fried chocolates are a pound from the chippy, or 50 pence if you provide them with your own bar.

Dead pets in bins? Which pet is the perfect size to throw in your wheelie bin? Or should you take it to the vet? Because his bins big enough to fit an entire horse. Chinese New Year was the year of the rabbit. And for those old enough to still appreciate outdated racial stereotypes, the Chinese don't throw away their dead pets, they eat them. Great opportunity to tell you the classic Chinese wheelie bin joke there, but I shall wait till the year of the cheeky monkey. The Whitby Gazette was full of news about the new charity shops window display, and some say journalism is dead.

Signature voice messages, ugly people who've got attractive voices should have a signature at the very end of their answer machine message that says, 'Oh, by the way, I'm a pig.' It takes away the shock when you eventually do meet them in real life. We also talked about Comic Relief as well. 365th of the TV licence should just go immediately to Comic Relief, on the understanding they stay away from everyone's telly. Because really, it's a full days entertainment completely wasted, isn't it? I'd prefer the zombie film to watching so called comedians on a messianic jaunt to save Africa.

I should be the last person to talk about great production. Can I just mention that what you can hear next is a snippet of last week's show, have a listen to the quality of it? There was a problem which was, the computers stand-by channel coming through the back of us talking.

Jamie:

You left the fader up with the computer playing the out of hours music mix.

Christian:

So, if you were listening last week, you heard the show at that quality. Us two competing to be heard over 'Just be good to me' by the SOS band. It was piped out on full volume. You actually heard two shows at once. I wouldn't care, but the music coming out at that exact time was the worst kind. Sod's law. I don't even think it's the SOS band. It's some punk street remix. It's awful.

I got home last week and thought, 'I'll listen to the show.' It usually gets me to sleep. I'm glad you find this funny Jamie. You're laughing at that rap song in the background. Boo-Yay!

Jamie:

In the foreground.

Christian:

The fact is, if someone was listening, they'd think, 'Are they just trying to be young and trendy?' It's 1Xtra. It is. It's Jules DJ Cool. Anyway, Jamie let's drop last weeks show like it's hot. A hot potato. Which do you prefer real mash or reconstituted dehydrated flakes with a nob of butter?

Jamie:

I like to feel lumps of real potato inside the mash.

| Christian: | Jamie, I've got a new book called, 'Quantum theory cannot hurt you.' I'm up to the part where the physicists start to argue with each other if light is a particle or is it a wave. That must have been a pretty tense moment. Who was the arbitrator to that ugly scene? 'Listen professors, why can't we just agree it can be both?' 'Because atoms can't emit light, dumbkoff.'

All of the following is true. Every Breath You Take contains an atom breathed out by Marilyn Monroe. There is a liquid that can run uphill. You age faster at the top of a building than at the bottom. An atom can be in many different places at once. The entire human race would fit in the volume of a sugar cube. 1% of the static on a television tuned between stations is the relic of the Big Bang. Time Travel is not forbidden by the laws of physics. A cup of coffee weighs more when it's hot than when it's cold. And the faster you travel, the slimmer you get. That is quantum theory. |

| Jamie: | Back up a bit. How do they know that every breath we take contains a particle that Marilyn Monroe breathed out? We live in England. She was American. |

| Christian: | Calculations. Billions of atoms that go into your lungs, multiplied by how many breaths you take over the course of a lifetime. And how those atoms are transferred around the world, then there's a high chance of probability, there's a bit of carbon in you that used to be in a dinosaur. The amazing thing about atoms is their physical properties, they're mostly space. And if you remove all that space in-between, you could fit the human population onto a single, very heavy, sugar cube. |

| Jamie: | There's space inside an atom? |

Christian: Imagine atoms are like oranges in a crate, all
               stacked up. And that's what makes different things.
               Inside the atom is the nucleus, the powerful part
               containing the neutrons and protons.

Jamie: And croutons.

Christian: That's what you see in shop doorways following a
               Saturday night out, full of vomit. The protons,
               they're positive, and the neutrons are neutral. The
               negative electrons circle the nucleus in the middle,
               like tiny planets orbiting the heaviest part with
               most of the mass. But what they've said in this
               book, is if you imagine your clenched fist, and
               you're standing in St. Paul's Cathedral, by the way,
               don't type into Google 'fist inside St. Paul', it may
               bring back unsafe search results.

               It's the same proportionally in distance of standing
               in St. Paul's, and a moth as the electron, flying
               around your fist as the nucleus, from the altar up to
               the top of the domed ceiling, as if the cathedral is
               the atom. That's the space inside the atom that isn't
               used. So, if you subtract all that space away from
               every atom inside our body, you could fit the entire
               human population into a sugar cube. Now that's a
               scary thought, isn't it?

               Do you know how they discovered molecules? A
               guy called Robert Brown who was a botanist
               looked through his microscope in 1827 and he
               observed pollen in water. And it was moving
               erratically. And it was only later Einstein solved
               the problem. And it was atoms, water molecules
               hitting the pollen from every side, like it's a beach
               ball being thrown around in a crowd and that's why
               it's going everywhere because it's just getting
               whacked by all these different molecules. Pretty

impressive. And that is what scientists now call Brownian motion, named after botanist Bob.

Jamie: It's weird. You just mentioned dinosaurs. I was watching a programme on the History Channel. It was this scientist in Egypt, and he'd found these skeleton remains of what he believed was a crocodile. But it was massive. And it was from dinosaur times.

Christian: 180 million years ago. There's one in the Pannett park, Whitby museum on the wall. I told you, 'You can rub it.' The sign says. 'Don't touch', but you can rub it. It's excellent. No one was looking.

Jamie: Well, this guy said that this crocodile was that big it actually jumped out of the water and grabbed the necks of T Rexes and pulled them down. And he surmised they'd killed a lot of dinosaurs. And of course, crocodiles are still with us to this day. They're good at survival. It can stop breathing for a couple of hours and it will slow its heart rate down to a few beats per minute, so its body doesn't need the oxygen when its underwater.

Christian: We should do a controlled experiment after they've tied the jaws up of a crocodile. And pulled all their teeth out to make it laboratory safe. Our hypothesis is tested by bunging some corks into their nostrils and stating, 'It'll be fine underwater because it can breathe for ages'. It just needs a bit of encouragement to go into hibernation mode. Come back in a few days and analyze the results. 'Its heart rate is so slow I can't even detect it anymore.' In conclusion, that's how they survived because they are a dinosaur. Yeah, they're the Tony Blackburn off reptiles.

I don't know if you'd be interested in this because obviously Valentine's Days been and went and you could have spiced things up with this new invention designed by Andrew Christian. It's a gel insert into male underwear called 'the shock jock flirt boxers.' These briefs apparently add the illusion of two inches to a man's anatomy.

The brand is called Andrew Christian, he's put his name all over the waistband which is a bit of a clue to anyone reading the pants that you're modestly endowed. Not a great marketing tactic there. It has an inbuilt enlarged shaping technology with the added bonus of helping protect against zipper injury. Now that might be worth it just in itself. Actually for £27 I don't think so. Cheaper to stick to using a rolled-up pair of socks.

There's a couple of things in the news. The teacher who sprayed children because they smell. The fact she teaches mainly an inner-city school in London, where I think 90% of the children are Bangladeshi, she's been accused of being racist. Surely the same could be said of any classroom where the majority are non-English speaking students. It's not a regular headline. Accusing someone of racism doesn't make the air in the room any more palatable. I think she should have sprayed the parents for not washing their children or their clothes properly. It's a sign of neglect. They should be ashamed of themselves rather than deflecting blame to the fed-up teacher.

I bought Peter Falk's autobiography for Joanne as a Valentine's Day gift. It's called, 'Just one more thing.' Everyone knows Columbo the detective has a glass eye and dresses scruffy so if they made a remake, they could have Gordon Brown or Nick Griffin play the character. Both have eye problems and don't wear a suit properly. Neither of them politically sees eye to eye. One of their eyes does.

Imagine Nick Griffin MEP with his trench coat on playing Columbo. You know who he's going to arrest at the end of every episode. 'It was Mr Patel who savagely ate the local vicar in a spicy ethnic curry.' 'But detective Griffin, he wasn't even there. He's still in the holding cell since last week when you charged him with stealing our jobs.' 'Just one more thing.' 'It's the same thing isn't it sir?' 'Yes.'

Equally we could have Gordon Brown as the slovenly sleuth, but he'd just let everyone off. 'We've managed to finally apprehend the rapist detective Brown.' 'Release him immediately, we can't be too sure he did commit those crimes because he had poor social mobility or some other lame excuse that doesn't make it his fault. In fact, increase his government funded handouts and ask him if there's anything else we can do to help with his rehabilitation.' 'Right away sir.' Roll credits.

Do you carry a book of stamps with you?

Jamie:	I used to. Now I use email.

Christian:	This is the sexist part of the show. I'm going to say it, I think more women carry books of stamps around with them than men do.

Jamie:	A female student came up to me and spilled out from her handbag lots of cards and a book of stamps was in there. She was looking for her ID card. So, it's an observation. More women are more likely to have stamps on them.

Christian:	I want to say double. No, no, forget that. Treble.

Jamie: Quadruple.

Christian: Don't be crazy Jamie. That's insane. Say treble. I'm
                gonna say for every man that has a book of stamps
                I think there's three women that have a book of
                stamps on them. That's the figures. That's my
                findings. If I'm wrong, then who's going to do this
                research anyway? That's what I want to know.
                Maybe the post office. Maybe they know who
                they're selling them too.

                Can you still buy them outside the post office when
                if it's closed, you just put your coins in the slot and
                pull your stamp book out? I don't think I've seen
                one for years. Do they still exist? When was the
                last time you used a public phone box as well? To
                actually use the phone Jamie, not to urinate or
                vandalize with half-digested croutons.

Jamie: Oh well, in that case, I can't remember.

Christian: If you look here, under my eyes, I've got bags. I've
                been having a lot of nights awake. Can you see that
                dry skin there? I pulled down my eye like that,
                made the skin taut, and then got my nail and
                scraped the dry skin off. It did smart a bit, but I'm
                pleased with the results. Otherwise, it was like
                white flakey skin surrounding my eye.

                Have you seen the procedure you can have on your
                eyes? I guess that's how doctors describe it, but it's
                cosmetic surgery. They get a hot needle and inject
                it into the bag under your eye, and it just melts,
                burns away the accumulation of fluid that's inside
                there. And you know, people do look better for it,
                but it seems a painful operation for vanity's sake. I
                think I'd rather look like Garfield then have that
                done to me. It just looks horrendous.

And of course, I've seen how they do liposuction. They don't seem to be too careful with the patient. It's all over the shop, like a loofa scrubbing your back. The doctor literally has a small vacuum sucking up fatty deposits under your stomach like he's cleaning toenail clippings from under the rug.

This is something I only found out from watching the preschool cartoon Peppa Pig. She goes to the dentist and you know there's a disposable cup that's there to rinse with. Well, I always thought when you swill out with it, it gets topped back up with water. But it doesn't. What's coming out of that tap is mouthwash. It's topping it up with the same mouthwash as I began with. I never knew that. I thought when I got to the end of the cup it was getting less and less dilute. Not realizing it's as concentrated as it was when I started. Peppa Pig goes to the dentist and I could see it getting filled up with coloured liquid. Whereas I thought the liquid that's coming out was just clear water. So, I've learned something new.

That was The Doors, Hello I love you Scooby Doo. I've been to Jim Morrison's grave I think it's in the same Paris cemetery as Oscar Wilde.

The grieving parents of a US Marine dog handler who was killed in Afghanistan are adopting his loyal animal as a tribute to their Son. He was among seven Marines killed in a December attack in Helmand province. He was obviously the canine handler. I think it's a great, if not tragic story. I read a Daily Mail headline, which still has to have some elements of truth. Apparently more of our soldiers have died in Afghanistan, then every other 26 EU nation put together.

I'm not suggesting any soldier's death would be any different, other than a huge loss. But the fact is, it goes to show where our soldiers have been deployed into these murderous areas, more than all these other countries combined. Something's wrong. Are they just there to police a lawless country? It's just horrendous. I'll tell you one thing that can make me upset. And that's seeing a coffin draped in our Union Jack. Because we've lost one of our own. And these politicians don't give a damn. You know, they just really don't care. Sorry, how can you sit there and see your men and your women coming back like that? For what? Good God!

Men who adopt the stiff upper lip approach. That's not me. It was about to wobble just then. *They are becoming a thing of the past research has found. Men are happy to show their emotions and even cry in front of others.* Have you ever been to the cinema to watch a bit of a weepy and blubbed?

Jamie:	I've cried in front of people before like a girl.

Christian:	What I was gonna say, before you destroyed my theory, was that I can watch something knowing it's upsetting. I know it's a sad scene. I don't cry at it though. Yeah, I'm not Mr. Stoney Heart. I know that something is sad. It's just not going to do anything to my tear ducts. I'm not going to blub. I guess I get a lump. Don't Jamie.

Jamie:	Is this you and your box of tissues while watching teenage slasher horrors?

Christian:	I think men get accused of being heartless when we're guilty of telling the difference between comedy and tragedy. But in order to prove that

we've understood the difference, I don't see why
we should be blubbing.

Jamie: The last film I cried to was 'Passion of the Christ.'

Christian   Me too. When was the last time you cried?

Jamie: I was talking about my Granddad.

Christian: A similar thing happened at work. We were
discussing favourite songs and I mentioned Bette
Midler, 'Wind beneath my wings.' And this guy
implied it was a choice only a nancy boy would
make. 'Oh, I'm sorry, that was what was played at
my Granddad's funeral. It has a special place and
meaning for me.' He felt so small, and then
allowed me the right to my musical opinion.
'Alright, well, that's okay then.' As far as real men
are concerned, you're allowed to cry over your
Granddad, that's fine, but nothing else.

What I really hate about Facebook is that people
your age. I say that, you're only a year younger.
Well, people our age, they'll send you a request.
'Jamie's bought a pet pig in Loserville and he
needs an extra coin for a cup of coffee can you
help him with a crystal?' I actually have no idea
what all these virtual farm games are. 'Jamie has
grown a prize-winning cucumber and he needs an
extra rake. Can you help him find it?' 'No, I don't
want to.' Delete! But I seem to receive people
wanting to send me extra coins so I can join their
game and plough a field. Don't play it if you need
more than one player. Don't play it. Play Tetris
instead.

CCTV cameras. If I was to smash your head into
the studio wall, there's a camera rigged up in the
corner that'll capture it all as evidence against me.

So, why will the police only release images of the violent assailants to the media months after the actual aggravated assault? They haven't arrested anybody for a crime, someone getting hoofed and boofed down the town on a Saturday night, so they eventually ask the local paper to carry a grainy image of the thug from the CCTV that captured it. 'On New Year's Eve, this thug blinded an innocent drinker at the bar,' so hold on a minute, it's two months later, why are you only showing me the image now?

Next time you see a news item that has accompanying CCTV pictures saying, 'Does anyone know this man? look at the date of when it happened. It'll be ages ago. I don't even remember what I had for tea last night, let alone if I was in a pub when somebody was hit with a snooker cue. I wouldn't have remembered any of that. But if I see it over the next few days I might. You can do the Colombo, 'Just one more thing.'

'Yes, what is it detective?' 'Do you recall a shop that was owned by the Drake family? They sold it a few years back and it's now a launderette. Well, before the national lottery started their son was working the late shift, he's married with kids now, but back then he was only a teenager. And he was robbed. This is the person who robbed him. Can you identify the thief from this CCTV camera photo? Think man. It's important you think back to that late night in November 1992. I would have shown you it earlier, but I've been far too busy. And we only asked to see the CCTV footage last week.'

Christian: Did you watch the Olympics opening ceremony?

Jamie: But you don't have a TV license.

Christian: Who's bank rolling this extravaganza?

Jamie: The government.

Christian: Right? So, I have every right to watch it. I've paid for some of that.

Jamie: You're right, so I've paid twice to see it.

Christian: I don't believe any of the TV license goes to fund the opening ceremony of the Olympics, so therefore everyone has a right to see it. In fact, a government funded committee should knock on working people's doors who don't own a television set, and get one setup on their doorstep and say, 'Watch this. You've paid for it.' Let's be honest, most of the celebrities that took part avoid paying any taxes. They should have not been allowed to watch it. Blindfold the buggers.

Jamie: Then put them up against a firing wall.

Christian: That could be the opening and closing ceremony all in one. Do our country proud.

Jamie: As long as we can get back the money in their offshore accounts. Paul McCartney will have an account bigger than the small island that protects it. And he can't sing any more.

Christian: Everyone's nasty about Paul McCartney. Do you know I went to the Lego adventure in Manchester?

And in there, there's a small little Lego replica of the Cavern Club in Liverpool.

Jamie: I've been to the Cavern Club in Liverpool.

Christian: You've been to the replica Cavern Club. The original was closed, blocked up, then excavated to replicate what it once looked like. It's mostly in the same place, but it's not. It has the same address.

Jamie: Not when I went.

Christian: Is that when you went to see George Michael's piano? Or was that his pianist? He was arrested for that. No, that was John Lennon's piano on loan from George Michael's personal collection on display at the Beatles tour.

              We go down into this Lego Cavern. They've got all the Lego Beatles in there. Of course, the drummer isn't Lego Ringo, because it wasn't him at the time was it? Paul McCartney should have had Ringo playing drums at the Olympic ceremony. Everyone loves Ringo, and it would have been phenomenal. But he didn't. Instead, it looked like an uglier Ken Dodd performing dreadfully. But I will say this again, 'You've got to walk only a metre in Paul McCartney shoes to realize you're beyond TV celebrity culture. You're something much bigger.'

              Now you be Paul McCartney. Basically, you can never do something right again. Okay, so he's not been relevant in maybe 20 years. And he was relevant for maybe 20 years, but a huge relevance by any stretch. All I'm saying is, 'Let's not knock the guy.' He might be a bit of a tightwad, a bit greedy. Doesn't give much money to charity. Yeah, I sponsored a security guard 20 quid. That must be the equivalent of Paul McCartney giving away a million pounds out of his money, everything being relative. But he would never do that because he's a bit greedy. And we know that. Yeah, you just hope the super-rich eventually do the right thing.

There was a great story in the news about the 13-year-old who was running with the Olympic torch and fell over because he'd lost part of his leg to cancer. And the couple in Scotland who won £161 million in the Euro lottery seen it, and bought him a new leg, which cost a five-figure sum. Now that puts Paul McCartney and David Beckham in the shade. Just a genuine slice of humanity. Why can't more people like that win the lottery? Or people who win the lottery become people like that?

Paul and Ringo appeared together at the opening of Liverpool's city of culture bid in 2008. So, I think we're going to forgive Paul McCartney for being atrocious at the Olympic opening ceremony, because he's Paul McCartney. I'd say Ringo is the Beatle with the biggest heart. And we love Ringo. And he narrated Thomas the Tank Engine, another reason why he's great. Have you seen videos of Ringo crying over John Lennon? Every time he's in an interview and somebody asks Ringo about John, you can actually, and this is no word of a lie, see the guy getting really upset.

It's not holding onto his coattails of success. He's genuinely upset. He gets emotionally choked up about it. And there's something quite endearing about that. I also think Ringo Starr was worth his weight in carrying the Beatles in interviews. He's got so much personality, so much drive, and he's lived so much more. His experience shows. Quick witted and cheeky. It helped sell millions of records. He certainly earned his place in the band.

I want to mention a DVD that I bought about the Victoria tunnels. No, that's **Victoria's**, a different movie Jamie. This is about the history of Newcastle. There was a pit at Spital Tongues and they wanted to get the coal from the mine to the ships on the river, but because it cost too much to transport the coal on roads, there was a road tax to pay. Also, it cost money to pay for horses to pull these carts up and down the streets each time. So, they built an underground tunnel all the way down, two and a half miles in Newcastle, all the way down to the quay.

There were no horses, no people, no overground noise. It was just a steam powered engine pulling the carts up and down with rope and eventually wire. Simply emptying and pulling it back up through this tunnel. We got to see about 700 metres of it, not all of it. Part of it's been taken over by Northumbrian water. But some of it you can still go into. And it was used as an air raid shelter during the Second World War. Fascinating. It was a two-hour experience. It lasted three hours because there were so many questions. When we finally got out, there was another tour waiting to start. Obviously, they were late, and this big fat chav young woman stood outside the door when it opened, and she went ape. 'We were supposed to be half 12, this is like two o'clock now, no way!'

This guy who was on the tour with us noticed he didn't have his money with him. He was totally embarrassed to tell the tour guide that he'd forgotten his money, I tell you this about my kind deed, after I overheard him on the phone asking a family or friend to come down with the money, it was only four quid. So, I gave him the money, but he insisted on paying me it back and wanted my address. I thought it was a bit dodgy. I said, 'No, if I didn't want to give you it, I wouldn't give you it.'

Just to add to the story, my kids were all hungry. They said, 'Let's have our picnic.' So, we went up this field where there's a little path leading up there to a bush and a bench. And Calvary who's nine, bless him, said 'There's a bench up there, I'll go get it for us.' So, he's sat waiting on this bench. As we approached closer and closer, you could see behind the bush, there was another bench full of drunks. There was about four skinhead drunks with their T-shirts off drinking bottles of cider and Calvary's just sat there waiting for his picnic.

I had to quietly grab him and say, 'Look, we're going.' Without explaining why his idea was a bad idea. It's that childhood innocence where he didn't understand. As far as he was concerned, there were just some people sat on a bench next to him. Good old Newcastle. So, it was a great experience. We bought the DVD, which looks like it was a college students project. A final year dissertation. A lecturer at the college must have said, 'By the way, Victoria tunnels want an information DVD creating, who can do it?' And some students must have put their hands up and said, 'We can.' Yeah, but they couldn't.

I got home and put it on. Some audio comes out one speaker, some audio doesn't come out at all. Then it goes to a still. Then it's muffled, you can hear traffic. The interviewer has this big boom microphone, and she's interviewing these women outside the house next to the busiest road ever. You can't hear a word they're saying. Later on, in the road, they're pointing at places that don't mean anything. There's no relevance to what they're talking about.

You know, people sometimes say, 'it's so bad, it's good', yeah, well this isn't that. It was that bad, it was just bad. Jamie, you reviewed 'Abraham Lincoln Vampire Slayer' and gave it a minus figure. Well, I can finally give a minus review, even though it's not a movie. It's an educational DVD about the Victoria tunnels, and it's minus 10. It's just horrendous. I don't know what they were thinking. Those media students should not have passed their course.

It shoots to some other footage that's in someone's house. And it looks like they're borrowed the scene from Tyne-Tees television because it's fine. And then it cuts back to this woman where they've used chroma key to stand in front of a picture of the tunnel. And there's even a point where she disappears off the still. It's only a split second, but it just looks so awful. She vanishes, then she comes back. And there's no reason for it. Someone clicked the wrong button and couldn't be bothered to do a retake.

| | |
| Jamie: | It's one thing for students to do the video project. But the tour operator shouldn't have charged for it. |

| Christian: | To be fair, they know. It was only £3. I noticed they didn't do any credits. No one wanted their names associated with it. 'We'll just leave it and call it a Victoria tunnel production.' But it is fascinating if you get the opportunity to go there. You've got to book it in advance, and it's well worth it. |

We had our picnic at Beamish open-air museum, because we've got the year pass. We tried the fish and chip shop, which is always closed when I've been before. They use a real Edwardian fryer. It's not fully authentic, the till is touch screen. But it's encased in one of those registers that pop up tombstone prices. We got some chips, and they were wrapped in photocopied old newspaper headlines, which was great. And the chips are absolutely divine. They are absolutely scrummy. I think our annual tickets expire soon, but we'll buy another one.

I also wanted to mention because I don't know about you, but I used to get a lot of spam email. Usually about genital cream, but that stopped since the recession. Russian servers have stopped spewing out these adverts. Is that the first thing to go when people are tightening the belt? maybe you have to weigh up what you truly need when finances are tight, you know, do I want to put food on my family's table? Do I want to renew my Beamish pass? Or do I want to make my appendage that little bit bigger?

Jamie: Well, now we all know what choice happened when your kids go hungry.

Christian: What's going on with the duck pond in Norton? It stunk the other day. I mean, like stink bombs. It's horrible, yet it'd only been cleaned recently. Is it too much rainwater? Is it people throwing too much bread in the water? Surely the bread that doesn't get eaten, begins to rot and turn the water manky. Then the rats turn up. Or is it the locals?

Jamie: Hey, I live in Norton.

Christian: That'll teach you for that 'bad dad, pitiful prong' remark. I saw a review of an MP3 pillow on the 'Gadget Show.' It's basically a pillow with an inbuilt speaker that you can only hear when you snuggle right down into it. Jamie bought himself one and rated it 10 out of 10 for comfort and usefulness. So, listening to repeat shows of mine gets you off… to sleep? Are you taking it camping with you? Won't it get wet? Couldn't it electrocute you? Does it plug into the wall?

Jamie: No.

Christian: It should. It would save time on having to change batteries all the time, wouldn't it?

Jamie: It doesn't have a battery.

Christian: I need to know what's powering the speaker.

Jamie: Nothing's powering it. As olden times, in the 80s, you could buy a pair of speakers for a Walkman.

Christian: The Walkman itself is the one with the batteries. So, where are the batteries on this pillow?

Jamie: It's coming straight from my mobile phone.

Christian: Right. Okay. So, it's the battery of the mobile phone that's powering it. It wasn't a difficult question. You were basically saying, or implying, the pillow had some kind of magical, renewable energy source.

                The other thing you could find out for me as a little love experiment, I think it's in a 'Friend's' episode, where Joey goes to sleep, and he's listening to a hypnosis tape but it's for the wrong sex, 'You are a strong, confident, independent woman,' you could learn French or Spanish or Indonesian. You could even listen to '50 Shades of Grey' on audio. I could read it to you in my manly sexy voice, 'I met the ruby team the week after, but that's another story.'

My boss said, 'I'm sure I've told you this story before.' But I think he added that to the beginning to escape any accusations of hiding secrets from the baying crowd. There's just no way he'd told us this story before. He apparently broke a rib, slipping on a puddle of urine when he was at the pub toilets at the Market Tavern in Chester-le-Street. There was a tiled step, and as he put his other foot forward his now wet shoe, soaked in urine, slipped the other way. His legs were already wobbly having ran the Great North Run, so that didn't help matters.

I did have to ask him, 'Were you tackle out at the time?' It's gonna be a bit embarrassing, someone's gonna come in and see you lying comatose like a turtle stranded on its shell in a puddle of pee, struggling to get up. And if you're, you know, presenting yourself, it's not gonna be a pretty sight. That's a little bit more additional embarrassment.

Jamie:	When I was epileptic many years ago. In 1993 I think this happened. I had a fit in the toilets, fell back at the urinal, tackle out. So, it can happen.
Christian:	And you were covered in your own urine?
Jamie:	Well, maybe it was my own. Some guy came and found me and put me away. I wasn't aware he did that. Zipped me back up. I'm sure I've told you.
Christian:	That's exactly what I mean. These are the stories you've hidden from me. Actually, I can accuse my boss of doing that, but Jamie's the kind of person who would definitely tell me about embarrassing stories. Like when you didn't get to the toilet in time at the bus stop. Jamie hasn't the good grace to

blush. So yeah, I've heard that story, but it's quite repulsive.

Anyway, to add insult to my boss who was now nursing a broken rib, he noticed there was also fresh paint on the door. So, not only was he soaked in urine, but he was covered in paint as well. Paint fumes probably helped with the smell to be honest. Quite a nasty result, I guess. And that's before he'd even managed to empty his own bladder.

Did you hear about that Olympic swimmer who received hate tweets? The police have said they're probably not going to arrest the tweeter, because if they arrested him, they would have to arrest pretty much everyone on Twitter. And anyone who's ever commented on a Daily Mail article. I believe the tweet said something along the lines, 'You've let your dad down.' And this swimmer's father is dead. To his defence, he could be a medium who was given the message from beyond the grave, 'Tell my son he's useless. Tweet him if you have to. We don't have internet access from the other side. I'm too disappointed to speak to him directly, I thought I'd do it through you, random stranger.'

So, the guy's not happy, move on. I mean, how do you define hate? I don't think it was that bad. It was a bit naughty. But was it really arrestable? That's the question. In all truth, did he hurt somebody physically? There are sex pests that walk free from court all the time. Why are we getting so worked up over a tweet? Things happen. I'm not justifying it, but I'm putting it into perspective. The rich and famous have been receiving fan mail since fame began, and not all those letters have been high praise.

Jamie: Is it because of who he is? If I had done it to you.
                  If I threatened to cut you up and bury you in a bin
                  bag. I say that as an example, would they come
                  round and arrest me? Is butchering a third-rate DJ
                  that much of a crime? They'd knock on my door to
                  thank me. But I wouldn't tweet about it. That
                  would be crossing the line of public decency.

Christian: We're quite good at hate in Britain, aren't we? We
                  could get a gold medal in that particular field. So,
                  our swimmers don't get gold. But the guy who sent
                  the hate tweet should have been awarded a gold
                  medal for such hatred. The police knock on the
                  door and invite him onto the loathsome podium.
                  'Look at what I won. I'd firstly like to thank that
                  useless, talentless swimmer who made this all
                  possible.'

                  You know all the empty seats at the Olympics?
                  Well, that's nothing compared to the empty seats
                  we have in the studio every week. No one wants to
                  sit and watch us present for two hours. We can't fill
                  our half empty studio. We've asked the cleaner to
                  stay, but she'd rather clean the toilets, than rest up
                  with us, drinking tea and pretending to find us
                  amusing or remotely interesting. She just wants to
                  empty the bin and leave. In fact, if she comes in
                  tonight, live on air, I want you to ask her to sit
                  down. I want to get a live reaction to what she
                  says. It might have to be edited. But we'll see.

                  Hardwick Park have introduced parking fees in
                  July, we've reached eight months of the year
                  already, and there were no pay and display notices
                  on there. They actually gave us a £25 ticket stating,
                  'If you don't pay it within 14 days, it goes up to
                  £50.' So, we've sent off the cheque, but I've also
                  sent a letter demanding my money back because I
                  don't think legally, they can do that. There's no

notices. It's like an illegal contract kind of thing. If it doesn't bring it to your attention, then it's not valid. It's one of those kinds of things. I guess we'll see.

One of my friends went to Rothbury and passed the area where Raoul Moat died. There's a shrine there next to the storm drain. He said he'd actually seen it. He just wanted to stand on all the flowers that had been left there, STOT! STOT! STOT! It's near Cragside the first house in the world to be powered by hydroelectric. You could use the moving waters from the storm drain and power a little eternal flame for Moaty, and the sick tourists who flock there. Or not. It would keep the chavs warm when they go on pilgrimage to pay their respects. Not that I'm suggesting people who go there would be chav scum Jamie, are you?

I'm fed up with children's fingernails. They grow so quickly, and I don't know what's underneath them. It looks like they've played with plasticine, but they haven't. It's disgusting. Cana's front tooth came out. I hadn't realised just how big adult teeth are by comparison to milk teeth. Massive. I talked about the old-fashioned tills that ring up the tombstone prices in Beamish. It's one of them, 'No Sale', hanging out of his top lip. Also, rounding of this section, after discussing Twitter, I found a few politically incorrect joke tweets that I think are worthy of sharing here:

I had my male to female sex change last week, and I'd say it was a success. I'm still trying to reverse out of the NHS carpark.

I used to think my son was a transformer - But then he was diagnosed with brittle bones and epilepsy.

According to a recent survey, Liverpool has the largest amount of people who go into small businesses, usually through the skylight.

What did the snail say to his ex-wife? 'I'm still leaving you.'

My physics teacher says my understanding of forces is the worst he's ever known. Personally, I think he's pushing my leg.

I've just broken the sound barrier or as the police call it - my wife's jaw.

Struggling to get your lizard up in the morning, you may have a reptile dysfunction.

Dyslexia cost me my job in IT, turns out my boss wants me to unzip his files.

Apparently, towels are the biggest cause of dry skin.

My neighbours listen to some excellent music, whether they want to or not.

Why is it, a TV in front of a shop window always looks so much better than the TV set at home? I want to know why? I was very conscious of it as I walked past a shop in the Metro Centre. There was nothing different, it wasn't a futuristic 3-D TV, it was flat screen plasma, same as mine, same size and everything, it just looked pretty awesome. Or is there something about a TV being placed in front of a shop window that makes it look terrific? It makes us want to buy one.

The behavioural science behind that positive impression I have for a piece of equipment, that I already have, fascinates me. What's extra and why am I attracted like a dog to a stick? Could it be its sparkly? It's got a sparkly sharp image, because I can't hear the noise. So, it's definitely a visual thing. They're all on mute. I think they're doing something hypnotic, like a lava lamp.

Now I want you to be very conscious of this the next time you walk past Rumbelows, have a look and tell me whether or not their telly looks more appetizing than the one you've got at home. Even though the one at home will be screening something you want to watch. The one in Argos is playing a movie you've never heard of or seen.

Jamie: I can imagine taking it back to Comet, 'The telly I bought in the shop, looked better in the shop. What happened?' But I think I know the answer. And you touched on it when you said hypnotic. 'You are a strong and sensitive woman.' All the television sets play the same video, and it's never a normal channel. It's usually a high-definition wildlife scene, or lots of colourful hot air balloons or umbrellas.

Christian: Yes, yes, it is. So, you're telling me there definitely isn't a magician working in the shop waving his wand.

Jamie: That would be a different shop entirely.

Christian: I got Masters of the Universe, PlayStation two game. It shows I'm still living in the old times, PlayStation two. When I was reading the instructions, it was bogged down with TM. Do you know what TM stands for above a word?

Jamie: Trademark.

Christian: Yeah. Above the word 'Eternia', 'Skeletor', 'He-man', 'Sorceress', 'Grayskull' - the entire sentence must have had about 10 TMs in it, so the font just looked terrible, all pushed up. Because everything He-man was doing, TM, rides Battle Cat TM, all the way to Snake Mountain TM, to fight Beast Man TM… Shut up! We get it, everything is a trademark. But no, it has to be spelled out on the off chance they say Trap Jaw, and you think that's a really good idea to title your next toy. 'But that's our trademark, we should have said.'

Jamie: Couldn't they have wrote the entire thing, and at the bottom simply mentioned the trademarks once?

Christian: Yes, I would have gone for that. Don't they normally say all insignia, logos and characters pertaining to – are the copyright or trademark of Mattel toys. Why didn't they just do that? Too simplistic? I think toys made in China as well, don't need a 'Made in China' sign. Like 99.9% of everything on the planet is made in China. From now on, stop telling us it's made there. Only tell us if it's made in another country like America or Britain, then let us know. Don't let us know, phone me, tell me, 'By the way you know those shoes your daughter's wearing? They're made in Britain.' 'No way.' I'm going out into the street, shouting it from the rooftops. 'We own something British made.' And then you double check, 'Oh no, sorry everyone, you can go back in, it was a false alarm.'

Jamie: It said, 'Made in Tibet.' Same thing, China. The monks won't be happy. What do I care?

Christian: I went to the dentist last week. The thing about the dentist is not only do you brush your teeth before you visit, so the dentist doesn't have to delve in there, but you've got to make sure there's no snot up your snout as well. Do you lean up against the bathroom mirror when you brush your teeth pre-visit? Or does your mobile phone have a mirror function on it? Trying to look up your snout.

If you were a dentist, would you tell someone in need of personal hygiene and grooming? You know when they go through the teeth chart? 'Okay, upper right, third molar,' and the assistant is busy ticking off your teeth. 'Small occlusion on upper left seven… Ooh, bogey up nostril, left. Mr. Morgan, did you not check before you came here? Your teeth are fine by the way.' I think they should turn your head and look in your ears and give you a thorough once over. You're paying good money; it should be part of the service the NHS provides.

You know we had a go at Paul McCartney, I was just thinking about The Beatles. If they were still hugely popular, which I guess they still are, and they had their own little pasta shapes in sauce, what would their shapes be? What would you find in The Beatles spaghetti?

Jamie:

Well obviously the drums. And a little Ringo shape. The tomato sauce has come from his loving heart. Yeah, and a wig. Not real hair from their heads. Actually, if it is real hair, it better be only from their heads. Ugly face shapes too. Yeah, Yoko. Shoes, platforms. Some sideburns.

Christian:

Now it's become Slade pasta shapes. Or is it Wizard from Telford, the birthplace of industry? I don't like this dish anymore. It's gone off. THROW! SMASH! WALL! CLEAN!

Stephen Hodson lost an impressive 16 stone in 18 months. Instead of celebrating his success, the 32-

year-old virgin, nice reporting Daily Mail, *has been feeling unattractive after the weight loss left him with huge flaps of sagging skin.* He could pretend to be Batman. All the ladies love Batman. *He consumed 6000 calories a day but decided to go on a diet to find love,* and live, I think. *Stephen hired a personal trainer after he got stuck in a caravan while on holiday.* This is a Mr. Man story isn't it? *After 18 months of eating just 1200 calories a day and exercising for up to two hours a day he now weighs a svelte 14 Stone 10 pounds. Stephen says he's still scared to go on a date in case his saggy skin repels women.*

Jamie: Just the idea of Mr. Fat stuck in the caravan.

Christian: Catch up Jamie. Do you remember the Winnie the Pooh story where he eats so much honey, he gets stuck in Rabbit's burrow? And Rabbit has to put a picture frame over his bottom, just to make do, because his backside is pointing into his living room. That's like this story, but less fictional with more baggy clothes to hide unsightly skin.

What kind of noise would you make with lots of loose skin on your face? Ask Paul McCartney. *'It affects my confidence. It's heavy and uncomfortable. And when I'm naked the skin hands down over my genitalia.'* That's Stephen, not me. I'm just reading it in my voice. I'm gonna get an MP3 recording of me saying that. Imagine Jamie all cuddled up in the fetal position lying in bed listening to me through his pillow speaker, *'It affects my confidence. It's heavy and uncomfortable. And when I'm naked, the skin hangs down over my genitalia.'* EXCITED SNORE! CURIOUS SNORE! SWEET DREAMS!

Stephen is shy and the thought of taking his shirt off fills him with fear, especially when he's on holiday with his friends. They're not really your friends than if they say something cruel. 'We use him as a windbreak.' *The NHS will perform the £10,000 operation and Stephen will finally go under the knife to remove his excess skin.*

They cut across your abdomen. Then they roll it out like dough. It sounds really crude, like some kind of pastry

<table>
<tr><td>Jamie:</td><td>They could cut it up into fat knacker pasta shapes.</td></tr>
</table>

Jamie: They could cut it up into fat knacker pasta shapes.

Christian: *'They have to take my bellybutton and nipples off and then reposition them.'* Yeah, and sew them back on. *'I won't have a body ready to show off this summer. But I'll hopefully look good in time for the Christmas party season. I just can't wait to start dating.'* Surely to be attractive, you need a belly button. Well, you don't need it. But you need it cosmetically, so you don't look creepy weird. Otherwise, you'll look like Adam or Eve walking around naked without a belly button. It's not gonna look right. And your nipples are on your shoulders. Something's gone wrong.

I cannot say 'No' to people giving away books. My Uncle comes round every now and again whenever he has a clear out. He brings bags of books or videos, arty-farty videos. And I take them in, and we watch them over the course of some time. And these are what he's recorded off the TV, some animations of Oscar Wilde and 'The devoted friend', 'The nightingale and the rose', 'The selfish giant.' These are stories for children. I have to sit there explaining to the kids what's what. It's a lot to take in for a child, symbolism and tone. But once you tell them what it means, then they get it, they really, really get it. They understand it.

It's really interesting to see a child enjoy something when a penny drops. It's like they've watched this really bad cartoon for half an hour. But if you're sat there telling them, 'Well this character is actually Jesus coming to take the giant to Heaven in the tree.' Then they start piecing it together. But if you just leave a child to sit and watch something without directing or instructing them, it's actually a wasted opportunity. And it's really a waste of their time. You need to engage them and ask them what they're thinking.

There are plenty of certificate U videos for them to sit and watch without interruption, like Ringo's Thomas the Tank Engine. You don't need to spoon feed them. But if you do want to give them something a bit more intellectually stimulating, they are up for it. Kids are up for it, but you've got to be as well. The problem with some of Oscar Wilde's stories, I didn't really get it myself. Like the nightingale kills herself by piercing its heart on a thorn to make a red rose. So, the student can give the rose to a girl that he wants to take to a dance. But she decides that she's got jewelry instead, so she doesn't want it. So, she throws it on the floor, and he decides to go back to reading his books. I summarized.

And the kids said, 'Dad, the birds dead. What was that about?' and I thought for a bit before answering, 'It's like, you know, it's man's folly.' I think if you don't know the answer, just be as pretentious as possible. 'Where the wild things are' is a crazy arty movie, but I explained the protagonist emotions are actually the wild creatures he fears. Some fairy tales I admit, even I don't quite understand. Maybe I'll wait for the graphic novel format to come out of Oscars stories. I can then read the comic book to my kids.

Jamie, did you draw on that photo of Boy George? Given him a moustache or something. Did you ever write speech bubbles that come out of celebrities' mouths in magazines? I'm hoping that's a speech bubble coming out of Boy George's mouth. We know what the caption would be for that particular photo. I was actually gonna say, 'Pasta shapes for Culture Club? They look like spaghetti hoops, but they're linked into chains. A chain to whip a male escort. And two hoops to make a handcuff.

If you ran a shop, would you sell things to people at different prices based solely on how they look? If I came into your shop, would you think, 'Well, he probably can't afford as much as the last customer judging by his appearance.' Positively discriminate for us common folk.

Jamie: The likes of you, I wouldn't want in my shop. So, I'd charge you the earth.

Christian: I see, you're doing the absolute opposite. So, if I came into your shop, you wouldn't sell me midget gems for cheaper? All of a sudden, the quarter of midget gems doubles. 'I can't shop here.' 'Good!' Are you allowed to do that? Negative discrimination?

Jamie: Positive, negative, it's all discrimination. In fact, calling discrimination 'positive' only adds further stupidity to an already out and out idiot.

Christian: Okay, I'll give you that. What about saying you changed the pricing policy when I happened to be in your shop.

Jamie: What, every time? And as soon as you leave, the price drops back down again. The door buzzes when you step back in and the price jumps back up. Back and forth. It's probably easier for me to put a sign on the door banning you from entering. Or a sign saying we've sold out of midget gems.

Christian: Pah!

You know the theme music to EastEnders, 'Doo, doo doo doo doo doo doo doo doo,' when it pans out to the map and we see the river Thames? What would the theme be for the river Tees? I think we should come up with a little catchy number. I want something unique. You think about that before the end of the show as I pan out with high drama. Maybe we should try to incorporate words like 'mega', 'proper' and 'mint.' Give it a real cultural celebration.

We went to the Baptist church because they did a summer club for the kids. And they'd learned a song about Jesus. And the lyrics had 'brill, brill, wicked, wicked, skill, skill' in them. And I was thinking, 'I haven't said the word 'skill' in donkeys, yonks. Actually, it was probably when I was back in school. 'Skill', 'smart as', 'man-head', I still don't say 'proper like'. And I think 'mint' is more scouse; 'What do you think of Paul McCartney?' 'Not mint.' That's just naughty, proper like.

Moonpig is a website shop where you buy personalized cards. I have a colleague at work who got an e-mail reminding him it was his birthday tomorrow. As if he might not have remembered. Surely, you'd know that? Who sends themselves a card anyway, except Mr Bean? Post it through the front door and pretend to be surprised, 'Yay! I remembered.' What would be the point?

News about fake laughter. *Even our most realistic efforts to feign amusement are easy to spot according to scientists.*

Jamie:

If I find something funny, I will laugh. If I don't find it funny, I won't. I'm not going to lie to them.

Christian:

But you're quite blunt, in a rude, on the spectrum, kind of way. I appreciate it, but most people don't like that.

Jamie:

Yeah, I've heard that before.

Christian:

The most awkward moments for me are when someone tells a blasphemous joke. I can honestly tell you this, if it's funny, and I hold my head in absolute sinful shame, I would still laugh. And if I don't laugh at a blasphemous joke, I get accused of being a religious killjoy. 'Well, he wouldn't find it funny, being a complete do-gooder.' They actually don't get it. I'm not laughing because it's just not funny. Period. Don't laugh at that Jamie, you're better than that. Raise that mirth standard.

I end up with people telling me racist, homophobic, sexist, religious, whatever jokes, and I don't laugh, then it's my fault. It couldn't possibly be because the joke wasn't funny. The problem is with me, the audience. I've even been accused of being left-wing and too politically correct. Can you believe that – me? Too PC? Now, that accusation hurts. But then equally, I've questioned my own thinking on this. What if, in age, I have developed a certain line of reverence, or dare I say, morals, to no longer allow me to laugh at the downtrodden, marginalized and suppressed? Just a thought.

Jamie:

You don't need experts to tell us when someone genuinely laughs and when it's fake. All humans can distinguish between the two.

Christian:

It's like the soundtrack to the Pink Panther cartoon or the Flintstones. Where do they get that from? Canned laughter. When was there ever an audience that allowed those laughs to be recorded? They're so fake. They even added them to sitcoms in pre-production. You're relying on the sound engineer to put the laughs at the right places. If it was our show, they wouldn't have a clue where to edit the chuckles. Just plenty of tumbleweed sounds added for comedic effect.

You know what I miss with the advent of the digital age? When a recording these days runs out of power it simply stops. We've lost the good old cassette recorder. When my MP3 player runs out of batteries, it just stops working. Whereas, if I was listening to a tape, you can tell the batteries are running out. The music or the voices sound strangled, and it keeps playing the tape, but really slowly. Kylie sounds like Rick Astley. I guess then, logically you would sound like me.

Jamie:

Slower? Definitely.

Christian:

How do you leave your body to medical science? And why do only medical departments of universities or hospitals get them? For instance, Jamie wants to leave his body to medical science and Teesside University gets it. How come I can't get it? You know, I've got a chemistry set at home. I've made a cream that can remove hair. How come

I can't get hold of your body and use it for my own experiments?

Jamie:

Well, your address isn't a medical establishment. You have to be registered with the correct authorities in order to legally dissect bodies. It's the establishment that then gets given the body. But why am I telling you how to get hold of my body?

Christian:

You could just leave your body to me in your last will and testament. 'I bequeath my CDs to Oxfam, my clothing to be recycled, and my books to be heaped onto the local bonfire. Oh, and by the way, Christian thinks he's a doctor. So, let him have my body for medical practice.'

Jamie:

CHOP! CHOP!

Christian:

We we're talking about the creams that get advertised from the spam servers in Russia. It would be like, 'Dr Frank's new growth remedy.' 'He's tried it on Jamie.' 'That doesn't look like a cream, that looks more like a weight pulling device.' 'I heard Jamie's dead and the alleged cream was used on his corpse.' I am naughty Jamie.

Jamie:

Well, it helps the show.

Christian:

We have clowns in authority for that. *The health services have removed the word 'Dad' from a pregnancy book for fear of offending gay and lesbian parents. Officials have decided the term 'partner' is less discriminating against same sex couples.*

Jamie:

Wasn't there a canned laughter, 80s sitcom, about my two dads?

Christian:	They could remake it with Elton John and David
	Furnish, 'My two partners.' A truly unfunny
	sitcom with a lot of tantrums and crying in it.

	I remember in the 80s there was this idea that there
	were enough nuclear warheads to destroy the world
	40 times over. These days there's enough liberals
	in Britain to bury the country 400 times over. It's
	scary.

	We're going camping on Friday. Last time we went
	away, it was a few weeks ago, and we went to a
	hotel. We had the shower, toilet and sink all in the
	same room.

Jamie:	It's called a bathroom.

Christian:	Imagine, half of its dedicated to the sink area, a
	quarter is dedicated to the shower and the other
	quarter, to the toilet. The shower was separated
	with frosted glass. So, when you're sat on the toilet,
	you can lock the door, but you can still see the light
	coming through the pane of glass, that's how you
	get the light inside the toilet. But people who are
	using the sink can see the pink silhouette of you
	wiping your bum. Which is disgusting. No one
	should be able to work out what's going on inside
	the loo. Or if you're sat in the loo and someone's in
	the shower, you can see the skin toned figure
	washing in the shower. Or if they press themselves
	up against the window. 'Brrrr! Glass is cold.' And
	you pay £120 pound a night for that. I'm not saying
	for that experience. I mean for a night in the hotel.

	Jamie very quickly, what was your theme tune that
	you wanted to offer us, as we pan out from the
	river Tees? I'm hoping to capture the emotions and

the energy of the people and the vibrant
surroundings. What have you got?

Jamie: Well, I think I'm gonna go along the lines of,
                    'Wuw-whockah! Wow-whockha! Chang-whackha!
                    Bom chicka wah!'

Christian: That's 70s porno music.

Jamie: Yeah. It seems dated, but people will still come to
                    see it. Teesside that is. I needed a bit more time.

Christian: And a bit more civic pride. Sadly, we've none left
                    for this show. Take care. God bless.

Christian: I can picture Victorian England. I can picture Tiny Tim on his crutches waving goodbye to his Dad who's trying to get to work early in the morning. Now, how did Bob Cratchit make sure that he got to work bang on time without Ebenezer having a go at him? That's my question. Right? If you know when bedside alarm clocks were invented fine. Basically, I'm asking the question, you give me the answer. And not in your usual Wikipedia response that's half-baked and made up.

You say, 'Oh, alarm clocks. They were mass produced in 1879.' I say, 'Okay, how did people make sure they were at their place of work before 1879?' Especially when you consider winter and how cold and dark it gets, it looks like night on a morning. Would they have to hold their time piece up to a candle to make out the time? Did the working man of the house get his wife to stay up all night, so he didn't sleep in? 'Here, it's time you woke up for your shift down pit.'

Jamie: That's what Captain Cook's wife done. Stood around all night looking at his clock. I said Cook.

Christian: Benjamin Franklin is quoted 'finding the key to success under the alarm clock' and he lived throughout the 1700s. This mystery has not been solved. What about your favourite Lionel? Is it Lionel Richie? Is it Lionel Blair? or is it Sir Lionel one of the knights from the roundtable?

Jamie: He sounds cool. I assume even though no one's even heard of him, he's guaranteed to win the poll.

Christian: I've heard of Lionel Blair. You go to a urinal,
               because you need to go. What I want to know is
               how come I can be standing there, and someone
               comes into the toilets, stands next to me, and
               they've finished way before I've finished? And
               they came in about five minute later.

Jamie: It just means you've got a bigger bladder. And
               some folks get stage fright.

Christian: One guy was answering his phone. I don't think he
               actually needed a comfort break. Do they try that
               on at college? Excuse themselves to go to the
               toilet, but sneakily taking a personal phone call
               instead? 'I need the toilet Miss.' 'But Jamie, we
               haven't learned how to tell the time using a clock
               face yet.' 'Yeah, sorry. I'll take less time than
               some other men take to urinate Miss.' 'Jamie we'll
               never know how clock alarms woke the industrial
               revolution at this rate.'

Jamie: 'Yeah. Whatever. Computer resets itself Miss.' Is
               she my Maths teacher or my History teacher? She
               seems a little confused.

Christian: Don't be sexist Jamie to fictitious women I've
               created to illustrate your skiving out of lessons.

               I wanted to mention 'Supersize versus super
               skinny' yesterday on Channel Four. The chubster
               has to eat what the skinny person eats, and the
               skinny person is given the fatty's food. That's the
               concept in a nutshell. One is supposed to pile on
               weight and the other shouldn't. At the very end of
               the show, they're in new clothes, the producer
               wants the viewers to see how their change in
               weight makes them look fitter and healthier. Okay,
               they're all dressed up. And as the credits roll, they

do a bit of a dance for the camera to show off their
new features.

Now these people are about 36 stone. They've been
on a diet for six weeks, and they've lost about six
pounds. I don't think that's any reason to have a
little bit of a jig and celebrate for the cameras.
Clearly the production company does. It's nice to
end the show on a high. 'Oh, you've lost six
pounds.' A chubster with actual will power, a rare
and precious thing. But that's probably just in
sweat. So, they get them in a shirt, probably one of
those homemade shirts they've had to have
specially commissioned to fit around their portly
frame.

Not only do they perform a dance at the end of the
show, but when they're in their underwear, getting
on the scales to get weighed in, they do a dance as
well, and it's disgusting. I think some things
shouldn't be pre watershed.

Jamie:	I think they should slow down the footage so we can see exactly what weight they need to lose.
Christian:	I should be thankful you're not the producer. I've heard you've not been doing a show on the weekend in a while. I don't want to give you a disciplinary live on air, but when was the last time you did a show?
Jamie:	Sometime back.
Christian:	There you go.
Jamie:	Thank you.
Christian:	I had to pick my nose there. You know radio, sometimes you don't need to tell people about it.

But I just thought I needed to share that. You know, you get one of those 'Joke-a-day' calendars, and you can go 100 days and not laugh once. I did get one though, and I thought it was funny. No one else laughed at it. But then I think it's a little bit too difficult for them. It's a bit like those small mini busses that drive around called 'community payback', and it's full of people who've been sentenced to work community hours. They're so thick they don't even know they're travelling in a bus titled 'community payback.'

A Yorkshire man takes his cat to the vet, and the vet says, 'Is it a tom?' He says, 'No, it's here in t'box.'

Jamie: I get it. I get it. I just… Tell me a funny gag instead.

Christian: *I once had a job cleaning up in a glitter factory, it was pretty rubbish.*

Jamie: *Michael Jackson could be attending the funeral of Jade Goody according to news reports. During recent visits to London to announce his final tour, the superstar has been in contact with Goody before she died of cervical cancer on Mother's Day. Jackson became acquainted when brother Jermaine appeared together on Celebrity Big Brother in 2007. Michael made Jade very happy during her final days, by calling several times to speak to her and leave messages of support.*

Christian: I'm sorry, I'm gonna ask you this. You're on your deathbed, and the phone rings. 'Yeah, I'll take it.' 'Hi Jamie, it's me Micky Jay, Shamone!' It's just not on. I'm sorry, but God's given me these last few moments to spend wisely with friends and family. 'Hee-hoo!' CLICK!

Jamie: *Sharon Osbourne has complained that her family's history of drug and drink addiction make her unsuitable to host a TV variety show.*

Christian: There are testing kits you can buy for personal home use. Do you know what 'adulteration' is?

Jamie: It's one of those adult party games. And there's a big punchbowl in the middle of the table filled with condoms and you put your car keys in it.

Christian: *'Adulteration' is the intentional tampering with urine. It's a sample by a donor to avoid detection. Whereby someone else passes the water for you. And that's designed to mask or destroy the drug.* You know, you get air fresheners and it just masks the smell. It doesn't make it go away. Because sometimes if you spray it, it still smells of pumps with a hint of peach in it. You need one that actually eats the odour, like odour eaters.

You can also buy on the internet test strips of paper that can detect if your drink has been spiked with a date rape drug which are easily added to flavoured drinks without the victim's knowledge. Most experts prefer the term 'drug facilitated sexual assault.' That's a mouthful, isn't it?

Jamie: Well, quite.

Christian: *The positives of drugs tests. Testing your child will discourage them from taking drugs.* Do you not think you're going to alienate your kid? 'Jamie, it's your weekly drug test.' 'But Dad, I don't do drugs.' 'I've heard the music you listen to, something's not right.' 'Dad, I've got my friends round.' 'They can do one as well. I don't want you knocking about

- 162 -

with potential drug users. Now come on everyone urinate in a test tube and give them to your Dad.'

So, if you're around Jamie's on a Monday, don't. It's when he does his drug test. 'Jamie, you know it's that time of the week. I hope you've drunk something more than a cup of tea.' Anyway, apparently it protects your kids. I'm not sure it protects rather than mentally scars them and destroys any trust you may have ever built up with them.

Employers can drug their employees, not drug them. Sorry. 'Hey, I was alright before dinner. What was in that cheesecake?' Anyway, *employers can drug test their employees. This will help decrease the amount of working days lost per year from drug abuse.* Imagine coming into work Jamie, 'Oh, not again.' It's Monday morning. You've just arrived, and there's your boss. 'Jamie, you were off sick the other day.' 'Well, yeah, I had appendicitis.' 'Yeah, we're kind of thinking it wasn't. Now fill this up.' *The latest data estimates that around 800 million is lost per year because of drug abuse in the workplace.* That was the BBC stats from 2004.

Drug testing in schools. Can they do this? Is this legal? 'Jamie just wee in this tube. Result. I knew he wasn't that daft for no reason.' *Currently, it's estimated that one in five children will have handled drugs by the time they're 13.* That's shocking, isn't it? We should remember, this comes from a website that's trying to sell drug testing kits. Okay, so they're obviously going to try and frightened you a bit. It's called 'marketing.'

A scheme was trailed in Middlesbrough. That's nice, it puts your town on the map Jamie. *If people are arrested for certain crimes, they are forced to take a drug test. If they failed, they are forced to go and see a drug counsellor. In 2004. The scheme was expanded to cover Hartlepool and Stockton.* I spoke too soon. *Refusing this test is a criminal offence.* Go Middlesbrough's mayor. He's like Robocop and he doesn't need oiling, because he's got enough grease to self-lubricate over a lifetime.

There's a prostate test as well you can order on the internet. 'What have you got me for Christmas?' 'A digital rectal examination, which I ordered for you online Grandad.' *It's recommended together with a PSA test to detect prostate problems.*

There are cholesterol tests too. Do you eat lots of cheese? You should eat lots of porridge instead.

Jamie: Replace cheese with porridge? That's crazy. It would put me off cheesecake.

Christian: Someone I work with; his girlfriend dispenses glasses. A mobile optician if you will. And she goes to… you can't really call them 'nut houses' these days. I don't know what the proper name is though, 'loony bin'? Can I say Madhouse?

Jamie: Oh, asylums.

Christian: So, she went there, and this patient sat within a metre of her face getting his eyes tested for new glasses. And he kept saying, 'Pie!' And every time he sounded the 'P' he was literally spitting all over her. That's why we have a spit guard over the microphone in the studio. Saves me from gobbing all over it. 'Pie!' and 'Porridge!', like that. And she was having to dab the spittle from her eyes and face, nodding, 'That's nice.' She knew this guy had issues and tried to hold conversation, or he might just attack her. 'Toast!' He kept shouting these words in a Yorkshire accent. 'Porridge!', 'Toast!', 'Pies!' That's all he kept saying.

She asked, 'Are you hungry?' Which would explain why he kept saying these specific words. Eventually his carer chipped in and said, 'No, that's what he'd had to eat.' Apparently, he'd been saying that all morning. She was curious and asked, 'When did he have his pie?' Because porridge and toast you can easily associate with breakfast, it makes sense. 'When did he have his pie?' Remember she was there visiting early morning. He said, 'Oh, he's looking forward to it.'

And I thought about this as a porridge pie parable. Crazy people sometimes aren't the mad ones. When was the last time you got so excited about what you were going to have for dinner, that you actually shared your saliva with others from the sheer passion? Out of the mouth of babes, and the mentally ill, sometimes comes wisdom, and a fair bit of drool that we can all learn from.

Jamie: Pecan pie sounds nice.

Christian: And sometimes they have nothing to offer.

Why is it taking Jamie so long to make a cup of tea? Do you remember the toilets at school? The hot tap was labelled with a red dot on the top of it. But it was just to trick children into thinking it gave out hot water. I guarantee, if you remember back when you were a child, those taps with the red dot never got hot. I don't think they even went lukewarm. They were just another cold tap. It's true. The teachers didn't trust kids with hot water. And to be fair, I don't know if I should be trusting Jamie with a kettle.

If you would like to win a watch, we're giving
away this watch here I found on the other side of
the mixing desk. It's probably worth a bit. There's
a swanky stainless-steel covering at the back you
could have engraved. It's a nice little watch. It's
even had hour hand moved forward. Jamie's
thought of everything. That's great. I better add,
'This competition is now closed,' just to make sure
no one phones down to claim Jamie's property as a
top prize. Also, Jamie's armed with a hot scalding
cup of tea. I don't fancy that knocked down me
back. Down my front Jamie, scolded nipples if you
do requests.

Speaking of winners. This Saturday Graham Mack
will be opening the newly revamped studio with
equipment donated from his commercial radio
station. Last year I done the Redcar half marathon
and before it started, I met him. And I hadn't meant
to fawn over a local celebrity, but I unashamedly
gushed, 'I listen to you all the time. I think you're
great.' I hadn't listened to him in a while, but he
didn't know that.'

He was handing out individually numbered cards
in an attempt to break a hand shaking world record.
Here's the thing, before a long race like a half
marathon, most of the contestants, certainly the
men runners go for a quick wee before it starts.
And of course, it's out in the open, behind trees
and bushes, so it's a quick shake, and away they
go. No facilities to wash your hands afterwards.
Graham Mack, unbeknownst to him, is shaking the
hands of all these men who've moments earlier
been holding their winkies. I didn't have the heart
to tell him. I'm sure his world record certificate
will be worth the health risks.

Jamie: Next week, we'll be broadcasting in stereo for the first time.

Christian: Can you get me Graham Mack's autograph? I can't be here because I've got things to do.

Jamie: 'Can I have your autograph for a friend, he really wanted to be here to meet you, but he went shopping instead.'

Christian: I don't have time for popping in on a whim. Like Saturday gone? What happened with my dedicated '15 years' service' certificate?

Jamie: I put down your 'apologies for absence'.

Christian: Dedicated, that's me. To my family that is. On Saturday the weather was freezing. We were all on our bikes, which isn't normally an issue. It's all to do with destination with my kids. Should we have been cycling to Toys R Us, no problem, 'It's a bit bracing Dad.' But when they're going to the dentist's, which is quite a distance, all hell breaks loose. Anyway, we bought these pocket heaters that work like magic. You crack them, by snapping this sachet of white gel and you put your hands on it. It's warm. It stays warm for a few hours. You can also buy some beads in a bag that you shake to activate them, and it stays warm for seven hours. Some chemical reaction. Whoever invented them should be millionaires. Don't eat them Jamie, unless you want to warm up your tum. Then you have to jump up and down to activate them. In which case just keep jumping up and down, that'll soon warm you up.

Jamie: I bought a £20 umbrella for the worst weather.

Christian: I remember accusing you ages ago of being a snob, and you got upset. Now you don't care. You go to expensive coffee shops and you buy 20 quid brollies. Normal people's stories, by the way, when they see the price at 20 pounds, they usually put it back. But your story isn't that. 'I saw the highly extortionate price and so I bought it.' It's not really a story is it? It's just you buying a brolly. You could just wear a hat. It'd probably be a bowler. An Earl Grey bowler hat. Mr. quintessentially British aristocrat, Lord Morgan of the shires.

Have you worked out you and your family's escape route if there was a fire in your house? Is it just doors? No little toffee mallet that you can smash the windows with, and jump outside onto a mattress?

Jamie: Below my bedroom is the downstairs extension.

Christian: If you jump on top, wouldn't you fall through the roof, into the kitchen, straight into the fire? Not just go into the fire, but actually feeding it.

The reason I ask is because we have an old mattress in the front garden, and I'm trying to justify why we've kept it there so long. I've now got one of those horrific gardens, all we're missing is loads of dog poo. I keep saying to myself, 'I'll take that down the incinerator soon.' And it just lays there day after day collecting rainwater. We've become the family with a mattress in the front yard.

I don't know how we went from having a nice garden, all looking lovely one day, then saying, 'We need rid of that bed. Let's take it down and we'll put the mattress there on the lawn, because it'll be gone soon. I'll take it to the tip next weekend.' I don't want to even touch the mattress now. It's horrible. I don't want it in my car. If I had to jump from my burning room, I'd aim to miss the rotten thing completely. Be full of slugs and snails now. You probably only had waterproof mattresses as a child Jamie.

Jamie: Mam called them 'shiny covers of protection.'

Christian: Imagine bringing friends back to your house and your bed squeaks. 'Hey, what's that Jamie? Why am I sliding about on your bed? Are they rubber sheets?' 'It's so my Dad can test my urine and make sure it doesn't soak into the mattress before he has chance to get a sample.'

Speaking of shame. Normally I wouldn't tell you this story because it's a little gross, and as Freud says, 'An admission of stupidity.' And as you know, I'm very sensitive to other people's feelings and I don't want to upset anyone, particularly if they're having their tea. Sometimes I spit. I snort it up, then with a cheeky cough and some well-practiced talent since I was a teenager, I gob it out. Completely unpleasant. I don't like to keep it in. A lot of doctors would say. 'There's no problem to swallowing it, you know, it goes into your stomach where it gets digested. It's fine.' I don't like that thought. It's disgusting. I'd rather have a spittoon.

Anyway, I didn't have that luxury on Saturday while riding our bikes. So, I'm heading straight into the wind when I decide to rid my throat of this lung butter. Have you ever thrown something out from your car window, like a cigarette butt, and it flies straight back in because of the wind? There was a little bit of that going on.

Jamie: So, it went smack bang, back into your mouth?

Christian: It wasn't as bad as that. That would have been
                    really impressive. In fact, that would have saved
                    face if I'd have managed to do that. It was like a
                    huge phlegm boa constrictor, that wrapped itself
                    around my face and down my neck. Like a slimy
                    viscous tie hanging down from my chin.

                    Now normally that would have made everyone
                    vomit, but they seemed to think it was quite funny.
                    I was like some sort of phlegm riddled clown.
                    'Dad, what's that on you?' A fluorescent, neon
                    green necklace. A snot dog collar if you will. I had
                    to mop it all up. Lo and behold, people from
                    church are driving over the bridge looking at me.
                    'Ewww!' That's sod's law - has to be.

Jamie: Or you could have used a tissue to cough it into.

Christian: Where would be the shameful story in that?

                    Speaking of coughing up. I managed to track down
                    the guy who I sold my Kylie records to and he's
                    decided to finally pay me. I'd sent him a nasty
                    email saying I'm going to relist them. I opened a
                    dispute with him on eBay. Everyone I work with
                    said I should open the dispute before I relist it,
                    because I would be selling it to someone else
                    which would invalidate the dispute. Confusing.

                    So, I'm chasing them for money, when I looked at
                    some email notifications on my account that I
                    didn't bother checking. He'd previously got in
                    touch with me saying he was finding it difficult to
                    pay for the records and he was gonna pay at the
                    end of the month. Funny the things you don't read
                    hey?

Jamie: Have you relisted it?

Christian: I've paid 22 pence to get it relisted and now I've
                    had to cancel it. No one bid on it though. It was
                    only put up yesterday.

Jamie: I'm going to down vote you now for not reading
                    your e-mails. I'm going to go on to your site and
                    just give you bad feedback.

Christian: You'll be able to see what I bought. You can see
                    my purchasing history and see if I've bought any
                    naughty products. Yeah, home testing kits, types of
                    cream or certain toys. You can click on it and see
                    who's been buying it and read their feedback. You
                    can also see their track record of purchases.
                    Sometimes quite interesting. Germans I find are up
                    for those kinds of products. Lederhosen.

                    I never thought of my Dad as the superstitious
                    type. But he's been sending me these e-mail
                    chains, whereby I have to forward them on in order
                    to keep the good luck going. Needless to say, I
                    delete them immediately. If you receive six replies,
                    you'll get a small GIF animation of a leprechaun
                    shouting at you, 'Good luck!' I'm sorry, but if that
                    makes your day, tough, I'm not passing it back.

Jamie: 'Send this within five minutes and your phone will
                    ring and whatever you wished for will be granted.
                    If you don't send it, the opposite will happen.' So, I
                    wish for everyone in the world to die before hitting
                    delete. Oh, there goes the population boom.

Christian: Very bizarre, isn't it?

Photo Break

Two bald men in a shed   With Graham Mack 04/04/09   Jamie chin-wagging with
With Simon Asker 2021   Official re-opening of Studio A   Graham Mack 04/04/09

Showing off Trinity at 3 months... almost 21 years later   Me & Joanne
                                   (with Nicea)

"Reporting live from Redcar!"   (L-R) Calvary, Emmaus, Cana, Nicea, Trinity

18-year-old me   Cana   Nicea

(Clockwise) Cana, Emmaus,   (L-R) Joanne, Nicea, Trinity
Calvary, Nicea, Trinity)

Me as a thumbnail   Emmaus   Calvary

Kids (L-R) Nicea, Emmaus, Cana, Calvary, Trinity with Nanna & Grandad Anderson

Christian: How are you finding the frosty mornings? I had to scrape the car already.

Jamie: Well, no, because I've got heated windscreens.

Christian: Do you park your car outside? You've got a garage.

Jamie: It's a three-car family. And all three cars are on the drive. The garage is full of stuff that no one bothers with, but no one wants to get rid of it.

Christian: I told you, make a list of things to do before you're 40. One should be to have a stall on Stockton market and flog all your junk. Also kill a bull in a bull fight. Actually, you should run for mayor. The one you've got at the moment isn't doing a good job.

Jamie: I heard. He's blaming Channel 4 for putting Middlesbrough at the top of the 'worst places to live in the UK' list. Shoot the messenger.

Christian: 'The buck stops here.' What's wrong with him saying, 'Hold on a minute. You've shown me a problem. Let's try and fix it.' Instead, he's asking the locals to boycott the TV station. Not sure how that will change the level of problems highlighted in the show. To be fair, I'm not sure how Nottingham wasn't crowned. Did you see it? I watched it on repeat.

Jamie: I watched a little bit. And it said, 'We've got an hour to get to number one.' So, I stopped watching.

Christian: Even though it was broadcast live, people knew
                already because it was in the news who'd won.
                Now this is the beautiful thing. My sister-in-law
                had a party on Linthorpe Road above a restaurant.
                Soon as it started, the presenter said, 'We're here at
                a secret location.' I could see where it was, I'd
                been there only a few months ago. We'd been
                upstairs in that exact place where the camera crew
                were sat. So, if it was live, and I was watching it
                live, I would have had enough time to get into my
                car, go down there and clock her one. That
                wouldn't help Middlesbrough look good though. It
                would just add to the statistics she was already
                quoting about crime.

Jamie: 'Local man clocks TV presenter Kirstie Allsopp.'
                If you can call her that?

Christian: What - 'presenter'?

Jamie: No, 'man.'

Christian: Cheek! I went for a manly run this morning and it
                was so icy that when I returned my neighbours had
                come out from their house and said, 'Hello', by
                this time my mouth had gotten so numb with the
                cold, I waved back and managed to reply, 'Hurgh!'
                I'll do anything to avoid people.

                My neighbour works in the same building as me,
                different company. He was actually standing
                behind me at a reflective vending machine. And I
                could see this guy behind me, and I thought, 'You
                loser,' because there's another vending machine
                right next to this one. 'You're not rushing me' and
                so I took my time. I looked a bit closer, and for a
                moment did think, 'He looks like my neighbour.'
                But what are the odds it was him? I couldn't turn

around because if it wasn't him, it was just a thug standing behind me, waiting to fill me in.

With this false delay, I must have looked worse knowing my neighbour obviously now had the upper hand and he leant into me, 'Hi!' Then I had to give it the old doubletake, even though I guessed that it was him in the reflection. I still had to go, 'Oh, hello there,' instead of going, 'I thought it was you.' Because if that was true, I should have turned around a lot sooner. I can think quickly, I just don't act out any of my plans with any urgency. I'll do anything to avoid people.

And after we'd went through the, 'I didn't know you worked here.' 'Okay, yes, we do.' It was, 'Well, better get back to work.'

Can you park your car on the other side of the street where the sunrise will be earlier in the morning as of next week? Can you do that?

Jamie: I could, but I don't need to because I've got electric heated windows remember?

Christian: Oh, yeah. Let me tell you something even better than heated windscreens, and that's heated chairs. You might be able to relate to this if it's happened recently. You take a pair of pants, these jeans, this very pair of jeans, I got out from the tumble dryer tonight. Joanne said, 'Check to see if they're dry.' So, I put them on, and it was exhilarating to put on a pair of warm pants. Thing is, it doesn't last long. I'm giving it about 10 seconds, maximum, of real joy. Its sheer snugness as it warms your legs as you sit down hoping that it lasts forever. I almost passed them back to Joanne and said, 'Here, put them back in again for another minute.' I liken it to your cups of tea Jamie. Your cups of tea are nice.

By the way, you know when we were talking about 'Location, location, location,' and we perhaps talked down Middlesbrough and the people, well we're allowed to have a go. It's a bit like having a crazy Aunt who needs a slap and someone chips in with, 'Yeah, you're right, she is crazy, and I'll slap her myself.' I'll say, 'Hold on a minute, that's my Auntie you're talking about. You lay one finger on her and you'll know about it.' Just so you understand. It's alright for us to have a pop at Middlesbrough, but it's not a free for all. This is our patch of Britannia, and we love her very much.

Come on Hartlepool, you can get yourselves higher up the list than 20. Again, I went there recently, so I consider her my other alcohol addicted aunt. The one that screams and swears at passing traffic and fights the arresting officers. Speaking of crazy, delusional women, Jamie is still looking for love. There could be someone crazy enough listening who might go on a date with you, provided we can get the straight jacket off.

What would you say are your interest? Do you like walking on the beach, drinking pina coladas and getting caught in the rain?

Jamie:	I do like walks on the beach except for my ankle, it's a bit weak. If it gives way, I'll end up falling flat on my face. I'll leave behind a trail of death masks in the sand.
Christian:	That doesn't sound romantic. But that's my opinion. And I'm not sleeping with you. So, are you looking for sympathy or are you looking for a little bit of love action, keep feeling fascination?
Jamie:	Number two.

Christian: I'm a bad flirter. I realised this recently. As an example, Joanne will say something like, 'Open that can of baby new potatoes.' And I'll say, 'Phwoar, I'll open your can of baby new potatoes.' Or it'll be something like, 'Help me take the rubbish out.' 'Cor! I'll take your rubbish out.' It doesn't make any sense. 'I've got to drop the kids of at school.' 'I'll give you dropping the kids off at school.' Anyone who does that to flirt, it doesn't work. Unless you're Sid James and you add 'Oo, er, missus!' We'll try it during the show. I'll try and flirt with you.

Oh, by the way, speaking of gay people, JK Rowling apparently 'outed' one of her characters, the headmaster Dumbledore from her wizard books as gay. *A prominent gay rights campaigner said, 'Having gay characters in children's literature is good.'* Which is what a gay rights campaigner would say. However, he also added, *'It should be more explicitly revealed in the books.'* Not something I subscribe to, but that's his opinion. I don't think it even needs approaching in a child's book. Let's keep children innocent from adult sexuality. I would say the same about an explicit heterosexual scene. It just seems perverse to me. 'Noddy was terribly naughty hiding Big Ears trunks in the sauna, and as punishment was playfully whipped with the grumpy gnomes warm towel in the Toyland changing rooms.'

Next week is Halloween. How would you kill a vampire? Garlic to trap them in their coffin and then fill it with holy water? Hammer a stake through their heart? Or get a priest to bless a silver bullet and shoot them dead with it? There are your choices, which one are you going for?

Jamie: I'll go for the bullet.

Christian: Yeah, I love the idea of waving a gun under a
                priest's nose saying, 'Here Father, bless this!' I bet
                you he will. He certainly won't dismiss you out of
                hand or call your idea 'silly' once you start waving
                the gun about. Anyway, if you've got a better idea
                of how to kill a vampire, without the use of
                sunlight give us a call.

                The listener could recommend a scary horror
                movie for us to watch. Although no zombie films
                please, they're jokes. And none with special effects
                that are done using plasticine. Have you seen the
                guy in 'Dawn of the dead' who gets the top of his
                head chopped off with a helicopter blade? You can
                tell his forehead is an extra foot high with
                prosthetics, just so he can do the scene. Not that I
                expected the actor to really get his head chopped
                off. But you know, you kind of expect it to be
                almost… I was going to say, 'believable.' Like all
                the dead are coming out of coffins and have come
                to eat and feast on your brain. So not quite
                believable, but at least watchable.

                Have you seen the dolphin that hasn't got a tail?
                They've made it a prosthetic one. They've
                performed marvels on this creature and gave it a
                new lease of life. Now I thought if it was a
                bottlenose dolphin and it needed a new cosmetic
                beak, they could let it swim with a real bottle. You
                know. like a fizzy pop bottle. Keep the lid on it and
                watch it come flying up to the surface. Have you
                ever tried to keep a football under the water? It's
                really difficult to get a football to stay under the
                water, a lot of force is pulling up, and it comes
                bouncing off the water surface. The dolphin would
                have a real challenge trying to jump through hoops
                and catch fish with a recycled snout like that.

It is getting colder; it is October after all. I had a
warm shower. I think it's the first signs of frostbite
when your hands go bright red and the layer of fat
on your tum-tum goes red and itchy. It's worse
taking a hot bath in winter, and you put your hand
in and mistakenly believe it's scolding hot, so you
put in more cold water. Yeah, you put your cold
icy feet into the bathtub, and have to take them
back out again because of the heat, and you
naturally think, 'a bit more cold needs adding.'

Yet as soon as your bottom makes contact with the
water's surface, 'Ooo-hu!' you discover pretty
quickly it's only lukewarm. 'What have I done?
I've been out playing in the snow and now I've
come indoors to get a freezing cold bath.' I blame
your deceitful hands. Once they get numb from the
cold, they really do feel like they're boiling in the
most tepid of waters. I'll give you 'cold bottom'
Jamie.

I didn't realise that when you go fishing you kill
the fish with a 'priest stick.' It's called that because
it's said to give the last rites to the fish. It's literally
a small baseball bat that you take with you when
you wade into the water with your big boots on,
and you beat the life out of the trout before you gut
it. Notice I didn't say, 'batter' the fish. It's the
most humane way to kill the fish. I'm not sure fish
have feelings as they have no central nervous
system. Although they seem to understand they
need water as they gasp and flip about desperately
trying to get back into the pond.

You would think this priest stick must be pretty
special if people are paying good money for them.
Instead, why not just go looking around for a heavy
stick. One you can find and pick up in the woods.

It can't be that difficult. A run of the mill twig to just hit a fish with. As long as it's a bit weighted at one end it'll be perfect. A torch would work just as well. I don't see anything special to these costly ones. We could be giving some weirdos excuses for hanging around forest areas alone. 'I was looking for a heavy stick to cosh my cod, officer.'

Jamie: I'll 'cosh your cod', ooer missus.

Christian: 'But can you explain the lump hammer in your haversack?'

Jamie: 'I'll give you 'lump hammer in your haversack,' sugar.'

Christian: Sounds like you've cracked this bad flirting thing Jamie. Another way to kill a fish would be to throw a big bag of plaster of Paris into the pond. Make your own fish fossils. Wait until it hardens, then chisel the fish out. Apparently in America it's called a fish whacker. They're not keen on labels. Why not shove your fingers under the gills and just pull the other way? What's the difference? The fish ends up dead in both scenarios.

Some people who fish, after taking a photo of their catch, they let the fish go again. Or if it's bitten this little finger on my right. How long can you hold a fish out of water before you need to put it back down again? I can assume it's been too long flapping when you put it back and it just floats on its side. You've got to check your watch. When did you last play that game where you try and stop start your stopwatch? You have to start and stop it as quickly as possible. I get about point one two seconds. Which isn't too bad for a real watch.

Jamie: You'll have to try it on a mobile phone stopwatch.
                School children are taking fish out of ponds all the
                time when they fill jars to see what's in them for
                science lessons.

Christian: You're talking about sticklebacks and dragonfly
                nymphs. I was thinking about record breaking carp.
                Did you see 'The One Show'? They were talking
                about bed bugs. They're not what you think. You
                know, those microscopic potatoes with matchsticks
                in them. They're not bedbugs, they're dust mites.
                Bed bugs are more like nits. And they suck on your
                blood and they can get really big, and you actually
                see them with the naked eye. I'm itching now just
                talking about them. Hopefully we've got none in
                the hospital.

                Do you remember the kid at school who was like
                the Nostradamus of the playground? In the days
                before the internet, he would say things like,
                'They're making three more Star Wars movies.
                They'll be the three episodes before the first
                movie.' No one knew they were going to get made,
                except for George Lucas obviously. 'They're
                making a Home and Away film.' And there was no
                way of asking Jeeves or going to Wiki to see if it
                was true. You had to gather round this loser freak
                in the playground, a self-appointed all-knowing
                oracle of popular culture with no citation needed.
                'In the film Bobby comes back. Alf's not in it.
                Yeah, Donald Fisher's in it. It wouldn't be Home
                and Away without Donald.'

                But anyway, that aside, have you heard they're
                making Coronation Street the movie? Apparently,
                Jack and Vera, they're in it. Gail's not. For a
                moment there you believed me Jamie. And that's
                how kids need no backup at all. Everything is
                matter of fact. It's like they have their own little

production ideas for their wild imaginations. And they had a gullible audience, so they got away with it. I guess it's different nowadays with easy access to check on these facts. 'Gail Platt is so in the movie you liar.' I imagine teenagers would be desperate to know the full casting to 'Coro the movie.'

Some news, *a teenager who had tattooed the word 'Mum' on her lower back, in Chinese letters was horrified to find that it said, 'friend from hell'*

Jamie: Where does your lower back end and your bum begin?

Christian: An important question. Let's see if the article sheds any light into those dark recesses. *The teenager only found out something was wrong when a passing Chinese woman shouted, 'Evil, evil, very bad.' She paid 10 pounds for the tattoo four years ago and has now covered the insult with a leaf design costing 40 pounds. The original tattooist did not know Chinese letters change meaning when they are put together.*

Let's go back to what you said Jamie. Why would a random Chinese woman come along and see her bottom and start shouting, 'You evil woman'? It doesn't make any sense.

Jamie: I'll give you 'doesn't make any sense' evil woman.

Christian: Keeping to the same culture, *a jewelry company in China has made a bra out of more than 2,500 diamonds priced at approximately 650,000 pounds. It was demonstrated by a small model.* Well, it would be. I mean, you don't want to get a bigger cup size, you'd have more diamonds to think about. *The maker said, 'The piece had 100 carat*

diamonds set in 300 grammes of white gold.' You
can see all the security guards protecting it. You
know, when I used to watch the 1960s episodes of
Batman, and there was a jewel that went on display
at the Gotham museum, they always had Batman to
guard it because the commissioner knew the Joker
would be there. So, imagine this little Chinese
woman with her tiny bra on full of diamonds. And
all of a sudden, the Riddler comes in and yoinked
her. 'Oh, me got glabbed by Liddler.'

I picked up a box of some Terry's York Fruits.
They were named after York, the place they were
made in. But it now says, 'Made in Croatia.' Port is
a wine made in Portugal and can not be made
anywhere else because that's where Port comes
from. 'Terry's Croatian Fruits,' doesn't sound as
nice as York. No thanks. See how many they'd sell
to the elderly for Christmas if they try that kind of
rebranding.

My final amazing discovery this week, is a losing
your finger story. The guitarist with Black Sabbath
on his last day of being a metal sheet worker before
going to start his career in the band, he lost his
digits in an accident. And he said, 'Oh, that's me
finished.' But he went and got melted, washing up
liquid tops, and shoved his fingers into them. Then
played the guitar amazingly. I think that's a pretty
cool thing. The drummer from Def Leppard very
similar story. I do like a bit of rock. And I think it
would only be right to play 'Paranoid' to take us
out.

Christian: How long would you listen to a radio station that you knew was just a test card? Just automated continuous output, song after song, looped with jingles?

Jamie: More importantly, how long can you listen to two people chatting continuous? You're sporting a Batman top.

Christian: Well, it's not the new movie one yet. It's one of those 60s ones you know, 'Holy smokes Batman' and all that, before Robin become a sex-comedy actor. The guy who played Robin, Burt Ward, not the superhero in saucy frolics. The Dark Knight, a lot of people are saying it's overrated. But if you admit the film should be certificate 15, and kids should never see it, then stop trying to sell toys to children when it's clearly a movie they should never see.

I think it's brilliant. I got it for Christmas on DVD. Unfortunately, the kids can't watch it all the way through. So, I let them have a look at some scenes where Batman's in it. So, they're watching scenes completely out of context from the rest of the movie just so they could see Batman's car. 'Wow! That looks cool.' 'Oh, anyway, that's enough. Get yourselves off to bed.' 'What happens next Dad? Why did the Joker just kill that man? And why isn't he breathing anymore?'

We were able to watch all of Iron Man with the kids. There's a bit where these refugees are being put against a wall and they're gonna get executed. Now before you start getting your Daily Mail out and telling me how good that would be. This is in their own country okay. And this father's getting taken away from his kids, and so my kids are bouncing about on the settee shouting, 'Come on Iron Man.' And he hasn't even arrived yet. And I don't know whether Iron Man is going to make it in time.

I'm thinking, 'I hope my kids don't get to see this guy get shot' because these kids are crying now on the movie. Iron Man is ages away, the kids are still jumping up and down cheering for Iron Man, you know, like the cavalry is coming. And the baddies are loading their guns and I'm thinking, 'Oh, this isn't good.' But Iron Man is there, and he blasts them. Screams of excitement go up from the settee, and even I'm like, 'Yes! Go Iron Man.' Now any movie where kids are that excited for a good guy to administer justice. And it arrives in the nick of time. And then destroys and lays waste to these evil people, is a good movie by anyone's standards.

I haven't seen a good movie like that since Biff got a good smack from McFly in 'Back to the future.' Unfortunately, Batman can't do that, and he lets down a lot of people in the movie. So, there's a lot of people who you think should get saved. Anyway, it's a good movie. If you've seen it, you'll know exactly what I'm talking about. Although don't rave about Keith Ledger as Jamie calls him. And then you correct him and say, 'Hey, Jamie, he's called Heath Ledger.' Only for his predictable reply, 'Whatever!'

I've been off work with the influenza. It's called Man Flu when others have to run around after you to make sure you're resting up and taking it easy. It's when you couldn't even pick up a biscuit by yourself without someone else doing all the lifting. 'You'll have to stir my tea; I'm feeling all peaky. I'm feeling all peculiar.' I tell you what though,

that was the only thing I done on Saturday, watch
Iron Man. I was sweating all day in bed. That's all
I done for the day. So, I thought, 'Right, well, I'm
not feeling 100% so I'll phone in on Monday and
claim the day back.' Well, you may as well, you'll
only live to regret it. You don't want to be on your
deathbed, even in your hundreds, going, 'Oh, tell
you what, I wish I phoned in sick that day.'
Although with the economy, as it is, I'm sure we'll
all have a lot of time on our hands soon.

Unfortunately, there's lots of good people losing
their jobs. Apparently, they've worked out a very
fair system of who stays and who goes. And we all
think it's to do with the amount of time they've
taken off on the sick over the years. Some of these
people really have been ill though. You know, bits
of foot missing from diabetes, kidney transplants,
cancer diagnosis. And they're getting turfed out.
Again, it's shocking. I think there was a lot of
people also taking voluntary redundancy. You put
your name down for it, and if accepted you get a
lump sum calculated on the years worked there.

They don't turn anyone down because they want to
reduce the headcount. So, they're gone. What I
want to know, are the people leaving through the
voluntary redundancy route having leaving dos?
Because they're happy to be going, they've been
paid out and moving on to greener pastures. So, if
you go to their leaving do and they've combined it
with someone else who was made compulsory
redundant, straightaway you'll appreciate the
added bonus - you've brought your own
entertainment.

'Aww, Claire this is a fantastic party. Good luck on
your first day at your new office. Oh look, there's
Anne, she was pushed. Here, Anne! Entertain me.'

'Who'll employ me at my age?' 'Your funny.' Hey Clare, fab idea on hiring the compulsory clown for your leaving do.' It'll happen to us all; you may as well laugh about it. A bit like death, it happens to the best of us, so treat it with derision, it's the only way it doesn't win. Jamie, what have you been doing this week? Anything good?

Jamie: I've been job looking.

Christian: Why? Not happy with the job you've got? Or are you one of those people at the party in the corner crying?

Jamie: I couldn't even afford to go to my own leaving party.

Christian: You could always go professional with your cups of tea. This one is particularly appreciated. And the cup did not smell of sweat. Imagine if machines could sweat. You know in physics there's these triangular formulas. Well, work itself has got a formula. It's to do with the distance a mass is carried and how much force it takes to move the object. I think calories or joules are the units burnt up doing the work. So maybe, if you applied that formula on machines, like lifts in this hospital, and judging from the people who were leaving as we arrived, then those lifts have had some pretty strenuous work. 'One at a time please!'

If you could speak to lifts in the future. We have this simplistic idea that anything robotic with a microchip you will be able to talk to. So, you'll say to the lift, 'Don't worry, most people will take the stairs because there's only two floors in this building. So, don't worry about having to work too hard.' What a lie. All the heifers and Billy Bunters that can't be bothered to climb say 14 steps, 'Take

the strain!' It's time to go out for the cigarette. It's
a vicious circle isn't it – they're fat because they
don't do any exercise and they're the first to climb
into the lift to reach the first floor. It's got to be a
lot of wear and tear on the poor old lift mechanism.

Although I suppose with compulsory redundancy,
they'll be saving a lot on maintenance to the shaft
of the lift there. That's what they based it on,
people who are using the lift. 'He's using the lift far
too many times, he's out.' And 'Her Body Mass
Index is morbidly obese, she's out.' Hold on a
minute, that's what I would do. I think that's the
friendliest, healthiest and positive thing to decide
on redundancies.

Jamie: Pulling someone into an office and saying, 'Right,
your BMI is extremely horrible. You're out.' Sack
them like Alan Sugar, 'Your fat, you're fired.'
They could complain of constructive dismissal, but
only if they had their interview looking like that.
Had them winched down into the chair.

Christian: Everyone goes on about how bad Bon Jovi are.
Well, I have pretty much all their albums. I don't
think they're that bad. They're one of those bands
you know, they have a few good songs and then all
the rest sound a bit samey. Although really in Bon
Jovi's case if all of them were anything like 'Living
on a prayer' that would be amazing. They peaked
too soon, and then it went downhill slowly.
However, I still like them. They're doing a couple
of gigs in order to raise money for Hillary Clinton,
after she failed in becoming the presidential
Democrat hopeful. Who would you have voted for
Jamie? Obama or McCain?

Jamie: I would have voted on the basis that lots of
celebrities kept saying, 'Vote Obama! Vote

Obama!' So, I would have voted for Hillary. If I'd
heard Bon Jovi preach to me about Hillary, I'd
have probably went Obama. Or neither to be
honest.

Christian: Bon Jovi with 'Last cigarette.' And just for those
people who said, '2009 was their last year of
giving up', remember, don't give up giving up.

Jamie: The thing is for me, to have my last cigarette, I'd
have to have my first one too. I've never smoked.

Christian: Goody-two-shoes Jamie. You're like a powerless
superhero, a boy scout Clark Kent in a pink
kryptonite thong. We were talking about Batman
before, and Joanne made a comment saying the
movie was good. The only thing that she couldn't
believe was billionaire Bruce Wayne would pay
good money for a cockney butler like Michael
Caine. 'Jellied eels.'

Christian Bale when he does Batman sounds gruff,
like he's straining on the toilet. 'Urgh! I'm
Batman!' 'Quick Batman's having a heart attack.'
Alfred the butler played by Michael Caine sounds
almost like, 'Knees up matha' braan.' It doesn't
make sense, you would just say, 'I'm sorry. You're
fired. You have a horrible cockney accent, take
your pearly suits and get back to the east end.'
For a super-rich playboy, you'd think hiring staff
shouldn't be a problem. You just can't get them
these days.

Batman literally is just a spoilt rich guy. If you
were to meet him in real life it would be Richard
Branson, spending his own money on gadgets and
ammunition. What a plonker. He'd launch himself
on a badly designed hand glider, crack a rib and
fall into a flower box, not saving anybody and

trying to make the headlines, smiling during a world disaster. A bit like when the Virgin train crashed, and a granny died. He was the first one to be flown out there to stand in the middle of a field. The only thing he was missing was the costume and utility belt.

Did you see him in the James Bond movie, going through the scanner? It's just sad. And he's in Superman as one of the pilots of the aeroplane. Still not as sad as him being on the news. Mr. Monopoly, 'I think I'll buy a magic bean factory, because I want Virgin brand magic beans.' What a loser. Everyone cites him as the world's most famous entrepreneur. He's just a loser. You heard it here first. Yes, he's very rich, but what else? He's lacking in a lot of other departments, isn't he? He's funny just because he shouldn't be. Anyway. I don't think I'd go and see a superhero movie based on him.

Jamie:

Windsor Castle had released a statement about Harry and what he'd said about his Asian chum, 'It was a friendly term used in context.'

Christian:

Apparently, they called a polo player 'Sooty' and that's a term of endearment as well. It's up to them, if he's happy with it. I'm gonna bring two different politically correct spheres together. Whatever the sexuality of an adult. And I use 'adult' to mean old enough legally to consent, whether or not it's in a loving relationship. They're adults. They're consenting. They have the mental capacity to agree to these things. Whatever the naughty shenanigans behind closed bedroom doors. It's not a TV programme, it's nothing for OFCOM to be complained about. It's behind closed doors. Do what you like. Go for it. I don't care. What's it to me? Why should I care?

So, what's the difference between somebody
calling someone a word that they don't have a
problem with? They're consenting to it. They're
happy with it. What's it to me? Why do I care?
Why should anybody care? All of a sudden, a big,
massive, politically correct nose has gone snooping
up the unpolitically correct backside of people's
private lives. And brown-nosed journalists are
pretending they're the moral arbitrator to the
nations lost way.

Jamie: It's just the 'News of the world' thinking, we've
                  came across this video, let's use it to make sure
                  Harry looks bad.

Christian: Aren't people more bothered that these are
                  parasites on the state, rather than saying a word
                  that no one cared about? I guess if you want the
                  title that goes with royalty then you also should set
                  a better example. I'm an ordinary commoner, so
                  people should expect me to have little to no regard
                  for calling people names. But I don't have breeding
                  like the royals, and when I say 'breeding' I mean
                  inbreeding. There's enough put downs the Asian
                  lad could have said to Harry though. He must have
                  been biting his lip thinking, 'I'd better not say
                  anything about his mam.' In the army that's the
                  kind of gallows humour they sport. It's healthy to
                  just put it out there.

Jamie: You say this like you know.

Christian: I'll tell you, if he dared say anything to me, that's
                  exactly what the line back to him would be. 'Yeah,
                  I might be that, but your mams this. Yeah, go on,
                  disprove it.'

Lemsips. You know when you boil vegetables, and you boil all the goodness out of them? Well, when you make Lemsips, if you pour boiling water straight onto the sachet of medicine, doesn't that damage its constitution? You know, it destroys the vitamins and some of the goodness that's in there. Lemsips are horrible anyway. Can anything good come from a Lemsip?

There's a blackcurrant one I was going to try. I try not to fill the cup all the way up. I don't like a full cup of the stuff. I have to knock it back like a shot of spirit. When it's less diluted it's a lot stronger. Like licking salt from your hand and biting the slice of lemon before necking tequila, but this is the other way round.

Jamie: You can add honey to it.

Christian: I'm sure you can add anything you like to it, lots of sugar for starters. 'The world's fattest man' was on TV on Monday at 10 o'clock. He could try eating Lemsip like sherbet. Lick his stubby finger then stick it in the sachet. That would be a quick lesson in giving up sweets. Remember, always read the label.

After they lose so much weight, they've got all this lose skin, which needs to come off. They look like a disfigured flying squirrel. Nice. What I'd like to do is take them to the top of a tree, then throw them off and see if they can glide safely to a lower branch.

Jamie: A branch of Sainsbury's.

Christian: Have you seen the porker in Mexico who's treated like royalty? He has a Cajun band play every time he leaves the house on his bed. They've got a reenforced four poster bed, that gets winched on a crane that puts him onto a four-by-four truck. And then he goes off for a picnic. As he goes out, he waves to everybody because he's just a big, massive fat person. And everyone comes out to see the local fat guy. He's a tourist attraction. A morbidly obese curiosity. The Cajun band plays music while he's eating spicy chicken wings.

I love the idea that Batman jumps off these buildings like Richard Branson on a hand glider. He could genuinely be a superhero. And no one would suspect the world's fattest person. 'It can't be him, because he's hideous and he sweats at room temperature.' But it is, because you and I know otherwise. Obviously, the lift has to do most of the work to move him up and down the building, 'WHEEZE!' But at night he comes out, gets to the top of the building, and throws himself off. Everyone thinks it's suicide, but it's not, because me and you know, he's got some kind of mask on. 'It's Fatman.' He just opens up his arms where all that loose skin is, because he's lost a few stone in a couple of hours between snacks, and then he glides down and lands, or bounces safely.

Jamie:	How would he save somebody? There's no point in having just a fat guy base jumping from tall buildings. He could glide under somebody falling and protect them inside his flabby bingo wings.
Christian:	Maybe the window cleaner leans over too far and slips. 'Help Fatman!' He gets rescued, 'How can I ever thank you Fatman?' 'I couldn't help but notice your uneaten packed lunch Mr Window Cleaner.' Cajun music plays with end credits, 'All in a day's work for Fatman.'

Now we've all fallen asleep on an arm, only to wake up and experienced pins and needles in a dead arm. Well, a lad I work with fell asleep with both his arms around his head, interlocking to prop his head up while watching TV. He woke up in the middle of the night and couldn't feel either of his arms. So, naturally he starts to panic because he's having a half asleep - half awake moment. And as he's struggling with his arms to make them move, one of them slaps his face, which I'm guessing will help to wake you fully from your sleep.

He dragged his arms down his body without any feeling in them and he's thinking something bad has happened to him like a stroke or some paralysis that he doesn't know about. So now he starts to shout his roommate. But then immediately stops shouting his roommate. The thought occurred that he was very unprotected, unable to fight anybody off. So, he was thinking, 'If I shout for help, they'll quickly realise I'm in such a vulnerable position, they could take advantage of me.'

Obviously, that sounds like he didn't trust his roommate that much. If you've got a really good friend, and you realise that both your arms are paralyzed, you're gonna shout for help. But to stop shouting, because you think they might get up to no good. There are some trust issues that need resolving. 'I think I'd rather wait indefinitely until my arms return to life on the off chance that my roommate might come in and go, 'Hey, you can't move. Let's have some fun.'' That's not a friend.

Jamie: That's a predatory pervert.

Christian: I was thinking possibly rummaging through his wallet. 'This is a job for Fatman.' Anyway, he doesn't go to sleep like that anymore.

When did it happen that we went from calling them Visual Display Units to monitors? At school we were taught they were VDUs. If I said that now it'd be like, 'What?' Anyway, at work the VDUs had a rhombus of light on them. So, instead of tilting their monitor or chairs, they closed the blinds instead. And we're talking about bleak midwinter, when water turns to stone. They close the blinds and you're in perpetual darkness. By the time you arrive in the morning at eight it's still dark, until the time you go home, you're in darkness throughout the working day.

Yet these people are in charge of the blinds at work. They can't be trusted. 'Oh look, there's a bit of sun.' CLICK! SHUT! 'Let's see it. Let's have a bit of sunlight.' 'No, no, we can't have any sunlight in here. There might be a glare on my monitor. Instead, we'll all live in darkness and walk about all bendy boned with rickets. Sunlight helps the body produce much needed vitamin D. Sadly, not while idiots are in charge of the Venetian blinds. They control them just because they sit closest to them. Sometimes even in winter the sun shining through a window is very pleasant and warm. That's how I'd decide on staff redundancies.

Nicea was in the Evening Gazette's top 10 of most bizarre names in Teesside for last year. Trinity made it into the list in 2006 yet our daughter was born in 2000. So obviously, even in 2006 it was a rare name. So probably all my children are in there somewhere.

There's a 16 - 17-year-old lad at work who got a tattoo of a snake coming out of a skulls eye socket with some water around it. And then he said the most bizarre thing while he was talking to a friend

on his mobile saying, 'Oh, yeah, yeah, I wouldn't
just get like a random tattoo.' And I thought, 'What
the hell!' A skull and a snake and a bit of water,
because that means something. Oh, yeah. It's got a
real hidden meaning, you've got a skull, we've all
got a skull. You might have once seen a snake.
And you drink water. I like it. I like the way you
went for the skull snake water motif.

He's gonna have that now for the next 80 years
permanently inked to his arm. I should say he's 18
to cover anybody who's tattooed him illegally. It's
up to his parents anyway to have a go if he's
underage. I said to an older colleague, 'What
would you have tattooed on your arm?' He said, 'A
picture of my wife's breasts, but they'd be all the
way down here.' Oh, how we laugh at work is just
a mere reflection of our real lives.

Ever been in the toilets at work and you thought,
'Urgh! Someone's died?' That was today. I walked
in, 'HOICK!' you sniffed up 'HAY-KK!' and you
know someone's dropped their entire guts in there.
As a sign of respect, everyone should chip in to
buy a communal incense stick just to burn in their
honour as a tribute to their lasting memory.
'Something's died in trap 3, lest we forget.' Like a
purifying vigil for the tormented soul who clearly
had stomach problems.

Jamie: I've had that. Listening to people retch while I'm
                    otherwise occupied. The last time - I was on a bus.

Christian: My five-year-old son went to play at the park when he needed the toilet, so I took him to the side of the field for a number one, before he went back to the park to play. A bit later he needs the toilet again, but this time it's for a number two. I said, 'Calm yourself down. Hold it in, we're going swimming anyway you can use the toilets when we get there.' We're making our way to the car when he makes these 'Uurrr' noises. I take his pants down then and there it's like a swiss roll just fell out of his bottom onto the car park.

Then he went, 'What am I going to do?', because obviously he needed wiping, you know, a bit sloppy. Considering he's only five, even he had the common sense to put his hands in his pocket pulling his trousers further forward, walking like Charlie Chaplin. Hey, I don't know, kids these days. Who'd have them? Speaking of which, will I be here next week? It's the ninth of May, it's the due date. Joanne always goes over though, about two weeks. I'll just do the show and she can call down to the studio from her bedside.

I got 1 hour 43 and 5 seconds in the Redcar half marathon. I don't know if you listen to local radio on a morning, but there's a presenter Graham Mack who hosts the breakfast Show. During my moment with him space and time broke down into small molecules in my body, and all adult dignity evaporated.

Jamie: He's not even a minor celebrity.

Christian: Anyway, there I was in a high-pitched voice, 'Hey Graham, I listen to you every morning. I think you're great.' Joanne probably not wanting to look me in the face at this point said, 'I think your race is going to start.' And I was still looking back to see where Graham had gone wondering, 'What's he up to?' Imagining what it must be like to have a real job in radio.

Jamie: How old are you?

Christian: Never give up on your dream Jamie. I do it for my teenage self. Me and him have invested too much in this already. Also, today I was at Castle Eden Walkway, and the guy that does the planetarium shows was locking up the visitor centre by the back door. I'd came in through the back and lifted the gate handle with a sign that said, 'wet paint.' As I lifted the gate an alarm went off and I thought, 'What have I done?' But it was just a wooden gate.

                Anyway, it was him, and as he came out, I said, 'I don't usually get an opportunity to say this, but you do some really good shows at the planetarium.' A bit of an icebreaker kind of thing. And I thought that was gonna be it.

Jamie: Did he give you a personal tour of the planetarium?

Christian: Oh yeah, wish he had, that would have been cool. No, I just wanted to acknowledge his work, 'I enjoy the shows. You have the audience in the palm of your hand. You do a good presentation.' That kind of thing. You say that to someone who doesn't get a lot of feedback at best, they hang around. He was a bit like, 'I was gonna lock up and head home, but someone here wants to massage my ego. I think I'll stay.' No, that's terrible. I'm belittling the exchange, even for comic value, because anyone who knows him, will know that's not what would have happened. He's a really nice guy. And if I could recommend the planetarium, as you know, I've recommended it so many times already, it's brilliant.

We had a nerdy conversation. He's telling me, 'Go on Google, and type in this application so you can go around the solar system.' And you just know he's more into it than me. And I felt like I needed to act more interested in it than I actually was. Have you ever had to do that Jamie?

Jamie: Yeah, your radio show.

Christian: Thanks Jamie. It could have been worse. I could have been wearing my National Geographic jacket, Lord of the Rings T-shirt reading a Spider Man comic outside the Planetarium. I was conscious ever since meeting Graham Mack, it's what helped me in that situation. And I managed not to gush all my feelings of admiration onto him like sugar coated vomit. I managed to keep it a level above.

Jamie: Congratulations. That's quite an achievement.

Christian: It would be wrong for me not to talk all over the ending to that song Jamie, 'Goodbye stranger' by Supertramp. By the way I got sent an e-mail from 'Essential radio skills.' It's one of the saddest things ever. I was about to delete it as spam, which is what it truly is. They targeted our email addresses here at the studio. It's really awful. If you require their services to make a show, you really shouldn't consider radio as your thing.

Having said that I think someone at the local BBC radio subscribes to it. *And this week, people are mainly talking about…* I should read this in my cheesiest DJ voice. *'Headlines - tell us all about the global credit crisis. What are you doing to cut back? Shopping bills are up, petrol prices are up, council tax, utility bills are all going up.'* Boring. *'Joe Calzaghe, should he retire now?'* Because good radio is mentioning a sport start that's not very good. 'Should they retire now?' Not sure who this Joe character is anyway. I'll say, 'No he shouldn't.' There that was top radio.

'This is moan day - not Monday. Get it off your chest. What are you not looking forward to today? Lots of kids go back to school today after the Easter break.' More of a statement, not really a talking point. *'The weather - four seasons in one day.'* There's not even a question mark there. *'Samuel L Jackson on those Virgin Media ads. Why is he doing those? Other topics. If you had a remote control for your life, what unpleasant event would you fast forward?'*

Jamie:	Reading this.
Christian:	We can easily have dull conversation without paying someone to write it. What's your favourite trilogy of movies?
Jamie:	Now, 'Back to the future' I think was excellent. Because it just was.
Christian:	Have you seen the kids that Professor Brown has, you know, when he introduces them, 'This is Jules, and this is Verne.' Something is wrong with Verne. Actually, I don't think Jules is all there either. Do you think they were just kids of the producer? 'Put my kid in the film.' 'But he's ugly.' 'Make him a star. Just like you did with Macaulay Culkin.' I think it's a touch further than ugly on those two. That could be the strapline to our show.

But really, it's an awful idea though, isn't it? The bits of scrap paper you write your radio show on, imagine trying to sell it to people? Random pointless conversations that don't go anywhere and have no educational value. Jamie, have you ever switched shift from an early to a late?

Jamie:

I have yeah. I've started work, and it's been short staffed so I've continued to work what should have been an eight-hour shift, turns into a 12-hour shift.

Christian:

I probably didn't explain myself. I mean, you're going from one day finishing early. You leave at around three. Next day, you're in and you're on a late shift and you finish at say eight or something. The worst thing for me is I get used to working the early shift all week, then all of a sudden, I'll be covering the late shift on Friday. And I'll arrive at work, but my body hasn't understood I've just got in. I'll be sat at lunch time thinking it'll be home time soon. But of course, that's no longer my perk of this particular shift. I'll watch the early shift go home and impending doom sets in, knowing I still have half a shift left to do. Have you ever had these conversations with security guards?

Jamie:

No, I just walk straight past them.

Christian:

Now there's a lesson in time management. Don't get me wrong, I appreciate them and they're great guys. But there's nothing worse, and there's always one, not all security guards are like this, but there is a type of security guard that bores the hell out of everybody. And that's the one who enjoys talking about his shifts. Doesn't matter what you're talking about, a quick reference to the rain outside as you scurry on by, 'It wasn't like this on Sunday when I was covering for Johnny. That's my second Sunday now. Still, I suppose Santa will be coming to my house this year. Worked the extra overnight shift because Paul was off ill after eating the curry I made him. Only managed to be at home for six hours before I was back here again this morning. And I'll have it all to do again tomorrow. I'm fed up of this place.'

They brag about their service yet slide in how much they dislike their job all at the same time. I guess that qualifies them for some kind of medal. Like the company cat who only gets put out at night. One of them left because he wanted to chase shoplifters instead of sleeping and raising the barrier every few hours. He said he'd had a calling in life. And this was to wrestle thieves to the ground for stealing selections of cold meat slices. He went to work in Hartlepool, so it probably wasn't real slices of meat, just a processed packet of offal with a disclaimer, 'may contain traces of other animal by-product.'

Jamie:	Same as those little muesli bars you gave me a few years ago that had omega three in, and it tasted of fish. They were a bit nasty.
Christian:	On the BBC website they had an article asking, 'What constitutes pornography? And when does it become illegal?' I think it was R Kelly related. And I said, 'I'd need to take a quick look at it, and I'd know the answer to both questions. I really didn't have a lot to say about it. If somebody owns something that I think is against human decency, then they probably need locking up. You'll have to employ your imagination here dear listener. Just suffice it to say if it's bordering on the abnormal or the unearthly then arrest them. But then people in the office argued with me about it being subjective. Let me share a great social skills tip here, for anyone who's gonna argue to defend sick perverts

and their collection of filth. Keep it to yourself.
Otherwise, people like me will forever think you're
also capable of being a monster. People are a bit
judgmental like that.

If I'm brutally honest, if I had thought it was quite
acceptable, I'd still have kept it to myself. 'Ban it!
Ban it!' SECRET STASH! SECRET STASH!
Why would I let everyone know my moral
standards are lower than an MPs? Some people
don't know how to go about their business without
informing others of their twisted tastes.

See that guy in Austria? Fritzl, he looks a bit like
Vincent Price. He kept his daughter in a dungeon
for 24 years. It's beyond disgusting. On a red top
tabloid, it stated he'd attacked his granddaughter.
The media keep throwing out these sick detail's
half expecting us to pick up the paper and go,
'He's crossed the line there.' We know what he's
done. Thanks for pushing it out further. Are there
still people unconvinced at how truly evil this guy
is? 'When he was 12, he kicked a puppy.' 'That's
it. He's taken the biscuit now. Something must be
done.' Sounds like a capital offence.

Jamie: I can see you as an executioner. You wouldn't
                wear a mask. The condemned would see you smile.

Christian: You know 'Popstars,' where everyone gets the
                opportunity to be a pop star, you could have
                'Hangman Idol.' All the contestants come in, and
                there's Simon Cowell, and some horrible criminal
                that you get to hang in front of him. NOOSE!
                PULL! TIGHT! And then Simon goes, 'Now I
                think you done that wrong. There was not enough
                passion in the knot making. The drop was too
                short. Not enough struggling.' And then you get
                somebody who comes in and hangs about10 Nazi

war criminals all in a row. 'Well, Mr Pierrpeoint it looks like you're through to the next round.' Like he did at the end of the war, but without the applause. 'That's nice, excellent, you owned the stage. Topped 10 Nazis all in one go! Beautiful work.' And the Hangstar judge is right of course, roping up crims is a dying art. I think it's a skill we can all master though. You bring me people like Fritzl and I'll master it. Bring me R Kelly and you can quite literally combine the pop star aspect with Hangman Idol.

I have an apple that wasn't vegetarian this week. A maggot was inside it. But that wasn't the worst discovery of the week. It was on my return to work all the e-mails that had gathered for me during my holidays. You realise how pointless your life is. E-mails that are rubbish. And that's your life. You don't notice it during the day when you're at work. But if you let them build up and then click on them all at once, it's very depressing.

Jamie:	'Has anyone seen a pair of glasses? I left them in the toilets.'
Christian:	Also on my computer I had a cleanup wizard pop up saying he's detected some unused icons on my desktop. I don't know if I need them or not. The cheeky wizard is telling me which applications I don't seem to use very often. It might be only once a year that I need it, but it's still mine. I know where it is, thanks Mr. Wizard. But the best nerdy discovery this week when it comes to technology was to do with the elections in London. I know you like Boris Johnson, but I can't suffer him.

It's gonna dawn on him, he's actually got work to do now. I wouldn't wish Boris on London, it's suffered enough over the years, but then again, the opposition Mayor candidate was just as bad, if not worse. David Cameron was at Tory HQ watching the results come in on the webcam, but it didn't say, 'webcam,' it said, 'web cam-eron.' Did you see what they'd done? The web Cameron, and it follows our David. That alone should cost them the general election, if not, then their policies.

You know the clear tube plastic canes that have got Smarties in them? Usually at the fun fair with candy floss. Well, my son thinks they're walking sticks for women, ladies walking sticks. If that were true, what is stopping us from taking real walking sticks, hollowing them out, and fitting Smarties in them, or chocolate buttons. Top idea. You've got grown men walking up into the hills, obviously not Robin Cook. I suppose he could have replaced his Smarties with heart medicine. And you'll never be too far from a tasty lifesaving snack.

R Kelly knows about pimp sticks, it's taking a walking cane and encrusting it in diamonds. If these rap artists used these small chocolate canes you get from Skegness, they'd have a natural hunched expression which they seem to favour in their videos, along with penguin tailcoats. And when they get aggressive towards the police, if they strike out at the officer, he'll be more than happy to have a chocolate bean fly out into his mouth rather than a nasty chrome polished cobra head.

I'm pretty sure I told this story before on air about someone falling on top of a helium canister, it inflated their leg like Tom the cat can blow up his own fist to hit Jerry. I can't remember when they got self-inflated, it's lost in the midst of time.

Jamie: Is it possible?

Christian: It must be, I vaguely recall. Our skin is like a
                sausage isn't it? Imagine your leg as a big
                Lincolnshire, it would swell up if a helium
                cannister nozzle was inserted under the casing.
                People get fat and it stretches their skin so I
                imagine it can happen. Helium, or for that matter
                any gas, is dangerous to be inflated in the skin
                especially if it gets inside your blood. Strangely
                there's a danger to breathing it to make your voice
                change. You don't want it in your lungs.

Jamie: My Dad was doing it at your wedding.

Christian: Well, I hope you got parental and told him it was
                dangerous.

Jamie: You must be fun at parties.

Christian: A friend got accused of bringing her Dad to a party
                once, meaning me. I would have been 15 at the
                time. They were doing the old condom over the
                head trick, and I said, 'You're being stupid.' You
                take the condom, stretch it over the head and below
                the nose, then you inflate it using your nostrils
                from air taken in through your mouth.

Jamie: You didn't con-dome their behaviour.

Christian: I'll overlook that pun, which was quite good. It
                takes a lot for me to lose my inhibition of common
                sense. And who wants to smell of spermicidal jelly
                and rubber latex for the rest of the night? Hands
                down Jamie. It was a party I was invited to, so it
                wasn't going to ever get used for anything else.

                *A priest who took off with hundreds of helium filled
                party balloons has gone missing off the coast of*

Brazil. He was reported missing eight hours later. The 41-year-old priest Adelir Antonio de Carli wanted to break a 19 hour record for the longest period aloft with balloons. Strange, he wants to break a record for 19 hours and he gets reported missing after only eight. Did they not think there's still another 11 hours left to go before he was clearly missing? *He's wanting to raise money for a spiritual rest stop for truckers.* Obviously because that's what truck drivers need most. I tried to find an update on this, but I couldn't, so God willing he arrives back home safe sometime soon.

'We have absolute confidence he will be found alive and well floating somewhere in the ocean.' That's a very tragic story, but you can't help but wonder, 'Jamie, you're always looking to do a little bit for this radio station. Get yourself some sponsorship. In fact, I will put down a full five pounds if you do that. Play to your skills, sitting down all day and doing nothing.'

Jamie: Lots of helium balloons would be expensive.

Christian: Actually, hydrogen balloons for you. They're explosive. Take a pellet gun and start popping them off, by the time you get down to the last few it would have brought you down in time for tea.

The priest had the common sense to wear a helmet. I used to wonder why I didn't have one over the years, as a child we didn't have helmets. Sure, they're safe, but if you cycle through a colony of Mayflies, they only live for one day, SWAT! SPLAT! You don't realise it, but eventually these insects eventually cover all your clothing. And when you've got your bike hat on. They've got those little grooves; little holes and the flies go through them. Then you can feel them crawling around on your head, but you can't scratch them because you've got to take your hat off first. You keep whacking the helmet until eventually for your own sanity you have to take it off and dust them all off your scalp. Horrible, horrible.

I want to invent or develop a cage. It would have to be made from very, very lightweight materials, so I can tether a few hundred birds of prey like an eagle or a falcon so it can't move unless I allow it. How many of them would I need to lift the cage with me sat underneath it in a little swing seat? The seat would be just a leather belt, the lighter the better. And all those birds of prey flap and lift me up. Imagine during the middle ages when we were still trying to develop flight, when the rich knew all about falconry. The falcons were trained to go off and get them small birds for their dinner.

I calculate with my weight, and my not so small ass slung into a leather loop, training one hundred birds, each attached to this wooden grid, and through metal rings to keep them all facing the same way, all flapping their wings together, will lift me up and fly me over some trees. I'll be like some medieval monk, in part because of my hair style, but also my commanding authority of the skies.

Jamie:	You'd have to be one of those monks who fasts for most of the time because you'll have to be exceptionally light. I don't think you can afford eagles and falcons, but we could tie a thousand pigeons and crows to a stick through some hooks.
Christian:	Okay, in my current state, perhaps we get a smaller person like a jockey.

Jamie: Technically you're a disc jockey, but you'd still
                  need to have your legs and arms amputated to
                  weigh a bit less.

Christian: How would I be able to get airborne with no arms?
                  I'd need at least one to whip the birds into flight.
                  It's how Father Christmas gets his reindeer to fly.

Jamie: Yee-haa! Yee-haa! You could deliver Easter eggs
                  to all the children of the world from the birds
                  carrying you.

Christian: And to celebrate, people could put up decorations
                  of me in their households at Easter, a bald one-
                  armed DJ torso guy brandishing a whip.

Jamie: Covered in bird poo and feathers.

Christian: Since Frank Whittle invented the jet engine, we
                  seem to have lost this drive for employing birds to
                  conquer the air. Did you see they're going to install
                  urinals on aeroplanes? Now that sounds like a
                  smelly bad idea. So, you're no longer sitting on a
                  toilet anymore, sat down squatting. The plane hits
                  turbulence while you're up against the urinal.
                  There's going to be spillage. There's an
                  understanding economy class, having to put up
                  with the stench from your slow drying trousers all
                  the way from Nairobi to Heathrow. Just have an
                  inflatable paddling pool on the floor and be done
                  with it.

                  Speaking of pools, somebody said Michael
                  Barrymore would make a good James Bond. I said,
                  'I don't see it.' He said, 'He always wears a
                  tuxedo,' Alwight! 'B for Bond, B for Barrymore.'
                  P – double-O – L. The only person who'd go and
                  watch it would be Stuart Lubbock's Dad. He
                  follows him everywhere hoping to uncover the

truth of what happened to his son through constant intimidation. And more power to him, but he's actually more like a groupie than a threating reminder for justice. A paid member of the audience with front row tickets. 'Would you like to come back to a party after the show? Why not? Your son did.' Perhaps a good James Bond villain.

A US woman has been arrested after chasing her boyfriend with a knife, thinking he was an actor in a porn movie. I think that's a compliment. You see the way I'm thinking here? It's alright looking a bit like him facially. She's sat there and thought, 'That looks like my boyfriend.' Now if me and the wife were for want of an evening watching some Frankie Vaughan, and Joanne went, 'Here Christian that looks a bit like you.' And then two minutes into the scene, 'Ah! It's not.' Straight away from her abilities of deduction she knows it's not me, even though we facially may look alike. The comparisons stop there. But this crazy woman after a while into the movie still thought it was her boyfriend. That's a compliment, because they don't let anyone into these skin flicks. So, I've been told.

The victim said, 'She suddenly snapped and went at me with a knife. She almost shanked me.' Sorry, was that not part of the evening's plans? *'She stabbed me in the face,' the victim told the 911 operator.* That doesn't sound terribly romantic. *And the dispatcher told the victim to keep running.* That's pretty good advice. 'Keep running.' I could do that job.

Jamie: Your US translation would have gotten the guy killed. 'She tried to shank me.' You'd be telling him to quit complaining the lucky devil.

Christian: Somebody once said, 'If you could get someone to play the role of Jamie Morgan in his life biopic, who would it be on the silver screen?' It's Dan Walton, here to fill his boots. Jamie's on holiday, he's gone to Grimsby. Grimsby in November does not scream out, 'holiday destination.' Although I came close when I went to Skegness during the last week of October.

Dan: Well, that's alright then. I'm sure that fortnight makes all the difference.

Christian: I used to use November as the month I went on holiday because it's always cheaper. And of course, I used to take the kids out of school, but now there's this big Hoo-ha about it. When they get into secondary school, I get it, it's important. But in primary school, they're little. They're gonna learn more by going out and spending family time together and doing different things. They only play in the sand pit, drink milk, and colour in at school anyway. And that's my fully informed opinion as a professional parent, and I'm entitled to it.

November a very cold month as the air temperature starts to drop dramatically. We've been a few times to Centre Parks in November. Whatever the local one is up near Carlisle. Always beautiful. And at this time of the year, they're preparing it for Christmas. So, there's a lot of cars going to and fro, in what should be a quite idyllic woodland retreat, you know, the hammering of nails into doors trying to put up wreaths.

It's a bit cheeky that they treat the cheap week customers as having to put up with all the surrounding work, as if it's why the costs are lower. Obviously when it gets to Christmas, that's when the sales go up again, and when they clearly try and keep the noise and traffic to a minimum. Of course, I wouldn't know, I can barely afford cheap week. You do manage to experience an outdoor swimming pool in Britain in winter. Something I guess was more common in the 1950s seaside resorts which had public lidos. I can stay in the cold water like a hippo with only my nostril poking out so long as my bottom is pushed up against the warm jets at the side of the pool. It's the getting back out that kills.

Dan: We used to have a lido in Hartlepool, but the great storm of 1953 destroyed it. We still have a child's paddling pool at the Headland which is ideal on a sunny day.

Christian: But would you have a dip in it in November Dan, if I sponsored you a quid for the radio station?

Dan: You haven't got a prayer in hell's chance of that ever happening. Even for cheap week.

Christian: You could always have a dip in the actual brine. The lido is next to the sea itself, isn't it? Although it's one of those areas that receive bad beach ratings.

Dan: I think it's unfair because it relies upon the people around the beach on how much they are polluted. It's not actually the beach, let's face it, a lot of these things are manmade problems.

Christian: But we still need to make an informed decision if I'm going to skinny dip because you've sponsored me 10p, I don't want to be standing on a discarded needle or a used condom. And of course you're right, these are manmade problems but it still needs fixing. We spend a lot of our tax money to have litter picked up. So why is it so polluted with litter? How many community hours are we owed back from all these lazy unemployable grifters in society? I never see them going around in chain-gangs like you see in America. Why don't we ever see them picking up the litter, paying back into the community and helping the place?

Dan: Because they're sat in a pub.

Christian: It feels like you've just sunk straight into Jamie's plimsolls. And I think you fit them very well. And that is exactly what I was thinking. They must be off somewhere else. Do you remember the guy who had a number one hit back in 96? Boo-yeah! What was he called? Boo-yeah! Mark Morrison. He got sentenced to community hours and sent a lookalike in his place to do it. He'd been threatening to use a cattle prod on people.

Let's be honest, a cattle prod sounds awesome. If you were a superhero and you wore a costume, very probably tight fitting, snug and obviously made from latex, and your weapon was a cattle prod, what would you get up to? You're going to go into a crowded area, because you don't want people to easily notice the guy in spandex zapping them. If you 'cattle prod' someone, does the person touching another person also get pronged with electricity? I assume it travels through them as well. You know, like a taser would. If you're in a romantic clinch and a policeman tasered your wife, would you feel the voltage as well? Would you go, 'Argh!' then tell your wife off for ever involving you in her nefarious activities? Could be a case of mistaken identity. You know what the police are like. Just ask Mark Morrison. Boo-yeah!

Dan:	In which case I'd be telling her off for hugging me. Divorce would be a bit harsh.

Christian:	I watched a fascinating NASA video of somebody on the international space station negatively charging a knitting needle by rubbing it with paper, then spraying it with water. And the water was positively charged, so the tiny water droplets orbit the needle. And you see it in slow motion as it goes around, more like a helter-skelter motion than a perfect orbit. And eventually it loses its energy and sticks to the needle. Anyway, it's pretty fascinating to see.

	Now if there's any physicists that might be listening, answer me this, gold, which has existed since the universe began, and came to Earth from outer space 4 billion years ago, when does the electrons inside eventually stop spinning around the nucleus? What's the law of physics that says it should slow down? I mean, even the Earth will one day stop spinning around the Sun, or be swallowed by the Sun. Is the mechanics inside an atom perpetual? Does the electron spin forever?

Dan:	Maybe they are slowing down. Where are they going to find readings from 4 billion years ago?

Christian:	I was watching a Looney Tunes cartoon. Can you do a Sylvester voice? You just put your tongue to the back of your teeth and start talking. It actually sounds closer to Jamie than the deth-picable cat. I didn't know this but cats every few months need to be dewormed because they can get intestinal worms, I guess through the meat they eat. And the medicine clears them up from these parasitic worms, roundworms and tapeworms. I just thought it's always Sylvester trying to eat Tweety Pie, but what if Tweety Pie was trying to eat the filarial worms that were coming out of Sylvester? And then of course the Granny will come in and start whacking Tweetie Pie with her umbrella handle. It's a nice twist, isn't it? Because all the kids are expecting Sylvester to get the usual drubbing from granny, but instead it's Tweetie Pie, that'd be great. And of course, the Grandma really should blame herself because she should have gotten the cat dewormed. I actually have a dog worm story but it's unpalatable even for this radio show. Now I think about it, I should have posted a photo and tagged you in it, but it would have been flagged as inappropriate content, which it was, but dog dirt blights us all, so why not on social media as well?

I was speaking to a guy at work, and he said, 'More dads need to get involved with their children at 'mother and toddler' level.' He's telling me he's watching these kids who are emerging as fresh new bullies, and bullies need smacking. I appreciate the irony in that statement, but they really do need a good hiding. And bullies start off from a very early age when they get away with their uncontrolled anger, especially if their parents aren't perceptive enough to notice that their precious little darling is actually naughty and demonic.

And let me be clear I don't mean naughty in a boisterous playful manner, knocking over a drink by accident, helping another child colour in a picture that wasn't called for. I'm talking about push, shove, take, kick, bite, yeah. Anyway, this guy from work watched as his son kept getting pushed constantly by another kid. And he looked over and he could see his mam, a big woman, watching it happen and not saying a word. Now this guy is small. He looks like a little Hobbit. And he told me he felt his stomach churning inside, but he knew he had to go over and say something because his son was shouting over, 'Dad what's going on?' And shrugging his shoulders not knowing why he kept getting pushed and not allowed to play with the football.

So, he went over and said, 'Is that your kid?' And she replies, 'Yeah.' He said, 'Well, can you kindly go over and stop him from doing that to my son? Because obviously he's not getting to play football, because he keeps getting pushed over.' And she went over and sorted it out. You were expecting her to be the antagonist in that story, but she wasn't. Don't get me wrong, he did think, 'You've seen that happening and done nothing until I came over to say something.' She sat there waiting for her bullying child to be named and shamed before she took action.

And I just thought, more dads are needed in situations like that, because speaking from experience, that story resonated with me. Men will choose confrontation quite quickly, usually in a civilized way. Whereas women try and avoid confrontation. I'm not saying they're not civilized. They're a lot more civilized than men. But women in general don't like confrontation, they'd much rather look the other way and hope it goes away. It's easier than having to tell them off. I mean no one likes to get told off, especially when you're criticizing their parental skills, and women are more empathetic to other mothers. The whole resolution takes much longer to achieve,

Men are like, 'Look Dan, stop belching, it stinks.' 'Alright, fair enough. I'm glad you told me.' Men are a bit more like that. From a young age as well, when they get into fights with each other. They can be the best friend the next day. With women, it's different politically, it's a certain click. It's different for men. They can have a go at each other, and then move on very quickly. And that's what I'm talking about here. I think if men attended more 'mother and toddler' groups, when this kind of thing happens, when kids are getting pushed and poked and prodded and shoved and unshared, the dads will just go. 'Oi! Sort out your young 'un.'

Dan:

I've been there done that, on Halloween morning. I took my child to mother and toddler. So, what happened is a child decided to swing other children around by their arms and legs while his parents were sat right behind me. You'd have to be completely blind not to have seen. And then he went for Matthew who's two and a half. He's a toddler, you know, this child was sort of four or five years old. I stood up and said to these crooks behind me, 'Do you want to do something about your son swinging my son by his leg?' And they just looked. I said, 'Well, you're not gonna do much stood there. I've just told you what's going on. And you're sat there as if you don't understand English. Do you need a good shake or something?' Yeah, it was just unbelievable. So she did get up and sort of disciplined him. And she said, 'Oh, I'm sorry, he's quite hyperactive,' or he'd been diagnosed with something. This is the problem, isn't it? You don't truly know whether it's a genuine reason.

Christian:

The truth or not, she needs to be more perceptive if her child is more prone to doing these things, she should be aware and watchful of other children around him. It's not the first time that would have happened. She was aware of it.

Dan:

Definitely. And the first time she didn't even get up. And she was sat with another woman, possibly her sister, happy to just ignore it.

Christian: Some are happy to sit there and gas to each other, play on their mobile phones and let the kids just do whatever they like.

Dan: But you know what, having said that…

Christian: You feel guilty?

Dan: I don't know. Slightly I do. There're external factors that you don't necessarily think about at the time. And when you do think about them you think, 'Oh, actually, you know, what if I was in that position, and I had a child that was quite difficult with learning problems.'

Christian: Bring back Jamie. He stands by what he says. Usually, 'Kill them all.' That's what we were trying to discuss, the difference between men and women, and you're becoming a bit of a woman Dan. You're trying to get inside the mindset of a woman, seeing if maybe there's other factors at play here, whereas a man doesn't think like that. We just want to sort people's horrid kids out as quickly as possible so all the children, even the naughty ones, can get back to playing happily together again.

Dan: No, I agree, but I think there's a difference between sorting a kid out and being fair. Because if you're not objective about these things you won't have the support from the other parents, which you might need if it turns ugly. And these hopeless parents don't need much turning.

Christian: I see. You don't want to come across as common? If you continue on your thoughts of understanding it'll boil down to one factor, feral parents haven't the education to raise children. Or themselves.

They're going to tax us as of October 5th for using carrier bags. That's going to be a new stealth tax. But if it stops the litter, although my solution was easier, wasn't it? Get everyone out of prison and get them to pick it up. And I don't mean everybody in prison. Not murderers. Just the people who don't want to work, get them hard at it.

Dan: Yeah, well, I don't know. I think this is stereotyping.

Christian: Oh, no, I don't mind stereotyping. It moves the plot along quicker. Why try to describe someone's character, when really all's you're meaning to say is, 'They're from that ilk.'

Dan: I know what you mean. And there will be people listening, saying, 'Hang on a minute. This guy's totally assuming that everybody who's unemployed doesn't go out looking for work.'

Christian: I'm not. I'm on your side. I know what you're saying. I agree with you. I've been unemployed and treated terribly by the job centre. But they didn't treat the other people that badly. I went there to search for jobs. I'd looked in the local newspapers, I'd been on the internet, I'd sent out CV's to different agencies. And I went presentable to sign a 'back to work' contract. They asked me how far was I willing to travel? What was the expected salary I was looking for? Then they completely knocked that figure down and extended the geographical range of where I was searching for work. And yet there was a lad in the queue with his hands down the front of his pants, paint on his clothes, stinking of body odour, and they just got him to sign on. They didn't give him any grief.

That's why I know there are people out there that we can stereotype because I've seen it. And I've experienced it. Those work-shy cretins can be out there picking up litter. And you were right to ask me, so now I can be justified when I stereotype people, because they exist. He was swearing his cap off while he was in the queue. He didn't even wait too long before they brought him straight to the front. He never had to jump through hoops. They couldn't be bothered with the hassle or a mouthful of verbal abuse.

Dan: You know what, that's a credit to you. They obviously thought that you were employable, and he wasn't.

Christian: The customer service I got from them was pretty deplorable. Also, while we're having this conversation, I'll put this out there, I told them I'd been offered a job. I said, 'I start in two weeks' time.' They said, 'Okay, then you no longer sign on.' I said, 'No, but I start in two weeks' time.' They said, 'Oh, well, you can get yourself an emergency loan.' 'What? No, I don't start until two weeks.' They said, 'Yes, you can get an emergency loan that you pay back.' Well, this is incredible. So, there's no benefit in telling them the truth. I may as well have just kept saying I'm unemployed until the start date and then terminated my signing off. It was absolutely unbelievable. I'm not saying you should do this, but if you're in a situation that's going to make you rely on handouts for two weeks. Just be aware.

Dan: It sort of incentivizes people to defraud.

Christian: I've got a family friend who works in a special needs school? Actually, more difficult children than children with difficulties. Those that have socially maladjusted issues. And they seem to know the entire benefits system. They know what forms they need to fill out. They know what their parents claim for them. They know that if they say they wet the bed, they get extra money for laundry, if they have asthma they claim extra in welfare. They play the system and know how best to exploit anything and everything that they perceive as 'their money.' They genuinely believe they're born to this cushy life of entitlement. They feel as if they're owed other people's money, a free house, health care, and top up the claim with another baby. Trust me, I haven't just stereotyped a whole class of people. They exist.

Dan: I am that woman at the mother and toddler, it's easier pretending not to look at the dregs of society pushing over the hard-working taxpayers, because it's too depressing to admit to.

Christian: Speaking of people who you might have thought didn't exist, this was in the newspaper. I haven't seen the TV documentary called 'Me and my sex doll.' It's basically these men in love with a realistic mannequin. They carry around these dolls with them, and they're not actual height size, which looks even more dodgy. These realistic silicon love dolls sell upwards of 1000 pounds and can reach 33,000 pounds for specialist models. I guess that's pushed you out of the market Dan? Don't dismiss the price just yet Danny boy. There's more than one way to deworm a cat.

Now I work with about nine other lads and I think if we all chip in, and possibly bring in Dan to this sex doll syndicate, then we're looking at no more than a hundred quid each. Alright, then we can knock up a rota and pencil in some dates, and then if you want every second Wednesday.

Dan: Oh man, you are sick.

Christian: Think of it as a comfort pillow, that just so happens
                to be shaped like a lady. Yeah, that sounds fairly
                innocent. I'll have it on the Thursday then if that
                helps. We don't want her to be spreading diseases
                around our little team. Germs could gather in the
                crack of her mouth. I imagine.

                If somebody said, 'We've made a Dan doll,' would
                you endorse it? You know, maybe just appear on
                the front of the box, grinning with your thumbs up?
                Official merchandise, like a George Foreman grill,
                where it's just a picture of you on the front with
                your signature? 'Inflatable Dan' as heard on
                hospital radio. Would you buy it?

Dan: I'm sure I wouldn't.

Christian: People use mannequins to drive in car share lanes,
                if you've got more than one person in the car, you
                can use the share lane. Roadside cameras won't
                distinguish between a real person and an inflatable
                doll. That would be my excuse. 'What are you
                doing with the lady?' 'Well officer, it's second
                Tuesday, she's my date. I wanted to avoid the bus
                lane.' They could use her as a breathalyser, by
                deflating a bit of air into their testing equipment to
                see if I'm over the limit. 'We'll be taking this doll
                as evidence Mr Frank. You can collect her
                tomorrow at the station. No, make that the day
                after tomorrow. We want to make sure we don't
                record any false positives.'

                How can people not realize they are dolls and not
                real people? Have you ever watched a Jeremy Kyle
                show where they've got someone like Chris who
                has a secret? Then this guy comes out and

immediately you know his secret. How could you not know? The entire audience has just watched Chris walk across the stage in the same certain biological manner a woman walks. It's in the hips. They've walked like a lady. Within the first minute we've worked out Chris wasn't born a fella.

He's dressed in his suit. You can see the eyebrows don't go down and slope over. There's no Adam's apple, the neckline is very feminine. The hands are delicate, the voice is soft. 'I'm Chris, and I'm here today to tell my girlfriend my secret.' The audience are more gob smacked that Chris actually thinks it's a secret. Even Mr Kyle wonders if it's worth reading from the autocue, 'Chris used to be Christine.'

Dan:

There's a gentleman who wears long flowery dresses. Okay, I have to say this right. There's two of them. There's one that makes an effort to look like a woman, but then there's this other bloke, who doesn't really dress up at all. He wears men's shorts and random flowery stuff as well. I don't want to criticise him, but he has no dress sense. Literally.

Christian:

I think that would be a barrier for me changing sex. I have no style. I would need a lady, not only to be understanding of my needs and wants, but she would also have to dress me. I wouldn't know how to blend in. As a fella, you get away with a lot. You just wear whatever you like, and no one cares. As a woman, you can't just throw on anything otherwise you get accused of looking frumpy. I'd be called the scruffy, dirty, smelly, bearded, jeans and T-shirt wearing woman. How long do you have to live as a woman before you can go under the knife? Is it about a year or more?

Dan:
I actually know somebody of that persuasion, who cancelled their NHS operation. This counsellor who I know said, the reason why he decided to cancel was because his father beat him up quite badly when he was younger and that had affected him in many ways. Even how he identified.

Christian:
Quite a serious issue for my show. I didn't realise psychologically domestic violence could damage your sexuality as well. I always take the opinion that people are born a certain way and that's just the way they are, but as you say maybe if you go through enough environmental trauma, I don't know.

Dan:
Women I've spoken to at work who've been in an abusive relationship have decided to turn lesbian.

Christian:
What women are queuing up to tell you this?

Dan:
We talk about it in a group thing. It's in our team brief time.

Christian:
I have meetings daily and I've never heard any gossip like that. What a strange work environment. I guess it's not gossip, its people's lives and it's true to them. Do they expect something out of you in return? You know, 'I've just told you my secret, now I want to know something about you.' Do you make stuff up? I think it's maybe worth bearing in mind that should you ever get given a massive slice of gossip like that again, always be prepared to back up your corner with, 'Oh, yeah, that happened to me too.'

Dan:
People are very open at work, in terms of what their backgrounds are. I don't know why that came up. There's a lot on my team who are openly lesbian.

Christian: So now what will you tell them Dan?

Dan: 'Oh, yeah, that happened to me too.'

Christian: Perfect. If we live to about 200 years old, do you think that there's a part of Dan that might think, 'You know what, I'm a bit bored now being a fella.' You might get to 150 and think, 'I might as well spend the next 50 years seeing the world through my wife's eyes.' It could be your own birthday present you give yourself. You just don't know. No one knows what life will be like if we live to be over 200. There'll be a whole new host of diseases that we'll be dying from. You'll start getting different symptoms and maybe the only cure is to swap sexes.

Dan: In a hundred years' time I'll remind you. The doctor can use the same knife you used for slicing up the birthday cake. 'Happy birthday Granny-dad!'

Christian: I'd rather die. I enjoy being a Dad too much. I got a big surprise at the parents evening this week that Calvary was doing a lot better than I thought which was nice. It was great because at baby school, there was a lot of feedback along the lines of, 'He does this, he should be doing that. He's not concentrating, he fidgets a lot. He needs to stop doing that.' Now, all of a sudden, it seems he's turned around a lot. And so that really is good.

                  The problem I have now is where he isn't using his ruler. It brought back a lot of memories of my own childhood when I looked at the pictures of his science laboratory experiments that he'd done. There's the Bunsen burner and the thistle funnel above the tripod. And Calvary had obviously thought, 'I'm pretty good at free hand. So, I'll not be needing the ruler.' He just started drawing it, almost without taking the pencil off the paper, and it was awful. It truly was awful. As a kid, do you genuinely think you're getting away with that?

We used to have a piece of dark lined white paper that would slide beneath the page you were writing on. It's like tracing where the line should be, so all the sentences are aligned nice and neatly, but magically without any lines. I think somewhere in his psyche, he thought to himself, 'Yeah, I don't need rulers. I'm already great at that. Move aside da Vinci.' Pretty much every teacher was saying he lacks presentation skills.

You don't realise just how many points you lose when a teacher can't see the answer because it's such a mess. Even if the answer is there, it's not for the teacher to be struggling to find it. I don't think I'd be the kind of teacher to find a hidden genius or the next prodigy. I would just simply give up, 'Nah! It's awful. Fail.' Even if they'd answered the question correctly, I'm not sieving through it. That's why I wouldn't be a good teacher. And I'm also quite strict.

To listen to me you'd think, 'Really?' But I'm not the strict Dad that I should be. I know. I know it's true my Poppet because I'll get home after being at work all day, and Joanne's set some boundaries for them, which is, maybe they've lost the PlayStation or the TV. And then Dad comes in. Dad hasn't seen them all day and wants to be their mate. And they'll come and play me off against Mam. 'Dad, can we put the telly on?' Straightaway, I don't know what's happened, I say, 'Yeah, that's fine.' They know they've been told not to put it back on. And then Mam will say, 'Why's the TV on?' 'Oh, Dad said we could.'

No one told me that I wasn't allowed to. So, now
I'm getting it in the neck. And I don't really know
why, but having said that, sometimes, yes, I know.
True story. Joanne will leave the house and say,
'Whatever you do, don't let them on the
PlayStation.' And I'll nod in agreement. Back in
the house I'll shout out, 'Is the PlayStation still
on?' You heard your Mam.' And then as I watch
Mam get in the car and leave, I lock the door and
whisper, just in case she can still hear me, she's
good at things like that, 'As long as you're quiet
you can have your games back on.' I'm negotiating
with them. As long as they're quiet, or they've
eaten all their food, or got ready for bed and
brushed their teeth. The list goes on. But I'm a fool
because they're never quiet and they always cause
trouble.

I asked them, maybe 10 minutes before Mam gets
back home, 'Mam's going to be home soon, can we
turn the PlayStation off now just so Dad doesn't
get into trouble?' 'Yeah, yeah. In a minute Dad. In
a minute.' And I always get rumbled. Joanne opens
the door and goes, 'Why are they on that? I told
them not to go on that.' I'm my own worst enemy.

Trusting them was my first mistake, and believing
they'd ever listen was another. I really ought to
support her more, I know that. But I'm terrible. I
crumble. That's what we should get told at parents
evening, not what the kids are doing, but what we
can do to improve as parents. Parenting is
something you mostly learn through your own
childhood. There's no exam on it so we get a bit of
imposter syndrome with the responsibility.

Dan: There's no one book for parenting is there?

Christian: That sounds like a cliché.

Dan: It's true, isn't it? Every child is different. Nobody's wired the same. And you know, what might work for one child might not work for another one. And it is all a learning experience.

Christian: Well, Calvary done PE and he had a pair of trainers that he lost. He said they were at the top of his bag and fell out. So, I told him he had to go and get them back. Many days past, and he didn't bring them home. Then after even more days he brought home a shoe. He eventually brought a shoe back home. I asked him, 'Where's the other?' 'I don't know. I'll go look for it.' Where would you go looking for a shoe that's been missing for weeks?

Anyway, I wrote an email to the headmaster. This wasn't done slyly, I told him, I showed him. I said, 'Look, I'm sending an email to your headmaster to tell him that if you can't do PE on Friday, it's because you've lost your shoes at school. Maybe they've even been stolen from out of your locker. We just don't know, because I'm getting half a story.' I actually instructed the headmaster, 'if you wish to discipline him, because he has no respect for his personal property, then by all means please do so.'

People at work said, 'Why are you expecting the headmaster to do your job? Why don't you punish him yourself?' I was lost for words, but now I wish I'd have come back, you know, like Ed Miliband tweeting Myleene Klass, a day later with a 'pure and simple' jibe? I would have said, 'Well there's no manual on being a good Dad is there?' You see how it sounds cliched? I don't think I'm gonna get away with that. I'll try it next time Joanne's about to crush me for disobedience. 'Remember dearest, there's no comprehensive unabridged book on parenting, so how can I be getting it wrong?'

Dan: And you know what, there never will. As long as you learn by your mistakes, because everybody makes mistakes. And that's the way you learn.

Christian: Teachers make a few mistakes. If a child does something wrong, like let's say Calvary didn't bring his shoes home. They don't blast him for being irresponsible, they'll have an assembly where the headmaster will address all the pupils, 'From now on, if anybody is caught carrying around their trainers, when they should be in their locker, you can expect a detention.' And all the kids in the assembly hall know who it's about. 'This is your fault we're here Calvary. Why doesn't Sir just speak to him?'

I suppose it gets kids used to the real world of adult management. Have you had the meeting where someone at work has done something like spat in the coffee or something, and instead of getting grabbed because they know who done it by examining CCTV, they instead get everyone together and say, 'This isn't about anyone in particular, but to the person who keeps urinating in the drinks machine, please stop.' Look, you know who it is, sort them out. Why is everyone getting tarred with the same brush? Have the cojones to stand by what you need to say. That's what I would do. I would single that one person out at the meeting and make it fairly obvious that it's them. Name and shame exactly like you would at the mother and toddlers. Nip it in the bud immediately.

Dan: I think the problem is that teachers face in this day and age, and I sort of blame society in a way for going too far the other way, they've got this thing now where you can't use any sort of real discipline as a teacher because you're suddenly a child abuser if you raise your voice. And I think that's ludicrous.

Christian: Speak English Dan. On a scale of 1 to 10, having the Queen as a 10, where are you on that scale? I just mean how you speak.

Dan: It depends on what situation I'm in.

Christian: Let's say you're standing in the docks accused of outraging public decency having been caught with this doll. It wasn't your allocated night, so another lad from the syndicate reported you. How would you plead? In English, not in a foreign language, so God himself could understand. Or would you try and get let off that way? 'Oh no, me no understand. Me no speaky Engleesh.' I'm there to judge your English. If you can give me some eloquent English I'll let you off, because that's the kind of judge I am. Yeah, because I'm gonna think you must be one of us, a public school boy.

Dan: Not guilty your Honour.

Christian: That's a 10 out of 10 old girl. Your English was rather spiffing. Not a pleb accent detected, what oh. Do you think I could borrow the dishy doll on Friday old bean sprout?

Dan: No, not at all. She needs me.

Christian: Judges are all up to that. I imagine they'll have money to buy the 30,000-pound model.

Dan: Stereotyping?

Christian: When Jamie does it, we call it casual racism. Don't pretend to be new here. You made an appearance

on my show a while back. And now you're wishing
you never popped your head in and went, 'Hello.'

Dan: I think that was the show somebody came down
                into the studio and thought you and Jamie were
                getting married.

Christian: We do have a lot of sexual chemistry. I'm
                wondering if the listeners gave much thought to
                which roles we would play. I assume Jamie would
                be the lady in our relationship. I'm just curious.
                The world is changing rapidly socially, sometimes
                for the better, and we should try and get in on the
                market for progressive wedding carts? You know,
                for same sex or interracial marriages. It's
                happening all over the world. Don't resist it, get on
                board. We could be in on ground floor.

                I imagine right, here me out, a white and a black
                get married, and they get sent a generic wedding
                card of two lovebirds on a perch, or a cartoon man
                and woman characters. How about black guy,
                white woman, on the wedding cake. And we
                charge an extra tenner because obviously, there's
                not that many out there. So, we exploit this
                situation while it's still a 'minority' thing. I'm not
                saying we should do it at a reasonable cost. It's
                good business sense, and we'll look good because
                when the couple open up the Christian and Dan
                tailor made card, and go, 'Wow, you found a card
                like this one for only10 quid! What a bargain. I
                can't wait to tell all my friends and family.'

                It's going to play tunes as well. Gay friendly disco
                pop and ethnic world sounds for hippies. I could
                base most of it on my own record collection of 80s
                synth. When you open them up you get a quick
                blast of high energy electro cheese. That'll be extra
                of course. I'm not made of whale noises and Euro

beats. We can really go to town on it though. We could have like, Chinese lady with white guy. Asian lady with white guy, old white guy. Yeah, really old white guy. Real bespoken products, like big British woman and Turkish waiter. Splatter their photo on the side of a cheap sponge cake from Iceland and jack up the price to a round fifty. All this is happening, and we could be making a financial killing. They'd pay the price for our services if they loved each other enough. That could be our guilt tripping strapline. Which is definitely our marketing angle.

Slightly topical and related is this interesting news article I got on my knowledge reference sheet, which I mention as we don't have access to the internet. I still like to get access to the facts. *New York Court of Appeals unanimously ruled Tuesday that uncles and nieces can legally marry in the state.* You thought it was going to be somewhere deep down south, like Green Tree, Alabama. "And that's all you can do with shrimp." *New York, which considered such marriages acceptable until 1893 apparently has joined Rhode Island in permitting them today. Judge Robert Smith*, not the lead singer of The Cure, *wrote in the ruling, 'I'm very happy for my clients.'*

This is their lawyer, now see if you agree with what he's saying, I think he's just making stuff up. He says, '*While laws prohibiting parent child and brother sister marriages are grounded in the almost universal horror, which is why such marriages are viewed, there is no comparable strong objection to uncle niece marriages.'* Really? I think there is. I think you haven't asked me. It makes me feel a little bit queasy, a bit 'Ewww! A bit of vomit came up in my mouth kind of thing.

When did you last have a good burp? Because I went out for a curry the other night. I had a prawn starter, I had chicken tikka masala, pilau rice. I didn't have any naan bread because I had chips. A lot of carbohydrates there. When I went home, I burped and it came up, you know, I could still taste the prawn. I could taste my starter. How good a starter must that have been if I could still accurately identify its taste after the curry?

I'm getting lost in saying all this. Let me get back to my reference sheet, '*People don't object with their uncle*,' which I assume therefore he's okay with nephew and auntie relations as well. '*For example, it really was the equivalent of cousins marrying which has been allowed in New York State for well over 100 years.*' As well as in the royal family in England. 'Yes, Yes, he is my cousin and I'm speaking a10 out of 10 in English.'

I remember getting bullied at school because I said that about cousin marriages, and someone actually said, 'My mum and dad are cousins.' And I don't know if he'd said that because he wanted to hit me, or he'd done that because he was defending the pride of his inbred family. I don't know what it was. I'm not upsetting you am I Dan? You've not got any webbed fingers or anything? Can you believe this is his other excuse? He says, '*As people are more mobile and living longer,*' this is going back to what I said, if you live long enough, you might try it. '*People are living longer, marriages are ending, and people are remarrying, and you get blended families, stepchildren, half children.*'

Family Law expert Michael Stutman told The Post, 'Following the same reasoning and given that same sex marriage as being legal in the Empire

State since 2011. This finding would appear to clear the way for uncle nephew or auntie niece nuptials as well. And I don't know if this is food for thought but New York has now given immigrants in America who want to stay a new option, marry a close relative.' That would make our wedding cards business too diverse, even for me. Surely, the genetic pool must throw out some mutated genes in New York? We should be repulsed from going with close family. Biologically we don't find them attractive, making us go elsewhere and help move ourselves forward in evolutionary terms.

Dan: Well, actually, if you're fancying your aunt or your uncle, get yourself that doll instead. You'll be doing society a huge favour. Doll marriage is less genetically irresponsible. The amount of children born with disability and birth conditions caused by close blooded parents is nothing close to shocking.

I remember watching Jerry Springer a number of years ago, and there was this chap on the show, and he said, 'Jerry I found the most beautiful person in my life. I fell in love and I want to get married.' And anyway, true to form, what came out was a horse with a wedding veil on. Of course, naturally as you would expect if it's going to get married. And he was kissing this horse, 'Oh darling, I can't believe I haven't seen you for hours. You look so good.'

Christian: Are they paid to do that?

Dan: No, no no, that's the problem. Sadly, if only they were, because why would you go on stage and marry a horse? Why would you? Even for a show?

Christian: We asked challenging questions. I mean, we want all the leading thinkers out there on these questions. What kind of sickness have you lied about so you wouldn't have to go to work? And I do remember being off sick. When as a kid, British TV has changed hugely. Now there's actual things to watch during the day if you're a kid. Back in our day, it was like schools and colleges. I remember being off for a week during my full five years of secondary school and I was actually sick, and I remember lying downstairs on the sofa watching schools and colleges thinking, 'This is rubbish.' Even then I knew it wasn't worth staying home for.

But they've changed now and of course you get kids cartoons throughout the day. Why would they broadcast during the day if they know kids should be in school? Is it for the unemployed who want to watch cartoons? I would probably rather watch Tweety Pie, seeing if he can get a filarial worm out of Sylvester's anus, rather than watching Jeremy Kyle. 'Whath's thith wurm hanging out between my legths?' Yeah, that's him.

I walked in Guisborough the other day and I didn't know this, but they do this in America, if you're a real estate agent or a realtor, they have a photo of themselves on the sign alongside their phone number. So there'd be a photo of Dan saying, 'Call me to buy your next house.' And I think the better looking the person is on that signpost, the more commission you can make. People are attracted to good looks whether subconsciously or consciously.

I think if you're fairly good looking, then that's the kind of career for you. If you were being honest, and I turned up in an interview and said, 'Oh, Dan, can I be a real estate agent? I've got the intelligence for it. I know all about the necessary property laws involved. I'm all right speaking to people and showing them around houses.' Would you say,

'Just hold it there ugly.' You know what I mean? 'You're not going to earn anything looking like a welder's bench. Go away.' I mean, that's not going to help me, and certainly not my self-confidence which will take a nosedive, but at least you've been honest and like you said, 'Honesty is the best policy.' I now know I'm not going to make a living out of it. I can move on to something else where my looks will be less of a contributing factor to the overall success of the business.

People have changed to become a little bit more conscious of looks these days. We're collectively a bit more shallow, a bit more materialistic. I'm the first to admit it. If I'm being shown around the house, it's quite palatial, it's quite nice, it's within my budget, and then I look at the real estate agent and they're a bit of a pig, I'm going to have to not live there, aren't I? I'm going to say, 'You know what, I can't go through with this house sale.'

Then all of a sudden, Dan comes in and seals the deal. You know, you say, 'Christian can I borrow you for a second?' 'Oh, sorry, I've just got to go and speak with my colleague Dan, I won't keep you a minute just have a look around and see what you think.' And then Dan says, 'Christian just go stand outside in the garden and pretend to be a gargoyle,' and then you go in and seal the deal with a firm handshake and a smoldering grin. I mean you've nicked my commission. I want to know statistically, does the person with their photo on the 'for sale' sign do better financially than the monstrosities in life?

Dan: Probably not. I think if you like somewhere enough, then you're only going to deal with that person for a number of times.

Christian: No, because I've said to the prospective buyers, out loud, 'I'll make sure I pop in and see you quite often.'

Dan: But you couldn't realistically do that unless you become their stalker.

Christian: 'You're a good-looking couple, and interracial I see. Have you seen my brand of greetings cards?' I would probably unnerve them. I'm just making them uncomfortable now. That's what it is.

Dan: Yeah, ever so slightly.

Christian: So, you're saying ugly people make just as much money in real estate as anyone else? We think so. We don't know. If we were a double dip, Dan and Christian estate agents, I'm going to sit at the office and take the calls while you field them out in the houses. I think probably they're more likely to take a shine to you rather than them thinking, 'What's Quasimodo got in his bag?'

Dan: What was Jamie's casual racism?

Christian: Oh, he basically mistook some Asian students for cleaners. It was a genuine mistake because there are Asian cleaning staff at the college he works at. I mean, for God's sake, the lad hasn't a racist bone in his body. But sometimes we can all say things based on stereotypes. I've produced weekly radio shows on it for years. There are even accusations now about Band Aid's song promoting negative stereotypes about Africa with poverty and disease. You can never win with some people.

My daughter is learning about famous speeches. She was tasked to name three important speeches from history, and then focus on one of them. Nine days after September the 11th, on the 20th, George W. Bush addressed the American public to unite the country in grief. That's an amazing speech. I said, 'Are you doing that?' She says, 'I'm not doing that.' Then she looked at the Beatitudes, the Sermon on the Mount by Jesus Christ, which is hugely important to Western history. I asked her, 'Are you going to concentrate on that?' 'No, no, I'm not going to do that.'

Do you know why? Because they're too long. She had a look at how long they are. So, she's doing Queen Elizabeth the first when she was at Tilbury speaking to the troops before they destroy the Spanish Armada. It's quite short. You know, it's like a two-minute thing. She won't tell the teacher why she really picked this one, 'It's not because it's the most inspiring, but I had a look at all the others. They were too long. I wanted to get this over and done with.'

Photo Break

(L-R) Calvary, Cana, Emmaus, Trinity (back) Nicea (front)

Calvary, Trinity, Cana

Calvary & Cana

Me & Trinity

Nanna with (Great Gran) Nanna Parkes

Emmaus & Nicea

Clockwise (Trinity, Calvary, Cana, Nicea, Emmaus)   Joanne teaching Nicea to ride

Nicea proving she has another coat   Emmaus & Calvary in matching Spiderman tops

Joanne with her niece Mollie   Auntie Jean surrounded by our love

Christian:	I'll start the show with an Oscar Wilde quote: '*I think it's very healthy to spend time alone. You need to know how to be alone and not be defined by another person.*' Which got me thinking, after last week's solo show, are you an introvert or an extrovert?
Jamie:	Oh, I don't know. Because I don't like people, I'm gonna go for an introvert.
Christian:	I'm with you. The entire office all went, 'That's a lie.' I said, 'No, you're basing it on shyness, which is a wrong factor when measuring introversion. I can quite happily get in front of this microphone with lots of people listening. I just don't want to be in the crowd meeting them. Big difference.
Jamie:	I like meeting people, I just wouldn't do it voluntary.
Christian:	I'm an innie, you're an outie. I got into Joanne's car and Olly Murs was up to level eight on the CD player volume. What level do you have Olly Murs on Jamie?
Jamie:	Zero.
Christian:	Yeah, wise choice. Don't pick at your scab Jamie.
Jamie:	Scabs don't picket. They go back to work.
Christian:	The teachers that don't go on strike are obviously scabs. Would you want a scab teaching your child? They're going to teach them all the wrong things.
Jamie:	I'm a scab because I went into work, because I'm not losing a day's pay. I disagree with it anyway. A

bit like doing this show. I cross the picket line of my moral compass every week. Except last week when I tumbled off my bike, hence the scabs. You done alright presenting on your own by the way.

Christian: Well, you weren't there to interrupt. We're like an old horrible married couple. Sexless but married. By the way, just so you know, Jamie off air said, 'I've got one small bit of criticism about last week's show - the energy. When you started off you started bouncing and got too happy too quickly.'

Jamie: After about an hour I thought, 'Ah, this is Christian he's calmed down. He's not hyper anymore.

Christian: I am on medication. I've got a throat problem. The doctor doesn't know what it is. He just gave me more penicillin. So that's where I am at the moment.

Jamie: I was with you in spirit.

Christian: I'm glad we're celebrating in fellowship together. I will let you wash my feet. No, no, no, I think you know, if it's good enough for our Lord, it's good enough for you. Wait till you see my bunions.

Jamie: Well, speaking of hurt. My car cost 590 quid to pass its MOT.

Christian: My car cost me 500 pound in total to buy. That's a lot of money. Do you think they know that we don't know, and so they exploit us? They can smell our lack of mechanics even on the phone. Okay, I'll be the mechanic. You just be you. 'Hello Mr. Morgan. We're gonna charge you an arbitrary figure of 590 pound.'

Jamie: Bargain.

Christian: You want to know what's wrong with your car
                first.

Jamie: Okay, well, hang on then. What's wrong with my
                car?

Christian: It's to do with the pumps.

Jamie: What? Can you be more specific? I've got Google
                here; I'm going to type in what you tell me.

Christian: That's what we need to start doing. We're getting
                taken for a ride.

Jamie: Actually, they've got my ride.

Christian: I seem to hear white noise when they explain the
                cost breakdown, 'This bracket needed replacing. A
                new valve had to be adjusted on the old piston.'
                Whereas I think the mechanics when they're in the
                middle of fixing your car, they all go off to
                Subway, and say, 'Right who's paying for these
                spicy meatball footlongs?' 'Mr Morgan. Just throw
                it all on his final receipt.'

Jamie: I'm taking it back to the garage because they do
                really good work on it. I said to them, 'Even
                though we're going to be living in Sunderland, I'll
                still bring it in to be serviced.'

Christian: You're banging on the microphone; we didn't miss
                that last week. So, you're going to travel miles and
                miles down the A19 just to get ripped off?

Jamie: He did say, 'Oh, we'll give you even more of a
                discount.' Because I do get a discount.

Christian: £590 is with a discount? Crikey! How much would it have been if it wasn't for the discount?

Jamie: Possibly looking at around a grand.

Christian: Okay, I'm going to be the mechanic again. 'So, you're saying it actually cost, with labour and parts £590 to the nearest penny? Oh, here he comes now, Mr. Morgan the cost to repair your car was over 1000 pounds. But I'm doing it for you for only £590. You won't find fairer than me.'

Jamie: There is another shop I used to take it to that would have charged a lot more.

Christian: We'll cover that story next week. Now I was thinking about discounts. Imagine you go to the tattooist, who also does piercings as well. Obviously, you're gonna get an Albert ring through your…

Jamie: Where?

Christian: Through your Prince Albert.

Jamie: Oh, that Prince Albert.

Christian: Is there another one you know of? We've mentioned these things before on the radio and it's been said, 'Is Christian maybe curious on the sexuality front?' And you've said to me, 'You're just comfortable in your own skin.' So, let me push that boat out a little further. You're talking to a friend, and your friend says he's going to get a gentleman piercing, and you've already got one. It's like having an arm tattoo. If you said, 'I'm thinking about getting a swastika.' And I say, 'Well, I've got a crucifix here, why not have a look at that and see if you like the tattooists needle skills first before you go ahead with it.'

Jamie: Oh, you mean show and tell?

Christian: Yeah, just saying, 'Well look, this is what it'll look like.' ZIP! Would that be morally wrong?

Jamie: It would be in the street.

Christian: So, if there was ever in context, a mate not even in jest, just flipping it out, would that be acceptable? You know, it'd be like, 'Oh, do you remember when Jamie took out his tackle in front of you?' 'I don't remember that, I recall he was trying to help me decide on what piercing to get.' You usually get a taster of the tattoo artists work, showing what it will look like in the front of the parlour window. So, your swastika could get photographed and put in the front window.

What I want to know, do they have a book with pictures of unmentionable piercings kept in a file that's left out on display on a coffee table inside the parlour? Do you go, 'Hold on a minute, let's have a quick look at these happy customers. I'm thinking about getting…' I was going to pretend to lick my finger there to turn the page. You definitely wouldn't want to be doing that. But would you start going through it and go, 'Hey, is this you Jamie?' Because surely the tattooist needs to build up his portfolio, and the best way to do that is to get willing customers to agree to be photographed.

Not many people would be willing to say, 'Have a picture of this.' But if he said, 'Here, if I put that bolt through the end of that, I'll give you a 20% discount off the price if you let me take a Polaroid.' And of course, you've probably got to know him a little bit while he's been down there doing his job. You may feel quite alright with it. As long as your face isn't in it. You don't want a full-on selfie. You just want the bit of the torso that people will want to see.

Jamie: The bottom of your gut.

Christian: 'Can you lift your stomach please Mr. Morgan, there's too much shadow?' I love the idea that Jamie's done this, yet he won't admit it on radio, and he still claims to be an introvert. Jamie, they don't call it being an introvert when you're doing it by yourself. That would be like saying Michael Hutchence was an introvert, behind closed door. It's great that we can still laugh at the death of Rock and Roll stars.

Jamie: Kurt Cobain next week.

Christian: I said 'stars.' There was a question I wanted to ask you. Say you're in a sex change clinic and you're sat next to Ringo. He's a good litmus test celebrity, you know, everyone loves him. So, imagine the doctor buzzes over the tannoy, 'Mrs Ringo, room three.' When you leave that waiting room, would you feel obliged to go phone a tabloid newspaper and give them a scoop?

Jamie: Max Clifford, Jamie Morgan speaking here. Guess which Beatle I've been sat next to in the sex change clinic?

Christian: Would you not want anonymity?

Jamie: They'll need my details for the £2000 I'll want for my story.

Christian: Why is it you're quite happy to have your name splashed onto these things? Have you no shame? 'An undisclosed source said', that's what I would do. 'No, I want my name printed if it's all in the same paragraph has Ringo's.' But my question isn't, 'Would you do it?' Because I knew you would, considering how shallow you are. My question was, 'Would you not be in breach of patient confidentiality?' Or is that only between the doctor and the patient?

When I go into a waiting room you sometimes see people who you know, then later on, you might bump into them at church, and they go, 'Ah, Christian, I seen you at the GUM clinic, has everything cleared up?' I'd be mortified, especially if it was shouted down from the pulpit. If you see someone you know, in a doctor's clinic, do you not mention it outside in front of other people?

Jamie: Well, it's kind of common etiquette not to.

Christian: Is it? You see, I think I need to be told. People are a bit ruder these days. We don't have social etiquette anymore. I don't think it would have crossed my mind if I saw a celebrity to not report their dirty laundry to the press for a big cash payout, a record token or even an official Evening Gazette pencil. If you don't share a celebrity story you could possibly burst. A guy from this station ran into the washed-up actor Robin Williams in the toilets at Disneyland. The world loves a good 'celebrity in the toilets' story. With Robin Williams it was really quite literal and also a little bit metaphoric, bless him.

I've got a really good wheeze that I'm going to do during the show that'll make you scared. I've been practicing my 'computer being turned off' noise.

Okay, 'BU-BOO-DEE-DOO!' Straightaway,
you're looking around thinking, 'Has that just gone
off?' So, during the show when you're least
expecting I'll go, 'BU-BOO-DEE-DOO!' And
you are going to have one of your episodes. We're
always getting technical issues in the studio, and of
course I nominated you in charge of all technical
issues for this show. Look around for a minute.
Can you see that postcard we received Jamie?

Jamie: Yes.

Christian: 'BU-BOO-DEE-DOO!'

Jamie: Oh no, what's just happened?

Christian: You see, I got him. The system is actually fully
operational for me to play you some more Jamie
Tipson. Who do you better know him as?

Jamie: I know him as 'Second Hand Poet.'

Christian: He listens to the show and he actually said,
'Fantastic show like always.' And we shall
continue to play his songs until we've bled dry his
album. I'm going to play the song that I've played
the most. You know you get an album, and you get
one song you can't help but keep playing. I do play
all of his album.

Jamie: Is it Roger Whittaker?

Christian: No, that's his album there. See the difference?
Jamie Tipson, young lad. Roger Whittaker, you
said, 'He's dead,' and I believed you. I've got to
show you this. This is 'The Skye Boat Song'
album, and Roger Whittaker is there, and he does
look very old. And he's wearing a pair of trainers
without any socks on the front cover, because he's

cool. And if you open it up, there's even a photo of him there with Des O'Connor. I mean, how cool is that? Trinity, who's thirteen, confessed to me, because we were talking about Roger Whittaker and she was playing Little Mix, and I said you'll get to an age where you'll begin to appreciate certain types of music. And she said something quite profound and mature, 'I want you to know Dad, I do like him. I just like my songs as well.' And so, I couldn't argue with that. I kind of lost all my thunder just when I was about to beat up on her musical tastes. She's a master at reverse psychology.

Anyway, she'll obviously love Second Hand Poet. Who doesn't? And this song for me is the one that I'm playing the most at the moment. It's called 'Back for more.' Love it. Absolutely love it. And I'll be going to everyone on Facebook and inviting you to like this guy's page.

Jamie:	I already have. Do you think he's an introvert or an extrovert? What would Cliff Richard be?

Christian: I'd say extrovert. Enjoys mingling at the after-party bash. I don't know. I'm only second-guessing here. What the hell would I know? I'd hate for people to think their ears are burning when we're off mic talking about them, because Cliff's at home right now going, 'Uh!' I imagine, sat on the sofa next to his live-in priest. That would be embarrassing for him if he heard us talking while he had his mouth full. It can be quite a shock to hear your name get mentioned completely out of the blue. Similar story, I didn't know I'd gulped too much tea in my mouth and so I wasn't sure if I either had to spit it out or swallow, scolding my throat in the process. I think Cliff would just swallow, rather than make a scene, staining his upholstery. It can hurt when it goes down, but I've got a bad throat at the moment, so it's difficult to know if it was too much, but it didn't spill out.

The doctor also recommended I keep a little cup of water to sip. Can you see the glass of water here? You know, like all children, it can be used as a magnifying glass. Behind the water, you can see the enlarged writing. So, what would you do if spectacles like those optics on the bridge of your nose hadn't been invented, and you had to go round using a little cup of water instead? You had to press the tumbler along the words in order to read. I'd gulp yours. Just before the show, CHUG! Blind you by guzzling your only lens to the world. That would be awesome, to have the ability to steal your sight at will. Although I could replace it quickly, SPLOSH! 'Is that paper yellow? What's that smell?'

There's an Asian guy we work with and he's never drank Dandelion and Burdock. And he said, 'So what's it taste of? I thought what a weird question. It's a bit like cough medicine, but then I have to end the sentence with, 'but it's nice.' Tasty cough medicine. It could help my throat. Is it just a British thing? We've not brought in fizzy pop for a while. It's been cups of tea lately. If there's a local fizzy pop company that wants to sponsor the show.

Jamie: Lowcocks.

Christian: Did you get yours delivered by their lorry on a Friday?

Jamie: Yeah, and a 10p refund for the empty bottle. I loved the American Cream Soda.

Christian:	It would go clear if you left it on your windowsill in sunlight for about five minutes. All the green colouring would go. Explain what it tastes like to people who aren't American.
Jamie:	It's soda and it tastes of cream. It really does have a creamy taste. It's weird.
Christian:	Hey, we're doing small talk now. That would make us extroverts. What's that about? I'm getting a bit sweaty in here. What I thought is, we could set up a bit of a strip troupe. Well, me and thee to begin with. And what we do is, well, we strip. Yeah, I don't mean for each other. We could do if you want. What we'll do is we go on stage. Yeah, because we're introverts, and we can strip and the good thing is, instead of always having firemen strippers, or policeman strippers, we can be binmen strippers, and we don't even have to bath. We can just turn up at a moment's notice. None of this fuss around cleanliness. No hygiene, or personal grooming. We just turn up, flick our tops off, dance about a bit. The women will be like, 'What's that smell?' 'It's the act.' Of course, it's gonna appeal to the lower echelons of society. A class divisional thing going on there. But you know, money's money. A bit of a down market thing, you start low and make our way up. Move up to fishmonger strippers, still covering a multitude of sins with that act too.

I was phoning the clinic for my blood test results and I kept getting hung up on. Do they have service level targets? That if the phone doesn't get answered in time, they're in trouble. Instead, they just lift up the phone so it registers as answered, and then put it back in the cradle again so it doesn't add towards their poor statistics on call handling. I was getting a little bit cheesed off with that.

Do you think that my tight throat could be symptomatic of a midlife crisis? You know, like the stresses of not achieving anything that I ever wanted to achieve.

Jamie: What did you want to achieve?

Christian: Well, nothing really.

Jamie: There you go then. All your aspirations have been met. Exceeded even.

Christian: Is midlife crisis then a well observed and truly understood phase of life?

Jamie: I think so.

Christian: So why is it women get upset when their husband starts having adulterous affairs, when really, it's just like a toddler going through a phase of breaking an ornament? 'Wife dearest get over it, I'm 42. It's a phase. They've done a lot of research into this. Speak to any cheating behavioural scientist, they'll explain that lipstick mark better than I can.'

Remember the monkeys that got their heads replaced? Possibly a failed Nazi experiment or something. They swapped the heads of two monkeys to do research into the possibility of head transplants and I guess the wider field of paralysis also. The monkeys were kept alive throughout the ordeal having their heads surgically sewn back on. But what I want to know is, how do I know they actually did the experiment? Because monkeys to me, all look the same. Yeah, so okay, turn around for a minute and I've got two monkeys… 'BU-BOO-DEE-DOO!'

Jamie: Oh, your computer's gone off.

Christian: Ha! I got you again. You'll never guess what? It
                was me.

Jamie: Was it? I can't believe it.

Christian: Oh well believe this. So, you've got two monkeys
                and I cut their heads off and I swap them. But all
                I've done is drawn some stitches onto their necks
                with a biro. And broke their back. Snapped their
                back over my knee so they're paralysed, because
                obviously that would give it away if they started
                jumping up and clawing you. 'Hey, they should be
                paralysed.' I'll be rumbled and my third Reich
                government grants would soon dry up. 'You can
                turn round now Jamie the procedure is complete.
                And pay no mind to the spine crunching noises you
                just heard.'

                If you wanted to know that the swapped monkey's
                head was definitely from the other monkey's body,
                you'd have to have subtle differences between the
                two. Maybe smash the teeth out of one of the
                monkeys.

Jamie: There's a lot of smashing sounds in your
                laboratory.

Christian: Probably drowned out with the much louder sound
                of crying and screaming chimps. Put a Prince
                Albert on the other monkey.

Jamie: A what? A Prince album?

Christian: Yeah, 'You will note the controlled animal has in
                his opposable thumb, a signed copy of Purple
                Rain.' No, I actually meant a Prince Albert ring. So

anyway, when you turn round, the monkey with the ring has no teeth. Ta-dah! Although you might suspect I've simply took a hammer to the second monkey's mouth. And you'd be correct. Seems like a lot of hard work just a swap a monkey's head to another. I don't think one monkey's thoughts are going to be wildly different from another. I assume very similar. I mean, I can't possibly prove that. But I'm assuming it probably wants peanuts. Then when you swap the head to the other monkey and it now appears to want a banana instead, I'd still say it's fairly similar to the monkey that's now dead.

Jamie: It's probably thinking, 'I wish they'd played Lovesexy instead of Purple Rain. And they hadn't cut my head off so I could actually listen to it.'

Christian: I'm gonna tell you about wee-wee. Phosphorus was the 13th element to be discovered. But do you know how it was discovered? By an alchemist from Hamburg called Henning Brand in 1669. He went to the toilet, I guess a bucket in those days, and he thought his tinkle looked a little bit like gold, ergo, 'there must be gold in it.' So, he left his chamber pot to stand until it stunk the room out, then he boiled it into a paste which left a white waxy residue, phosphorus, 'some would even say it glowed. Then one foggy Christmas Eve,' he named it phosphorus mirabilis, 'miraculous bearer of light' and of course, Lucifer is Latin for 'light bearer.'

Jamie: Imagine if they were the lyrics, 'Lucifer with your pee so bright, won't you guide my sleigh tonight.'

Christian: Ironically, Hamburg was bombed by phosphorus bombs during the second world war, the same place it was discovered in 1669. This wasn't derived from urine, it was from rock by then. It takes 1100 litres of urine to make about 60 grammes of phosphorus. So, if wee was still our only source, they'd have to convert York public toilets into a munition factory to get the goods out. The floor spillage alone would wipe out Dresden. They eventually discovered that it was unnecessary to allow the urine to rot before boiling, as sterile fresh piddle was just as good. That would have saved on the nose pegs.

I'm thinking of that saying, 'I'm so angry it makes my pee boil.' Imagine going into the lavatory at night with no lights on, you'd be able to see wee glowing from those stressed individuals. Stressed so much it went all over the seat instead. What's that luminous paint they used in the war? Radium. Marie Curie discovered that, sadly with no toilet or slop bucket to her story. It did tragically cause a lot of jaw deformities, making people look like Basil Brush from all the radiation it emitted.

Robert Boyle in 1680 was the first person to use phosphorus to ignite sulphur-tipped wooden splints. These were the forerunners to our very own John Walker's friction lights. White phosphorus was first made commercially in the 19th century for the match industry and then they realised they could use bone ash. There's always some dirty scientist out there who's gonna think, 'Well, what's this made from?' As Plato himself said, 'Filthy bored geniuses are the mother of invention.'

I've got a best Facebook comment this week. I was reading a friend of a friend's page when I noticed someone had posted, *'I can't believe what's going on in the world today.'* It was all to do with children behaving inappropriately having been sexualized at an innocent age. As usual, everyone was blaming the parents, the teachers, wherever they'd seen this in the first place without parental guidance. There were comments about the parents looking to blame everyone else. There was a great one, '*Wake up people. Sex has been pushed on our children any which way they can. Start asking questions to where it's all coming from and who backs it? There's no smoke without fire.*' And we would probably agree with most of these comments, but there was one insightful one from another friend that I thought, 'Interesting!' '*Something very wrong folks. Mercury is in retrograde but planets, moon, etc. has gone crazy. New Moon Friday, Saturday, first of March, all will calm down. People getting worried that all our world's going through a massive change.*'

Of course, when kids are acting out lewd scenarios, it'll be the stars and the planets. Yeah, that's what it is. Blame them. You know what was even more incredulous? The fact that this woman who had put up the original post, liked that comment. To be fair, I was half tempted to click 'like' as well because I was laughing at the sheer absurdity of it. I would have liked to think it was typed completely tongue in cheek, in which case it was comedy gold, but it wasn't. It was just another random crazy nut job out there making social media hell on Earth.

Do you know men go under the scalpel to get their body sculptured? There's an Australian man who's famous for having pectoral implants. You know, they slide a silicone six pack under your skin to give the illusion you've got toned abs. He looks good for his age. Could have made page seven in The Sun. Would you do that now vanity's becoming more common for men? You know, have it made a bit bigger?

Obviously, you get told the risks associated with plumping up the meat. You could come out from the operation with one that doesn't work. Yeah, it might be big enough to trip over, but it won't work. I'd rather have a tiddler that works than a silly sized prop. But some people will happily get cut open just to have, you know, their sausage stretched. And if it breaks, the only work around medically at the moment is a little pump. The kind of pumps women in the Victorian ages sprayed perfume onto themselves with. FHUH! FHUH! You'd have to reach down and FHUH! FHUH! FHUH! FHUH! How many pumps would it take for yours to be inflated?

Jamie: Oh, not many.

Christian: FHUH! 'Oh!' I love the idea that when your date hears that noise, she'll think you've farted, 'Pish! Such vulgar accusation directed at such a worldly gentleman as myself. My dear, it was merely my penis deflating.'

There was an opposite sex story to this one tragically in the news. A lady called Blondie Bennett who is so obsessed with the image of Barbie dolls, she pays for weekly therapy sessions to make herself dumb. The exact words in the paper are '*sessions designed to make her more easily confused and vacant.*' Honestly, she could just listen to our show. Miss Bennett also changed her name and spent thousands of dollars on five boob jobs with regular Botox and lip fillers.

Miss Bennett said, I'll do it in her voice, '*My obsession with Barbie began at a young age when playing with the child's doll.*' You're obsessed with He-man, Jamie's real name is Herman, he just smudges the 'R' into a hyphen. Yeah? I've heard lots of Geordie people call you that – 'Wee-aye ya great big Herman.' Miss Bennett doesn't have a job but supports her lifestyle by selling sexy pictures of herself dressed as Barbie online. She said, *'People can criticise me but this is who I am. I want to be transformed head to toe, inside and out.'*

Jamie: How is your throat after that?

Christian: Remarkably good.

Jamie: Talk like Barbie for the rest of the show.

Christian: And my body feels at rest. 'BU-BOO-DEE-DOO!'

Jamie: Oh, oh, as someone knock the power cable?

Christian: You'll never guess, but I've just went and had you again.

Jamie: You swine.

Christian: It is the end of the show and I'll be powering it down anyway.

Jamie: 'BU-BOO-DEE-DOO!'

Christian: Awww! You double-double got me.

Christian: I was driving down the road tonight and there's still a Christmas tree up in someone's house. If you were the neighbour of that person, would you politely ask them to take it down? Actually, you'd be terrible, I could barely hear you knocking at my door. Your wrist must be very limp.

Paul: I couldn't hear my own knocking. It was drowned out by Cliff Richard.

Christian: It was his new album. I bought it for Joanne. She loves him. I think that's what keeps our marriage together. Some people base their relationships on other mutual interests, even sometimes sexual, ours is Cliff. It's gave us a strong foundation for a marriage anyway. Maybe not for your generation, perhaps you could pick a current pop sensation like Rick Astley. Maybe if you had done that you wouldn't be in the mess you're in. Does the new year bring with it a new Paul Miller? To be honest, there's nothing new from my side of the desk. I've had a look at the full show, and it's all the same as before. My holidays were like that, all the days merged together, I didn't even know what day of the week it was. It was a beautiful December.

Paul: I've been at work since November. I did have one half day off. I had some bad chicken. I was ill.

Christian: Oh, was it? Is that true? Or was it when you were in London?

Paul: No, no, that was a bit later.

Christian: I must quickly tell you, because it's not an in-joke, Paul drove down to London on a whim. And when he got there, 10 minutes in, he got a phone call from his boss saying, 'You're at work tonight.' So, he had to get back in the car and drive back up. Regardless of how much it cost in petrol to do that round trip, you would have still saved an absolute fortune on parking charges. Those car parks in London cost quite a bit. Speaking of the boss, I had a very awkward Christmas greeting from a big, big boss at work.

Paul: Let me guess. He went in for a handshake and you went in for a cuddle?

Christian: He wishes. I stood there making myself a cup of tea and he came over. I thought, 'That's the big boss who doesn't speak to me, ever.' Sometimes he comes into the office and chats to other members of management, but he never bothers with me. And he just came over, and it was seriously awkward, he went, 'So you and the family will be having a good Christmas, I hope.' And then he said, 'Well, let me take this opportunity now, to wish you all the best, because I don't know when I'll see you again next.' I just thought, 'You don't bother with me for 364 days. Who are you?' However, instead of saying all that, which I'm sure it was expressed through my eye lids moving in amazement, I just went, 'Okay, same to you.'

Paul: I bet he doesn't even know your name.

Christian: You know what? Now you mentioned it. He didn't actually say, 'Christian.' He just came over and was very kind of generic. You know when an old man throws a coin from the top bedroom window and says, 'You boy, go buy me the turkey as big as yourself'? You know, it feels as if he's been visited by three spirits to try and mend his ways. And he clearly thought, 'I'll try it with him first, the bald fat one. See if it's okay to be nice.' And so yeah, maybe he's a changed man. Maybe he's going to be friendly to me all next year. Although I'd rather he didn't. I'm happy to wait for my own ghostly visitations than suffer such insincerity.

Paul:

Perhaps you're too alike to be friends.

Christian:

Could be. I got a handful of cards from people at church. I've been attending there since May and I still don't know who any of them are. Do you think they're sending me cards because they want one in return?

Paul:

Maybe you're over thinking this. I was gonna say they're giving you cards to make friends. Are you just sort of sitting in your corner and being a loner?

Christian:

Well, I have been doing that for a while now. Over 18 years actually. But they did ask me if I'd like to do the Christmas family prayer. So, me and the family had to get up in front of the church and each say something appropriate. I asked Joanne and the children, 'What is it you would like for me to include in the prayer?' And they said, 'Dad, just write it, we'll read it, we don't care.' I thought, 'Well, at least you're supporting me.' So I wrote this prayer with us reading a little paragraph each.

You know, some modern churches have the technology to broadcast videos onto the wall. So we're watching these puppets projected on a giant screen. And it's the same music to 'Video killed the radio star', but it's called 'Wise men looked up and followed the star.' It was great, everyone really enjoyed it. Then they went, 'And now Christian is going to do the family prayer.' I thought, 'I'm not following that. Those puppets will completely show me up.' And they probably did.

It wasn't the only time I was entertaining an audience this Christmas. I went to pantomime in Richmond at the Georgian theatre. I'll be honest, as much as people say, 'You must be a slight extrovert to do radio.' The difference is, I'm not in front of any crowds right now. I'm okay with a few select people or just you. And if there was a million billion people out there listening, they could quite easily tune in and I wouldn't get embarrassed. But to be on stage is a different medium. The pantomime dame asked only the men to stand up.

Paul: So why did you stand up then?

Christian: I turned to the people I was with, my mother and father-in-law had paid for about 13 people, so the two back rows were booked with just our family. And I turned to my sister-in-law just to make whispered small talk, and make sure I wasn't getting looked at by the dame. Oh, audience participation, it's a struggle. And I had my bauble top on, which he said, 'Can the man in the romper suit make his way to the front?' I thought hopefully he's referring to someone else. Until everybody started looking back towards me. I could see there was a sigh of relief on every man's face in that theatre when I got called up. 'Phew! It's not me.'

Paul: I love getting called up on stage.

Christian: You've mentioned on previous shows that you don't like getting your bits out in front of the doctor. Now to me, it's the equivalent of getting my baubles out. I just thought when I got up there, 'If I struggle here, it's going to be ten times worse, because that pantomime dame is going to tear into me.' It's a bit like going into the doctors, get it out, let him see it, get on with it, get your medicine and get out of there as quickly as you can. And that's what I was doing on stage, trying to get my antibiotics and run. But it felt like an eternity up there.

Paul:

It was ten minutes.

Christian:

About three. It felt like an eternity for you to watch it.

Paul:

It did look like you enjoyed yourself. You tried to get a bit handsy with her.

Christian:

He told me to try and be sexy, and so I thought I was doing a Rik Mayall impression, but when I watched it back on video, I looked more like Frank Spencer. It's amazing what you think you look like compared to what you actually do. Anyway, that was my festivities. It just felt like it went by so quickly.

When you were a kid it took a long time from one Christmas to another. And sometimes in the middle of the year you would get a little bit festive, and maybe read a Beano Christmas edition?

Paul:

What's a Beano? Try and 'youth-ify' it for me.

Christian:

Or maybe watch 'Yogi's first Christmas' in July just to get a bit festive because you're missing Christmas. It's still such a long way to go.

Paul:

Yogi? You're not helping here.

Christian:

I don't need to do that anymore because the years fly by so quickly, before I have chance to start missing the season, it's festive again. Isn't it?

Paul: You'll soon be cashing in your pension and taking
                    out your teeth before you go to bed.

Christian: What did you get for Christmas?

Paul: My Mam got me a stress ball shaped like a boob.

Christian: Only one? You'd have thought she'd have splashed
                    out and bought you a pair.

Paul: Last year she got me a lolly shaped of a male's
                    equivalent.

Christian: Oh, yeah, I've seen that. It's not really what your
                    Mam should be getting you. Although it explains a
                    lot about you. And which one did you enjoy the
                    most? Last years?

Paul: I was gonna say I liked the lolly.

Christian: My daughter got me a Scooby Doo onesie. Quick
                    joke, what's the difference between Scooby Doo
                    and Michael Jackson? 'He would have gotten away
                    with it too, if it weren't for his meddling with those
                    kids.' You could probably pull the plastic mask of
                    Michael's face and reveal the villain underneath,
                    'Zoiks! It's Black Michael Jackson! Run Scoob!'
                    'Roiks! Raggy!'

Paul: I bought an advent calendar in the middle of
                    December for half price.

Christian: Do you go for the one at the back of the shelf? Not
                    the one all the kids have touched. The box less
                    molested at the back, untouched. It doesn't have to
                    be an advent calendar. It could be a board game, an
                    ornament. And you say, 'I'm gonna buy that jig-
                    saw puzzle' then you put the one in your hand back
                    down, and you go searching for the one right at the

back. If you worked in a shop, would you put the poked ones at the back? Just to make sure they eventually get bought by people like me?

Paul: Well, no, because you want the good ones at the front.

Christian: You don't own the shop. You just work there.

Paul: Oh, well then, I couldn't care either way.

Christian: I went to the cinema to watch 'Bumblebee' the Transformers movie and it was in 4-D.

Paul: Is that the one where you get the 3-D glasses, and they spray liquids over you, so you feel like you're actually in the movie?

Christian: I suppose the liquid would depend on what you're going to watch, say Bohemian Rhapsody, the Freddie Mercury biopic, 'What's that smell? Is that lube?' as theatre mechanics are spraying it into your mouth?' Would that happen on the love scenes? Would your buttocks start vibrating in the seat?

Paul: I wouldn't want to watch '50 shades of grey.'

Christian: It would smell of leather and you'd get whipped?

Paul: No, I hear it was an awful movie based on an awful book.

Christian: I'm getting distracted. You know, sometimes people kick your chair in the cinema, usually disrespectful youngsters who are sat directly behind you? If they continue, you complain about it. With Bumblebee, you pay good money for the experience, like 13 pound a pop, just to have your

chair moving around a bit. I could have watched
the movie in 2-D and allowed the young thugs to
rest their feet on the back of my normal chair for a
fraction of the cost. But it really does move, it tilts
in the direction of the on-screen action.
Unfortunately for my family, I'm a bit of a giggler.
When I'm on a roller coaster I just giggle, it's laugh
rather than cry. And so, I'm in the cinema and my
children are sat next to me and they're getting
embarrassed, because dad's making a bit of a
scene.

Paul:

And this was after you'd been on stage and fondled
with a man-woman.

Christian:

Good point. You'd think their threshold for shame
would be relatively high considering I'm their Dad.
There's a great scene in it where Bumblebee gets
given a Smith's cassette, and Morrissey starts
singing. And the robot just spits the tape straight
back out. I couldn't stop laughing about it. And the
kids were like, 'Dad be quiet.' It was genius. It
was a real laugh, it's not like a Shakespearean play
where you pretend pretentiously to get the jokes. I
was genuinely laughing because it was a funny
scene.

So, there's air that blasts against the back of your
legs and it had a forest smell, because the
characters in the film were walking around a
wooded area. Again, I could have remained in the
2-D theater if forests were naturally scented of
sweat and popcorn. But the movie itself is very
good. Someone gets zapped and turns into water
and the audience gets sprayed? Oh, maybe that was
a spoiler for anyone going to see it in 4-D. If
you're viewing it in a London cinema, you'd best
make sure it isn't an acid attack first. Actually, that
reminds me, they had a lifeguard on patrol inside

the 4-D theater. I guess they're still called ushers, but without a torch and ice-cream. They sit on a chair facing everyone, I assume in case of a heart attack or you're pregnant.

Paul: You'd have to adjust the chair if that's what you're after. Sounds more like 5-D.

Christian: Sounds Creep-E.

Paul: No, it's 6-E.

Christian: Very good. The chair itself is huge. A lot of leg space. And my other interesting cinematic point to my mentioning of this invention, is from a Columbo episode from the 1970s. You probably don't remember it, but projectionists in the old cinemas had to change reels of film.

Paul: Yeah, when they see them blips in the corner.

Christian: Have you been looking at my notes? It actually says, 'cue blips.'

Paul: Do you know why I know that?

Christian: Is it because you're an untrustworthy little sneak?

Paul: No, it's in Fight Club. Brad Pitt mentions the three dots in the corner are to signal the projectionist to change the reel.

Christian: If you were that usher in the lifeguard seat, would you encourage the audience to get out of the seats and applaud the movie once the credits started? Dumb them down and make them act like Americans that whoop and holler at anything. Also, it encourages them to exit the theater quicker before the cleaning staff arrive. It might leave you with enough time to see if anyone's left behind any uneaten sweets. What abandoned sweets would you eat if you worked at the cinema?

Paul: Is it still in its wrapper?

Christian: Sure, why not.

Paul: What film has it been discarded from?

Christian: You ask too many questions for an opportunistic confectionary forager. Would you eat a melted chocolate coin that's been found on a chair to the previous showing of the Freddie Mercury movie?

Paul: I do like 'Choc Lick,' I had some about a week ago.

Christian: Oh, 'Choc Nibs'?

Paul: No, no, the 'Lick'.

Christian: I said, 'Choc Nibs'! Speaking of Transformers, have you seen these toys that help little boys with their maths? They teach you to count from zero all the way through to nine, then each one turns into a robot or a helicopter or a tank. They're called 'MagiDeal Numbers Armour Team.' You've even got an 'X', a plus, minus and a divide sign. And they all go together and make a massive robot. Would you have made the number three your crotch area? The robots now got big childbearing hips.

Paul: They should have gone for number one.

Christian: That'll be a bit skinny. Not much of a Voltron type of toy. But anyway, I just thought I'd mention that, and maybe if you're lucky this year, I might get you one to help you with your counting. I've already decided you're gonna get number three. Anyway, speaking of great things that we've got to look forward to, we've some top tunes coming up. What have we got? What's the first tracks we're gonna play tonight?

Paul: A 60s classic Dusty Springfield, 'Son of a preacher man', and then we've got this week's pop graduate which is The Vaccines and 'All my friends are falling in love.'

Christian: Here's the section of the show we call 'The lion's mouth,' where we throw items or people or pretty much anything into it that's annoyed us or needs destroying.

Paul: I had this one written down. I was at work, right? I'm always at work. And this guys in a wheelchair.

Christian: It's not a funny story then? The last time you told me a story we have to edit it out. I started laughing and it was about a child with a genetic disorder. I start smiling because I'm expecting your stories to be funny and then they disappoint. So, is it a tragic story or a comic story? Because I'm going to have the correct my expression for its duration. And try not to let it drag on.

Paul: No, no, definitely comedy. So, this guy is in a wheelchair. He comes over and he says, 'Can you put a song on for me? Ed Sheeran, 'When your legs don't work.'' Which is the first line to 'Thinking out loud' by Ed Sheeran. He started laughing and I'm feeling awkward. He went, 'No, I'm only joking. I do that all the time.' So, he goes away and then the song comes on. Then two of his mates pick him up out of his chair and carried him around the dancefloor. Dancing around with him.

Christian: Without the listener knowing, Paul just moved as if
               he was sat in one of those 4-D chairs watching
               Bohemian Rhapsody. Your bum started to move
               when you were describing them dance.

Paul: I didn't know whether to be mad at them. They
               probably do it to him all the time. It's not like he
               could put up a fight if he wasn't happy with being
               man handled.

Christian: So, did they end up throwing him around so much
               his penis poked out or something?

Paul: No.

Christian: You promised me a funny story.

Paul: I couldn't stop laughing. I guess you really had to
               be there. But if that's what passes for comedy, I
               also have another pre-Christmas story that ticks
               that box. I was helping a mate out on the door,
               when this drunk turned up and he'd wee-weed
               himself. I said to him, 'You can't come in, you've
               soiled yourself.' And I worked out later that
               'soiled' is when you've pooped yourself.

Christian: I would have allowed that word to describe this
               gentleman's situation.

Paul: He argues back, 'No, no, I've wee-weed myself.'
               He then proceeds to get his little Ed Sheeran out,
               and no one wants that, and pee.

Christian: There's nothing funny about that either. Why are
               you telling me these stories that are clearly more
               tragedy than comedy?

Paul:

I got peed on by a grown man. That's pretty disgusting, isn't it? And it's illegal. It's indecent exposure. So, he can go into the lion's mouth for urinating on me.

Christian:

Remember urine is sterile, so you'll be alright.

Paul:

I don't think this was. It smelt like beer. His kidney's must have stopped working.

Christian:

Speaking of drunks, I'm also going to throw one into the lion's mouth. My wife won two tickets to go see Boney M. So, me and my son Calvary went to the Sage in Gateshead, it cost six pounds 30 just to park the car there, which is a cost in itself. If we had bought the tickets, they were about 30 pounds each. It's a nice futuristic building they have up there. I did say to my son, 'It's like one of those places where they park aeroplanes.' He said, 'You mean an airport?' Yeah. It's like an airport.

Paul:

Hangar.

Christian:

Yes. Now why weren't you there to defend my limited wisdom. It looked like a futuristic hangar. Somewhere you could park a shiny rocketship. So, we went in. Nothing worse than getting in too early because everyone else is still getting to their seat. And it's always the stragglers who are still drinking at the bar. Yeah, they're coming in, and you have to keep standing up to let them walk past to get into their seat.

Also, I didn't want to miss the support act, Odyssey. They had a hit with 'Use it up, and wear it out.' Anyway, these drunken women who may have been on a hen night were all dressed up in disco threads. And they were handing the air microphone to me. 'Rivers of Babylon' is getting played, and I'm singing with my son from the terrace, and he's grooving away. She puts the air microphone right up to my mouth. And for those not understanding, she's literally holding her clenched fist a few inches from my face, but I guess it's all done in a flirty, yet still threatening manner.

It's not a good sight. My son's there and he's looking at this old haggard woman shoving an air microphone into his dad's mouth. And I told this story at work, and the colleague said, 'What you do with people like that is, you take the pretend microphone from them, and snap it.' But you run the risk of getting a slap from a drunken cougar type woman, don't you? Would you risk it? I just finished singing into her wrinkly hand. It stopped me singing after that. She kind of spoiled the disco atmos.

Towards the end the band left the stage. They unplugged their guitars and everything. Calvary says, 'Are we gonna go Dad?' I said, 'They haven't done *Mary's boy child* yet. They're gonna do that for their encore.' I sounded quite authoritative. He said, 'How do you know these things?' It's like I'm a wise oracle of all knowledge. I said, 'Because we're at a Boney M concert with one week till Christmas, and it's one of the biggest selling songs of all time ever.' And lo and behold they came back on stage to perform that exact song as a finale. I felt like I was Daddy Cool.

Disco is now Calvary's favourite genre of music, so I don't know if I've kick started anything that I shouldn't have by turning him into a disco diva. He was actually ill that day. First thing he said when I picked him up from school, 'We're still going to see Boney M aren't we Dad?' I said, 'Not if you're ill we can't.' He said, 'I'm feeling better now.' He desperately didn't want to miss the troupe. That's dedication. Even Boney M wasn't all there. Only one original member was on stage, Maizie Williams, I believe. Same goes for Odyssey.

I wanted to mention the toilets at the Sage as well. They don't have any doors on them. You can walk straight through the toilets and look at people urinating if you wanted to. I find that a bit weird.

Paul: Watching people pee? It is a bit weird yeah.

Christian: I should also thank all the diversity in our culture. I noticed at the York Christmas market there was plenty of armed police officers guarding the place. And this has been happening since all these terrorist attacks have taken place. I understand we want to be safe, but we've lost our identity as a cost to having that protection. But I guess it's like Sadiq Khan says, 'It's part and parcel of living in a big city.' But York's not like London, where I assume Santa drops knives down the chimneys to all the youths there.

Paul: I went into a shop in London, around the corner from the new Wembley Stadium. This is what I spent my 10 minutes doing. I literally went into a shop to buy a can of pop, and there were two security guards for this one little shop about the size of your front room. This was Saturday at 4:30 in the afternoon.

Christian: There's a shop in Hartlepool, where they don't let more than two children in at a time during school lunchtime, because they don't want all the kids in there shoplifting.

Paul: The KFC in Middlesbrough has plastic sheets on
their windows so drunks can't attack them for fried
chicken at three o'clock in the morning.

Christian: I guess it's not just home-grown terrorists that are
changing our society beyond recognition. There's a
much bigger generalization to be made here, but
it's far too depressing, especially at the beginning
of a new year, where I should be feeling full of
optimism for our country's future, so I'll try to not
utter those words.

Speaking of 'future', have you seen this? I picked
it up from the Sage. It's a 'Back to the Future' in
concert. The basic concept is they mute the
volume. You're watching the movie with no sound,
and an orchestra plays instrumental pieces
throughout. What is the point of that? The Czech
National Symphony Orchestra will reimagine the
original score. Huey Lewis isn't even there on
stage with them singing, 'That's the power of
love.' Not even one member of The News. It's
worse than Boney M's original line up. I'll be
interested to know if that sells out.

You know, shopkeepers, you mentioned them
about five minutes ago.

Paul: I've slept since then.

Christian: I'll say, 'sole traders.' I was in Whitby by the way,
and the moment I put my foot out of the shop door,
she closed and locked it. And I thought, 'Why
wouldn't you have the decency to wait until all
your customers have actually stepped away from
the shop front?' In a supermarket they'll say, 'Can
you start making your way to the checkout now
please,' with about ten minutes before the actual
closing time. Instead, this little shop in Whitby had

her looking over her glasses thinking, 'Get the hell out.' I didn't buy anything.

Paul: I'm on this lady's side now. Maybe it's the vibe you give off, and she just wanted you out of her shop. You know the people you get on the street corners picking up cigarette ends from the floor, asking if you've got a spare 20p for the bus fare back home?

Christian: Oh yeah, I'll be one of them, 'How mate, have youse got a twenty pence so's I can get a bus home?'

Paul: No. Where are you going?

Christian: 'I needs to gets to Stockton at this times of nights.'

Paul: I tell you what, right, since it's half twelve and there's no buses running, I'll give you a lift.

Christian: 'Erm, naw, it's alright mate, I'm good.' How dodgy do you have to look for a drunken chav to run away from you when you offer them a lift? I mean, your face screams 'stranger danger' even to drug addicts. 'Oh, mate I don't wants to get in your car, I can't imagines what'll happens to me next mate.'

Paul: He can see your 4-D vibrating leather chair in there and Queen's 'Radio Gaga' playing away in the background.

Christian: I wouldn't be trusting him to touch the buttons on my chair. You can stop it from spitting out smells if you want. You know, I think there's options. But why would you deactivate your chair? You're paying 13 pounds for the experience.

Did you hear about this crazy campaign to change the calendar?

Paul:

Is this 'Dry January'?

Christian:

There was gonna be 28 days in every month, and have13 months, which is 364 days. That was a new one. There was also one where they add 10,000 years to our calendar to incorporate all our known cultural history. So, we'd be living in the year 12,019 just so they can get rid of the Jesus birth link to our calendars, because they don't think that's important.

Paul:

So, the end of the Stone Age is now year zero?

Christian:

It's called the Holocence Epoch. When farming began once the ice glaciers had melted. I guess the calendar could be calculated by carbon dating rocks.

Paul:

What would they do with BC and AD?

Christian:

Get rid of it, even though Christ is culturally the most significant event in our history. That's the plan from these Marxist scholars. I find it strange that up in the Cleveland hills they've got these cairns, 4000-year-old burial mounds, that has a sign requesting people don't add any more stones to it. A cairn, by the way, is literally a pile of stones stacked up on top of each other. That's it. And if you add another stone to it, you're basically in effect, vandalizing this ancient monument. Some hikers sit on these things and have their picnics.

In the Shetland Islands there's some Bronze age housing, and 4000 years later when the Vikings came they graffitied the walls. I think one of the jokes is like, 'Redbeard was this tall', when really he was standing on someone's shoulders when he actually etched it into the stone. So that act of vandalism has become part of its history. Knights who've been on crusades have actually vandalized St Hilda's in the Headland at Hartlepool when they stayed overnight in the church. They kind of struck their sword onto the pillars. Now it's historic, but at the time, it was just mindless vandalism.

Paul: Like, you could put another rock on top of this cairn and carve 'Kyle was here 2019.'

Christian: I think there's an element whereby we want to be remembered. I think that's why Stonehenge exists. A quick way of marking our territory is to add a noteworthy sign of vandalism to an already recognized achievement.

Paul: Is that why dogs pee on everything?

Christian: If that were the case, why was the drunk leaving you his calling card? Marking you out as his territory. Paralytic drunks must see you as a human work of art.

Paul: It's true, I did feel vandalized and I suppose now I'll always remember him. Your theory is correct.

Christian: *BBC wildlife expert Chris Packham has offered himself as a hunt. I did say, 'hunt.' He's going to be the first human quarry in a bid to stop foxes being chased.* Now I've got to be honest, I hate fox hunting. I absolutely abhor it. But this - I could kind of get into. If they're going to chase after Chris Packham and have the hounds tear him to pieces, I could watch that. That'd be all right to see.

A 40-year-old Dominican man had emergency surgery to remove a can of Glade air freshener from his rear. Do you think his pumps would smell nice? *He was rushed to hospital to undergo emergency surgery after his wife inserted it, which she claimed he'd requested.* What kind of pervert wants a canister of air freshener shoved up their bum? Now if it was a Glade plug-in, that's a whole different question.

If this kinky incident had happened at Scarborough General Hospital their bowel surgeon may have told the patient to 'assume the George Michael position.' *Dr Serban Gheorghiu apparently shocked colleagues when he carried out intimate examinations and made references to the late singer's sexuality when he asked patients to get on all fours to perform colonoscopies.* I'll be honest, I kind of laughed a little at that. It wouldn't trouble me in the slightest. Maybe put me at ease while I can hear the rubber gloves being stretched over his hands.

Don't you just hate people who get offended over nothing? He's either doing his job and saving lives, or he isn't. Whether people think he's making a lighthearted comment or not, it really isn't worth getting rid of an NHS staff member who otherwise is doing a good job. Just say to him, 'Don't do it anymore.' Is it such a problem?

Paul: It's snowflakes. That saying could be applied for anything like, 'Stand up straight and lift your arms to your side like Jesus.' And the celebrity that gets arrested for lewd acts in a public toilet is quickest to get defended.

Christian: There was a certain toilet, not where I work, but another place of work. And they had a picture of George Michael above the sinks with a message saying, 'George Michael is watching you, to make sure you wash your hands.' And that was back in the day of him being caught by the police officer. The general public turned that into a joke. Is it because he's dead now, it's no longer funny? I don't understand. The joke, from what I understand of comedy, is poking fun at celebrity, which is what we do as a nation, rather than sexuality. But I admit society is changing. *A comedian had to cancel a university show after students forced him to sign a behaviour contract so he wouldn't offend any of the students with sexism, classism, ageism, ableism, transphobia, and seven other isms. It was at the School of Oriental and African Studies.*

Paul: A dyslexic man walks into a bra. That's the joke. But I guess it would now offend anyone with disabilities. So, how about a non-denominal human, somehow transports himself either with their legs or with a wheelchair into a trans gender neutral toilet? It's not funny.

Christian: Unless you have them assume the George Michael position. Then it'll work.

Paul: Okay. So, I went to the doctors the other day. He said, 'Mr Miller, I'm the doctor and I'll be doing the examination today.' He puts his rubber gloves on and says, 'Right, trousers off and lie on the table. Please assume the George Michael position.' So, I done what he asked me to do, before he finally said, 'Mr Miller, you can put your trousers back on again. I'll be back in a minute with your test results.' A moment later the nurse walks in and says, 'Who was that?'

Christian: Can I tell you a story about my great grandmother who I lost when I was about 13, so she would have been almost if not a Victorian. My Nanna Parkes had what you just described 'an old gas metre that took shillings.' And she used to cut out like 50 pence piece sizes of lint to pop into the metre to get it to work. She wouldn't rip people off, so when the guy came round to empty and collect the money, if he seen one or two in there, he knew times must have gotten tough, so bad in fact she was desperate enough to use them. And he would hand her them back. That's what the people of Middlesbrough done back then when times got hard, cut out fake vinyl coins from lino.

Paul: My aunt had a TV that you stuffed with pounds to keep watching it. It was how you paid the rent on this thing. It was like a pound an hour to watch it. She bought it from a dodgy shop called something like 'Crazy George's'. And she ended up putting bits of stuff into the payment slot that registered. So, when the guy came and emptied it on the table she would have to distract him with a cup of tea and take away the buttons and folded up paper clips.

Christian: I could easily live without TV in general. I hear more and more people are beginning to disconnect from TV, more specifically the news. They can't suffer it. I don't want to suckle at the teat of Donald Trump when he talks about 'fake news', but he's correct. There are so many clickbait articles out there, which is how they generate revenue, through the traffic on their web sites.

So, as long as the online newspapers are making money they don't care if the article is factually or grammatically incorrect. As long as readers are clicking on it, they don't care. And that is irresponsible sensational journalism or 'fake news.' And what's interesting on BBC news, where they don't rely on advertising revenue, is their complete disregard for remaining impartial on certain

subjects like Brexit and Trump. It's not news
anymore but dreadfully slanted opinion pieces
created to work as propaganda for what the ruling
elite insist us plebs should conform towards and
make their lives easy. No dissent in the ranks.

Paul:

Did you hear about the real newspaper that had
abstracted something from Wikipedia or another
internet site, because printed on the actual physical
newspaper page was, 'Click here to find out more.'
Can you imagine how many people reading were
tapping the paper with their finger? 'It won't do
anything. Why's it not working? That's weird, my
Wi-Fi must be down.'

1st June 2011

Christian: To celebrate the Progress Live tour kicking off in Sunderland at the weekend, this is going to be our Take That special where we're going to play their best tracks, their greatest songs, their most brilliantly written lyrics.

Jamie: Take That haven't done anything.

Christian: Yes, but if they did, we'd play them here on this show. Everyone in the area seems to know at least someone who went to the Stadium of Light to see Take That's opening concert of this tour.

Jamie: I know three or four people.

Christian: I know two. Oh, we've got half a dozen people just between us two here. The price of tickets is ridiculous.

Jamie: Well, over a pound is too much. I think we're talking about 50 quid.

Christian: The support act, by the way, is the Pet Shop Boys. However, support acts don't get the full stage. They don't get to use all of the lighting. The sounds aren't as amplified as the main act. So, they've got a restricted area, restricted sound, and a restricted set. Yeah, just so they don't blow them out of the water. Even though they're not allowed with those restrictions in place, I bet Pet Shop Boys still manage to bowl everyone over.

Jamie: Take That rely on gimmicks. They came on stage in a big robot and stuff like that. And Robbie Williams done his own set. And they also had an elephant on stage with them.

Christian:	Robbie's lost a lot of weight since then, so there's no need to call him any names Jamie. Me and the wife were talking about Mancunian acts. Obviously, we didn't get into the Smith's - New Order debacle, Oh, the Stone Roses, they rock. But we talked about Take That and Oasis, neither band Joanne would give a rats to see, but if she was forced at gunpoint… You begin to realise me and Joanne have a lot of 'if you were forced at point of death' scenarios. But to be fair, you've only been given two choices, and you've got to decide one or the other, otherwise you get shot. I love arguments like that because there's none of this safe middle ground business. Do you go see Take That or Oasis, Lock! Load! I said, 'Oasis.' Joann went with Take That.
Jamie:	I would favour that as well, because I can't bear the Gallagher's.
Christian:	I had to say Oasis for the simple fact I actually like a few of their songs and I have all their albums. Anyway, this is now a Take That special, and if any listeners think they've penned a song worthy of an Ivor Novello or done anything equally or remotely remarkable, please let us know so we can include it on tonight's tribute edition. The fact we've put the inclusion bar above mediocre means we'll not be troubled by middle aged women for the remainder of the night. That goes for our partners too.
Jamie:	And you like awful music like Bros.
Christian:	Exactly, so I don't think I'm being unfair here. I had two of their albums, 'Push' and 'Time'. I have no Take That albums, not even a greatest hits collection. I've known a lot of boy band pop music over the years. I can quite happily listen to most of

the manufactured bubblegum pop sound, but we're talking a few singles here and there because I'm not going to know certain album tracks. Let's say Greatest Hits of Westlife. There's probably one or two that I wouldn't mind, 'Flying without wings', 'Queen of my heart' to name but two.

Jamie: New kids on the block.

Christian: Quite a few. They were my teenage years. I guess we can do a Take That special and play New kids tracks and of course Bros, a couple of them.

Jamie: So, we're asking ourselves really, 'What Take That track could we bear without vomiting blood?' Once we decide, we should play it, or be shot.

Christian: Take That special notwithstanding, this is the part of the show where I say, 'Jamie, what have you done this week?' Do you enjoy, by the way, working within the education sector? Especially during the week where all the students are on their holidays?

Jamie: I love it. It's a lot easier. College would be so much better without students.

Christian: Do they smell? Because it's easy to imagine the collective student body being described as 'the great unwashed,' not just as a slur on their low social status, but a very real physical stench.

Jamie: Some of them smell worse than bins.

Christian: Does anyone politely inform them, 'By the way, you need to change your festering clothes due to an unaddressed personal hygiene problem'?

Jamie: That would be down to human resources. And I
                 don't think they'd do that. In fact, I know they don't
                 do that, because we constantly have to grin and
                 bear it. But the big news is I'm moving out. We've
                 found a place we're going to be around the corner
                 from my folks.

Christian: What does that mean to you? My mam and dad
                 lived, as the crow flies, 170 metres from our house.
                 We bought it because it's a cheap area with good
                 schools. It's what we could afford. There was a
                 part of me that thought, 'Are they going to bother
                 me? Am I making a huge mistake?' So, everything
                 being equal and you being of sane mind, I put it to
                 you, do you think, 'Oh my God, I hope they stay
                 away'?

                 There's nothing worse than, Knock! Knock!
                 Knock! 'Who's that? It's Mam. That's great you
                 made us casserole.' Okay, that's all right on the
                 first night. Second night, Knock! Knock! Knock!
                 'Who's there? It's Dad. What do you want?' 'I was
                 just passing in the area Son, thought I'd see how
                 you're doing?' 'Oh, that's really nice you've asked
                 Dad, but no, everything's fine.' Next day, Knock!
                 Knock! Knock! You're tipping buckets out of the
                 window onto them, 'Go on, clear off!'

Jamie: No, I know full well it won't be like that. We're
                 about three or four estates away from each other.

Christian: But have you had the conversation, 'Look just
                 make sure you sling your hook'?

Jamie: Yeah, they've told me.

Christian: Oh, it's the reverse. There's your parents saying,
                 'Jamie you do realise, once you're leaving, you're
                 leaving, there's no coming back. These bridges are

burned.' You've now got to fly or drowned. What is it, 'sink or swim'? I liked the 'fly or drowned' options better if I'm honest. I'm sure you'll do well, but we'll have a new section of the show called, 'Jamie, is he dying?'

What was it that you used to watch? It's called 'Hammer' or something?

Jamie: Sledgehammer.

Christian: Yeah, it's making a comeback on TV.

Jamie: Really? When?

Christian: In the autumn, I think once all the new schedules have been done.

Jamie: Because it didn't do very well, when it was out in 1987, but that was because the network's were playing with it.

Christian: Well, there you go.

Jamie: It's had a massive following when it came onto DVD. So, this is good news. Is it with the original characters?

Christian: Oh, that was it, 'Tell someone their favourite TV programme is making a comeback. Then later admit you made it all up.' That's what I wrote down as my first thing to do. I wanted to do that on the show live. It's horrible, isn't it?

Jamie: Yeah. I was really excited for a moment there.

Christian: Somebody said to me, 'I think some superhero is going to make a comeback.' And then they realized they'd just misread it. And I thought, 'What a horrible crummy thing to do to someone.' Note! 'That was a cruel experience, getting my hopes built up like that,' hold on a minute, 'let me just jot this down. This dreadful thing you've just done to me.' Write, write, write. 'I'll see how that goes down when I do it to someone else.' Scribbles Jamie's name. To have your high expectations so quickly dashed like that, it's a horrible thing. Can you describe to the listener exactly how gutted you are?

Jamie: I'm so gutted, I think you're gonna be walking home tonight.

Christian: The next few weeks, it's going to be a heatwave, that's according to the untrustworthy met office. I think the Daily Mail called it a 'scorcher,' but they try it on just like The Express, 'Oh, we're gonna be minus 40 this winter.' And they've still got a photo of Princess Diana on the front cover. There's no story, just a picture. 'We thought our readers would like this picture of Princess Diana. Please go and buy our paper.'

There was a list of famous people who've been suggested to be put on bank notes. Wogan, Jimmy Savile, David Beckham, Robbie Williams. Hardly what I'd consider potential banknote material. And at the very top of the submissions page, it says, 'The Bank of England reserves the right to say no to any of the suggestions. They also need to make sure that they're not going to offend anyone. They must be a person that most people know.' Now I don't believe that's fully true. Elizabeth Fry is on the £5 note. But seriously, who knew who she was before that? I think the Bank of England don't obey their own rules.

Why isn't Captain Cook, our own local hero, not on
a note? He's on Australia, Canadian and New
Zealand, but not here. And of course, George
Stephenson was on the £5 note before being
evicted by that Elizabeth Fry. Why? She reformed
prison services. Did she give them all plasma
screen TV's and make sure they all have their
European court of Human Rights protected so they
can still vote in general elections? I have a story in
the news about this that'll make your urine boil.

First, I wanted to chat about diabetics who feel sick
whilst at work. Do you know anyone who's
diabetic at work?

Jamie:	I notice a few diabetics using the shoot-up room.

Christian:	Interesting colloquial term. Why can't they just
administer the insulin to themselves there and
then? I just done an impression of someone pulling
up their shirt and injecting their side discreetly.
What's the problem?

Jamie:	I don't have an issue with that, but some people
don't like the sight of needles. Welcome to the
world where breastfeeding offends people. Have
you just arrived here?

Christian:	It's you who came down in the last shower? Jamie
slowed down to let a police van out. You never do
that unless you want to get pulled over.

Jamie:	Mind you, they did follow me for a while. Hot on
my trail, the swine's.

Christian:	It's probably because I was shaking my fist, 'Go
on, get out of it.' And so, diabetics. I spoke to him
and said, 'What's wrong?' He said, 'Actually I felt
really sick.' He had to leave the office and eat a

Mars bar. It depends on what type of diabetes you've got. Obviously, he knows if his blood sugar level runs low, and what he has to do to correct it. I said, 'How do you know other than checking your blood sugar level?' He has a battery powered portable device that reads from a droplet of blood from a finger prick test. He said, 'If I didn't have that equipment I wouldn't know.' I said, 'What about working with someone like, I do a radio show with Jamie. If I'm diabetic, right? And I've got a low blood sugar level. How would I know that I'm feeling ill from an underperforming pancreas, and it's not Jamie just knocking me nauseous? How would you know?'

You always talk about the people you work with and they make you violently ill. How would you know to separate the fact it's just your boss talking to you? 'Urgh!' Or you genuinely need to go and fix yourself up with some sugar? Dan le sucre. How would you know it's something built within you?

Jamie: It must be an instinct thing.

Christian: Yeah, it's like, can I go and look at this wall for a minute. One minute later, I'm still feeling ill, it's going to be the diabetes. See, there is the alternative option to having a gun against your head. It's either going home on an evening and looking at a bit of wet paint and letting people know once it's dried or watching Oasis or Take That. 'It's dry!' I know which one to choose.

On Thursday, I said, 'Oh, I really wish it was Friday today.' And somebody said, 'Why not Saturday?' Good point. If you're gonna make a wish, what a bad wish that would have been. I would have sat there on Thursday going, 'I wish it was Friday.' I don't know why my brain didn't catch up to the fact I was making a wish. No one makes half a wish. 'I wish I was financially well enough off.' You don't think like that, you go, 'I wish I was a millionaire.' Not, 'Oh, I wish I had enough to pay this month's bills.' What a waste. Imagine the magical genie's listening to you that one time you make the pointless wish. 'Oh, I wish somebody would close that door, only halfway. Oh, I'll have to get up and close it fully now. If only I'd have thought about my wish. Poof! It's Friday. 'Oh, I wish I had my wish again.'

A prisoner is being allowed to father a baby from behind bars. Strange position, perhaps it's a euphemism. It's a decision based on human rights laws to have a family life, according to justice secretary Kenneth Clarke. You'll remember this incompetent guy who said anyone caught with a knife will receive a mandatory prison sentence, and then decided all the prisons are full, 'Alright, well they'll get told off at the very least.' And if you're a convicted criminal he'll approve your request to have a child with your partner by artificial insemination. This guy knows how to get tough.

Jamie: In the TV show 'Sledgehammer', that you duped me earlier with, there's a quote, 'a prisoner loses their rights when they break the law.'

Christian: Have you been to the website of the month, sexy MP dot co dot UK? I guess it's like 'Hot or Not?' but for politicians. You rate the MPs basically to decide which one you'd sleep with. That's what it says, '*It's a way of trying to be proactive for us to get to know who's our members of parliament.*' To be honest, it's a gun against the head decision. Although it's more likely to be a machete if Ken Clarke is kept in charge. Now that's satire.

Jamie: Do you do it or not?

Christian: Yeah, well, he's Liberal Democrat. They'll
                probably do more without a fuss. Although Mark
                Oaten has left the party now.

Jamie: What about Harriet Harman?

Christian: Am I feeling the sickly onset of a diabetic coma or
                is it from looking at Harriet Harman's face? Do I
                take sugar or watch the paint dry?

                Mike, the guy I work with, he was talking to me
                about children. He says to me, 'Are your kids
                thick?' I said, 'Well, I don't know. I wouldn't think
                so. Because they're my kids and I'd probably
                delete it from my mind.' And he's telling me about
                his holiday to Australia. His son's a highly
                intelligent lad. He said they're visiting these
                Jurassic caves, and as you enter, there's lots of
                information panels about all the different dinosaurs
                that the archaeologists have found and how far
                back, natural history wise it dates to.

                And so the woman tour guide is talking to his son
                as he's reading these introductions about the finds
                and digs there. She's saying to him, 'If we go back
                65 million years ago, when there were plenty of big
                reptiles, does anyone know what they were called?
                What big animals did we have here in these
                caves?' He only had to say the word 'dinosaurs.'
                There's loads of other kids there as well. And of
                course, all their parents. An Australian cave full of
                adults and children, and she says to Nick, 'So do
                you know what type of animals we used to have
                living here?' He went, 'Skunks.'

Mike said he wanted to kill himself. 'Why would you do this to me?' He actually felt like going up to the woman who was doing the tour guide, and explaining to her, that his son's not normally that thick. 'Do you know what type of big reptile lizards lived here 65 million years ago? 'Skunks.' He could have pretended to be foreign, 'Ah, me no speaky Engrush.' I mean she'd only heard one word spoken by his son.

Jamie:

How dark were these caves if he's trying to pull off a Chinese man? Actually, that didn't sound right.

Christian:

I was thinking the other day, if you take all the curly C's out of Cliff Richards name, that's what he gets called in China, 'Liff Ri-hard.' Which ironically is the mandarin word for 'dinosaur.'

I arrived at work a little bit later than normal today, because I'd a late night. I had a late-night doing work for work. I didn't just waltz in whenever I like. Have you ever had those mornings where you get in and everyone's demanding of you in the first 10 minutes? You haven't even had time to log your computer on or sit down or swear at anyone. People are going, 'Can you have a look at this problem?' And 'Oh, by the way, such and such wants you to give them a call.' And 'There's a post it note, can you get this fixed?'

'Hold on, I'm going back outside.' What a horrible feeling that is, all within the first few minutes of arriving. It's all sorted and dealt with in the first hour, but it's that initial harassment. What's everyone doing to me? Why am I being attacked from all sides? I guess that's real popularity. And I don't care much for it.

Jamie:

I find that happens when I'm about to leave work. A few minutes before I'm able to walk out of the door, someone bothers me. The irritation is that I was free for the last hour to have helped with anyone, but they wait until the last minute.

Christian:

I'll tell you what else is guaranteed, incorrectly dialing a long number. It's like a teleconference and you dial the international code, the area code and then their meeting invite code. Why is it, the last digit you press, you always hit the wrong button? So you get up to 12 digits perfectly right, and then, when you concentrate towards the end, 'It's definitely a 9… Oh, I've hit 7.' Start over again. And if you don't, you end up getting put through to some random stranger, 'Harrow! Is that Riff Lichard? Solly, you have the Wong number.'

I wrote this down because it was quite funny. The Daily Mail was suggesting that Colonel Gaddafi has gotten paranoid. That people are out to get him. And I thought to myself, 'No, paranoid is when you think someone's out to get you, but they're not.' Colonel Gaddafi has every reason to believe that they're out to get him. There's NATO forces circling over and snipers hunting him down. There are bombs dropping all around him, he's not paranoid. What they should have said was, 'Colonel Gaddafi is very sensibly taking cover.' Instead, the headline reads, 'Paranoid Gaddafi on the run' with an insane picture of him. To be fair, any pictures that exists of him, he looks a bit crazy. But the fact is, 'paranoid' is used incorrectly there. He has every reason to know he's getting attacked. Under the insane photo it should have the caption, 'sensible Gaddafi yesterday.'

We went to Bede's world this weekend to learn all about the Venerable Bede who wrote 'the

ecclesiastical history of the English people,' and
he's done some other things as well to do with
calculating seasons. So, he was a very clever man
and he lived in Jarrow pretty much all of his life.
But you get the idea, he was a very intelligent, well
thought off man and that's why he's got Bede's
world named after him as a kind of celebration to
all things Anglo Saxon.

Now because it's in Jarrow, you don't need to go
through the Tyne tunnel. But there was so many
roadworks outside the tunnel, which is also the
Jarrow exit, I seen the temporary signpost they'd
put up and shouted to Joanne who was driving, 'It's
that way. It's that way.' And before we knew it,
other cars were queuing behind us, and we had to
go down into the tunnel. Once we got through, it
cost £1.20, which we should have never needed to
pay, because it was the fault of the construction
company for confusing the road layout, and now
we needed to get back again.

Jamie: Thanks Joanne.

Christian: There was a lot of that. I told her to drive through
                    some of the bollards at the side and get back into
                    the other lane and go back down the tunnel once
                    we'd come out on the other side.

Jamie: Sounds a bit illegal.

Christian: So is not paying for using the tunnel. What's
                    worse? Anyway, we got to the kiosk where you
                    throw the money into the funnel for the barrier to
                    open its arm and let you out. But we didn't have
                    enough money. Joanne only had a quid. We're 20p
                    short. So, I get out of the car shouting at all the
                    traffic behind us, 'Go back!' I'm getting angry
                    now. 'Go back! We haven't got any money.' I'm

just a mess of anxiety and adrenaline. 'Go back!'
The kids are hysterical in the car. 'Dad's gone ape.'

Then this woman in a car behind us, she says, 'Do
you need money?' Like you'd ask a tramp in need
of a cup of tea. I lean in through her window,
'Well, I need 20p.' So, she gives me 20 pence with
an expression of 'don't hurt us.' The weight of the
world was suddenly lifted from me in that one kind
act. Joanne was still sliding further down in her
chair, away from the rearview mirror in case this
lady could see her in it and begin to ask questions.
'Is that your carer?' Are they all hostages?'

But I did lose it. I was frothing at the mouth. I
genuinely believe I'd have stayed at that kiosk with
the arm down for the rest of the day until the
owners of the tunnel had resolved the issue. But
thanks to this understanding lady we got out. We
had to go to North Shields and buy a can of pop
just get some change for the return trip back
through the tunnel. But it does beg the question,
well it doesn't, because no one in Jarrow works, so
they won't be commuting, will they? They all just
sit around in their little Anglo-Saxon huts.

Seriously, I need to apologize for that last remark.
Just from my retelling of that story, it's gotten me
all hot and angry again. The people of Jarrow are
an especially hard-working breed of fellow
countrymen and women that should be rightly
proud of their industrious heritage. My problem is
only with the roadworks and not the good people
of South Tyneside. Bede's world is well worth a
visit.

<table>
<tr><td>Jamie:</td><td>Same with the Humber bridge you pay on the other side after you've gotten over it.</td></tr>
</table>

Christian: Financially the Humber Bridge is different with how it was built. The company that runs it still owes millions to the construction company. So, it was like a big loan. And in order to pay it off as well as the interest, and keep maintaining and repairing it, they'll probably have to charge a toll to cross it forever.

              The governments keep getting us into debt as a nation. They promise to build new schools, colleges, hospitals and other NHS facilities by allowing contractors to do it on the same terms as a big mortgage, to be paid by the rest of the country over the next 50 to 100 years. It might win votes to build new things, but in the long run, we're all paying them off. And of course, the Humber bridge is an example of that type of funding, where you've got a necessity, really to make the road network more efficient, but someone has to pay for it. And of course, the builders, at least the company and their descendants, rake it in.

Jamie: There was a picture in Private Eye, you know, the ones with politicians talking with speech bubbles? And they had one of Gordon Brown when he was Prime Minister, looking down at some school kids and the caption reads, 'What are you going to be when you grow up?' 'In debt because of you,' came their reply.

Christian: Dry wit. If I got to do a speech bubble coming out of an MPs mouth, it would be something rude. Do you remember doing that in a magazine, doodles? Make the front cover star on the Radio Times, like Lofty from Eastenders say, 'Bum Gravy' and then colour-in his teeth. Yeah, I'm gonna make him smoke a pipe. 'But that's not a pipe shape.' Well, he's smoking it anyway.

So, I was 20 pence up from this charitable lady, but in reality, it had cost us £2.20 extra for the pointless jaunt through the tunnel. We finally arrived at Bede's world and the receptionist said, 'If you've got English Heritage cards you can go in for half price.' We did, but they'd expired, but because they didn't look close enough at them, we got in for half price. So, in a way we managed to turn our fortunes around. Although It didn't last long.

There was this Cockney guy who was a volunteer there. He must have drunk a lot of strong coffee because he had vile terminal coffee breath. And he's telling us a bit about the exhibition. We had hoped to hang out together as a family, so the last thing I needed was this loud tag-a-long pointing with his walking stick, 'Awight me old China! Have ye seen the Anglo-Saxons, God love 'em. Yez, seez tha' dustbin lids exhibition of the auditowium tweacle? Would you Adam and Eve it, auditowiums are Roman, but its Anglo Saxon.' Phew! A bit of coffee going on in my eyes there.

'You see, this was a king. He's all powerful. He's all mighty.' 'A bit like Beowulf?' 'No, not him. Someone else?' 'Well, I don't know anyone else.' 'No, neither do I. Knees up Matha' braan.' It came to a point where I was actually cheesed off with him and I involuntarily rolled my eyes, genuinely wishing him to leave us alone. But the thing is, we're looking in this glass cabinet, and if you're looking at the display, fine, but if you're looking at the covering glass, you could just see me gnashing my teeth and silently cursing. He must have seen my streaming eyes from his breath rolling right back. 'Hey, are y'all right? I said Are y'all right?' Phew! Then he seen some nuns and followed them.

Speaking of Beowulf, which I did, which I kind of threw in there, a CGI movie has been done by Robert Zemeckis. Okay, so apparently, it's like the oldest story that's ever been written down in the English language or claiming to be the forerunner to the English language, ye olde English in Saxon runes, and it is very, very good. It's excellent.

It's still got a certificate 12, and there's a reason why, because Grendel the monster. He's literally ripping people in half. As an adult you know it's CGI, so it's okay to call it animated, but to see the men rowing the boat and they all look real. So when Grendel starts picking up these men and biting their heads off and ripping them in half, I'm looking at my kids and their little mouths have fallen open in disbelief at what they're watching.

They are quite sheltered, but I thought we'd do an Anglo-Saxon weekend. We had gone to the Kirkleatham museum which now has an Anglo-Saxon princess exhibition, well worth going to. They unearthed a princess near Loftus, and it was probably one of the last of many great pagan burials in the area because Christianity was coming to the northeast. They've reconstructed the wooden bedchamber that she was laid on in her shallow grave. And you can see the actual jewelry they found. One of the pendants was already 600 years old when the princess wore it. So, the pendant is almost from the time of Christ.

We attended the opening day of this exhibition and I even got my guide signed by the guy who wrote it. My daughter took it over to him and he said, 'Who do you want it signing for?' And of course, Trinity just shrugged. So, he just wrote, 'Best wishes' and added his signature. So, I've got an autographed copy by the author.

Jamie: Why didn't you go to the guy and get it signed?

Christian: Because sometimes I feel like I might not be on the same level playing field as a lot of people. I know this sounds like I've got a lack of confidence, which I don't, but when it comes to things like that, I do. I'd feel like if I went up there to meet him, I'd feel the need to speak to him and his professor archeologist friends about Anglo-Saxon Britain. And I don't really know that much, I'm still learning about it myself. I mean, look at me, I know about Grendel biting off villagers' heads. If I talked to him about that, and what little I do know about the subject, he'd think I was a phoney. Which is exactly what I thought of that coffee mouthed Cockney. So, I suppose I did learn something from him after all, intellectual modesty.

Jamie: I would say you know quite a bit about history. I'll be the author of the books about archaeology. 'I see you're interested in royalty from history.'

Christian: Yes, in 1976 the Queen pulled down her knicks, she licked her bum and said, 'Yum! Yum! It's better than Weetabix.' Although I must admit to not being a hundred percent sure of the exact date Emeritus Professor of European History at Oxford.

Jamie: I don't think you should speak to people, not just authors of clever books.

Christian: Have you heard about the whale situation in Redcar? Do you know anyone who's laid eyes on it? I think the dead whale body has been protected probably in case locals go out and try to eat it. I would. I've always said that to you, 'I'd eat whale meat.' I think it must be yummy, enough Japanese eat the stuff. And let's be fair, it's dead anyway, so why waste it?

The Evening Gazette wrote a piece: *Hundreds of Teessider's including many children on their school holidays made their way to the beach to catch a glimpse of the enormous mammal. Many took photos of the whale while others marvelled at its size.* I would presume the people photographing the whale were also marveling at its size, if not more so, hence them taking a photo. Did you know you can open the head of the whale and take out an oily oiliness that you can use to make soaps, its lovely.

Paul Waugh, a volunteer at British divers and marine mammal medics, was involved in the operation. 'It could have been ill,' he said. 'Maybe that's why it has come ashore.' You see, if I'd have read that I wouldn't try and cut myself a steak from the rotting carcass. There's a guy who could write a whale book, sat there and autographing them. Jamie comes along to buy a copy. 'Are you gonna' ask him to sign your copy?' 'No, he might ask me about whales.' 'Go on, sit down, don't be daft.' 'Who do you want it signing for?' 'To Jamie.' 'So, do you know much about whales?' 'You can make them into soap.' This guy's trying to conserve them, and you're wanting to make them into soap. Big huge blocks of soap.

The voluntary organisation advises members of the public to take the following steps when they come across one of the stranded animals. This is class, we've had one standard whale in how many hundreds of years? Anyway, just on the off chance you might be the First Aider to a whale, don't worry about CPR, because what are your chances of needing to revive another human? Something that might actually happen, no, here we learn how to revive a whale in a few easy steps.

Alright, you come across one of these stranded mammals. Okay, *step one, make sure the blowhole is not covered. Step two dig trenches under the pectoral fins. Step three keep wet by dousing with water. Step four cover with damp towels or seaweed.*

Jamie: And if you haven't got any?

Christian: It doesn't matter. It's not like I've got time for digging trenches around the whale with my small plastic spade. Hopefully it doesn't fall into the trench and squash me. *Step five remain calm and quiet so as not to distress the whale any further. Step six keep away from the tail as it can inflict serious injury. Step seven make a note of the whale size and any markings to give rescuers an idea of the breed before they arrive.* That's a lot of things to remember.

It might be easier just to take a photo of the whale and marvel at its size. I know that sounds flippant, but seriously if you come across a whale, what are you going to do? Even the fire brigade and specialists in marine conservation, people who know what they're doing, and they still couldn't save this whale. So, it's not a case of you jumping into action with your bucket and spade. An amazing animal, nonetheless, and it is a shame that it ended it's time on Redcar beach.

Christian: Hopefully that'll be the last cough we hear from Paul. What's going on? Have you picked up some viral infection?

Paul: I woke up yesterday and I was coughing me guts up. I've been having cough medicine, but I couldn't find a spoon, so I've been using shot glasses.

Christian: That's too much. You're supposed to only take like two teaspoons, around 10 milliliters.

Paul: I've been doing 25 mil which is a hell of a lot more.

Christian: It's called 'overdose.'

Paul: So, if I pass out during the show, you'll know why.

Christian: Yeah, and then wake up in the gutter. Has that happened before? You've woken up in a place where you didn't actually remember being?

Paul: I woke up on a night out once, key still in hand, outside the gate to my house in a puddle of rusty water.

Christian: And you don't recall it raining?

Paul: That's the only thing. But to make it even better, I lived underneath a pharmacy and they left me a bottle of water and some paracetamol next to me.

Christian: Didn't they try and disturb you to make sure you weren't choking on your own tongue or anything?

Paul: No, it was a pharmacist not a paramedic.

Christian:	I would probably have taken the key from out your hand and tried the door. It's probably why I don't make a good neighbour.

Paul:	Neighbour? Try human being.

Christian:	I'm looking at last week's show and it's got your birthday jotted down here, so you're a week older?

Paul:	We're all a week older.

Christian:	I've got some lion's mouth that I didn't use, 'Pringles, two for £2, or £2.49 each.' That was advertised at a petrol station on the roadside when we were on holiday. I just forgot to mention that.

Paul:	And you heard it here first for breaking news.

Christian:	What a strange bargain. If you worked there, and a customer took just one tube of Pringles to the counter, would you go, 'Alright, that'll be £2.49 please.' Or would you tell them to get another tube and give him back the 49p?

Paul:	Look, the advert was big enough for you to see from the roadside. If they missed it, bigger fool them. Let's move on to this week's show.

Christian:	I am a bit late because I had to swap shifts at work for a colleague pretending to be on his sick bed.

Paul:	I was waiting outside the house for like half an hour.

Christian:	Did none of my neighbours offer you a cup of tea?

Paul:	No.

Christian:	Good. I don't want to have to thank them.

Paul:	I thought I saw your car coming down the street, so I got out of the car, locked it, and thought, 'Oh that's not Christian.' Went to get back in the car, and the alarm went off. Then these kids on bikes start going, 'Nee-naw! Nee-naw!'
Christian:	That's brilliant. Did you notice one looked a little bit like you? I did. I thought if Paul sowed his wild oats, that could be his child. Did you see the stumpy fat kid with the little diamond stud earring in?
Paul:	No.
Christian:	I guess you have to say that to avoid paying any child support.
Paul:	Sounds like chunky Paul junior can sell his earring first.
Christian:	Before we opened the microphones I said, 'I've got some sweeties.' Have one with your cup of coffee. Now normally I buy raspberry flavoured Ruffles, which is a bar of raspberry flavoured coconut covered in chocolate. These ones are peppermint flavoued. I had one. And it's fine as you're eating it. But as you breathe out, there's a little vomiting texture to it. You know? Like baby formula milk? I can't really explain it, it's unpleasant but manageable. My son brushed his teeth over a urinal when we went camping because they were a few sinks short. Not sure how he was able to do that, but you somehow get through these things. And peppermint Ruffles are one of them. Another mystery happened on a recent family walk. I'm walking along, and let's say you're part of the family Paul. So, I'll catch up with you, 'It's

great to have this quality time spent together as a family. Anyway Paul, you know Rowing Clubs? Do you think it's a sport only for toffs or is that Badminton?' Then you say, 'I'm just gonna stop back and wait for someone else. I'll wait for them to catch up.'

Paul: They might have a better conversation. You go ahead.

Christian: But I'm already at the front. Yeah, it happened several times. That's why I was amazed that every time I caught up with someone and started talking to a different family member they kept looking behind and saying, 'I'll just wait for such-and-such, I don't want them lagging behind.' 'Yeah alright, I'll wait with you.' 'No, best you go ahead. Please go on ahead.'

Paul: Okay, try me. You've caught up to me, 'How's work been treating you Christian?'

Christian: There's a lad at work and he was telling me he watched someone standing at the urinal, then literally with one hand he… Which hand would you hold your mobile phone in if you were at the urinal?

Paul: Probably the strongest one, my right.

Christian: They are quite expensive. You wouldn't want to drop it into the yellow trough. First of all, he thought, 'What's he got his mobile phone out for?' It's a bit dodgy isn't it? Mobile phones are basically cameras these days. So, he's thumbing it, his phone. And he said, 'With one hand, and a single smooth movement, this guy was able to shake and tuck away.'

Paul: Wow!

Christian: ZIP! And then while he's still holding his phone, he's washing his hands with one hand. Yeah, to be honest, if you can do the putting away side of things, the washing of the hands is easy. But this colleague was very impressed. He wasn't sure if he should have been watching. That's what he said. He said, he felt a little uncomfortable at first. But I guess that passes quite quickly.

Paul: I suppose it does.

Christian: Practice makes perverts.

Paul: After eating that sweet right, I've got all this coconut stuck in my teeth. I can't get rid of it.

Christian: You are going to review that chocolate bar. I would have given it 1 out of 10. It was that awful.

Paul: I quite liked it.

Christian: You did say you like Hershey chocolate.

Paul: I do. I'll tell you what, you go ahead. I'll wait for such-and-such to catch up. Speaking of phones at the urinal. The new iPhone's getting released.

Christian: There's an iPhone fanatic camping outside Sydney's Apple Store for 10 days so he's the first in the world to get the new handset. He said he wouldn't give up that spot from being first in line for $50,000. Would it not have been easier to pay a tramp 10 Australian dollars or maybe just a warm conker to sleep in the doorway? Can you push in a queue by using a tramp as a decoy? That's the question to the listeners, would it be classed as pushing in? Or would it be classed as saving you a spot?

We've all been in a situation where the person in front of us has saved someone else a spot. And sadly, there's no laws surrounding this annoying practice, otherwise the police would be getting called all the time. Now, if they save a spot and they're behind me, it doesn't trouble me in the slightest. I probably don't even notice. But if you plant a tramp in front of me, I've got to now wait with that tramp for 10 days. That's going to be a problem.

Paul: You could blame him for all your smells. I mean, 10 days standing in a queue with no toilet facilities.

Christian: If you get to the front, can you buy them all.

Paul: Usually when a supermarket does an offer on beer it'll say like, 'eight max per customer.' And remember the tramp is at the front of the queue, so he's got dibsies.

Christian: Assuming he's got any money, I don't think it would help him in any way shape or form. He's got one hand on his genitals, and he can do everything else with the other. Practice, practice, practice.

Paul: I go through phones like underpants. I break them all after not long having them.

Christian: There's something simple about you, isn't there? Oh, I hadn't finish talking about toilets. After standing alongside another gentleman at the urinals, he goes to the door to leave, before washing his hands. And he actually held the door open for me, as if, 'come on, we can both escape without anyone knowing.' I stood there for a split second of indecisiveness. You know what? I said, 'I'm gonna wash my hands first.' Really, I should have replied by offering him some soap. As he's opening the door, shout out, 'Hey, what about some soap and water?' But he left. So, I guess by proxy, I kind of touched his penis, because I touched the same door he was holding. Imagine how many unwashed hands have opened that door?

Ever used a Gregg's paper bag to wipe your mouth? I can't think of a bag that would work. But if you had one made from tissue paper or baby wipes, that would be okay. But the Gregg's bags are a little bit laminated, it's grease proof paper. So, after I've eaten, and it's very rare that I have a mince and onion pie, because the pastry crumbles everywhere and the gravy inside is so hot it drops out of my mouth back into the tin foil tray making a complete mess.

But once you've enjoyed it, and it's all over, the only thing you've got to wipe your mouth with is the bag. I could feel a bit of gravy at the corners of my mouth, and by the time I'd finished wiping, it was on my forehead and everywhere. It spreads like my face is a baking sheet. If Gregg's is listening, and I know that you're a former employee Paul. Where you ever 'employ of the month'? When your little photo gets moved up higher on the 'meet the team' poster of recognition.

Paul: Maybe they did, and I was just useless I never ended up on it.

Christian: But if you'd have suggested they give a spoon to customers who purchase savory pies, you'd have been called 'head help' for at least a month.

Paul: They could give customers a spork.

Christian:	Now you're looking for a regional title with that 'mention the invention.' Something like, 'subordinate star,' and you get your little photo replaced with a photo of you actually meeting that months nationally recognized King of Gregg's, who presents you with your sash and sausage roll.

There's a picture of some old dead people from the 1890s. These were chamber maids, and tweenies, as Victorians called them, between maids and other domestic staff who lived and worked for the lord of the manor.

Paul:	Tweenies? I thought you meant the kid's programme.

Christian:	Yeah, a pre-school show based on scullery maids and butlers now all dead. So, there's this black and white photo circa 1890, and let's just say it was taken somewhere in Wales because I seen it at the Welsh national folk museum. It must have been taken during a holiday or celebration because all the staff are happily posing in front of a fortified manor house. Not to be confused with a castle. My point being their image and likeness are being used, even though they're dead.

Where are the royalties going? Because in the gift shop, you could buy an apron with the same picture of all these servants from their household. When they got that photo taken in 1890, did they have to get the domestic workers to sign a photo release form to say, in over 100 years, you can still use a picture of me dead on your hot water bottles. And whatever money you generate, keep for yourself. I'm guessing they didn't. If you trace back your family history and discovered one of them was a parlour maid to Lord Snot, would you receive some cash from all the merchandise? I'd at least want a lump sum, 'It's what great-great aunt Fannie wanted me to have.'

Have you ever looked at these old Victorian pictures, and judged who's the sexiest? Who's having an affair with each other? Who's the tallest? You look at the faces and you judge. Yeah, we all do it. I know we've got technology these days that can read our face and they know if you're a criminal, or your sexuality. But I don't think they need those controversial applications. Just hire me. I know, I judge everyone. So, I'm looking at them. And I'm thinking the old woman, actually none of them look young, she was probably getting it on with Roscoe the head footman. And I've watched Downton Abbey, so I know a little of what I speak.

If you could go back in time, would you try and relieve them from their lowly lot in life, by giving them an invention, like a spork? You could say, 'Look, make yourself famous old crone. Here's a spork, it's the future.'

Paul: But the servants work for the landed gentry, so obviously if the butler invents the spork, the owner of the manor will be like, 'Yep, I'm having that.'

Christian: Good point. And they wouldn't be able to tell them about you, because I imagine the time machine is more important than the spork. You're gonna have to take a mind wiping device with you in case the snobs claim intellectual property. You know in Superman one, where he kisses Lois, and she forgets his secret identity with a sloppy French kiss. Would you do that to the old crone? Then when you're finished, ask her if she still remembers. She's got a big wet slavered mouth and she goes, 'It's a spork isn't it?'

Paul: I think I'd go down the Men in Black route. Don't kiss anyone. Not even great aunt Fannie. I'll tell you what's worth licking, a dairy ice cream from the Jersey farm in Darlington.

Christian: The milk comes from Jersey cows, right?

Paul: Absolutely amazing.

Christian: I assume the cows are kept a distance away from the ice-creams being served? That would suppress my appetite, lots and lots of cow pat smells. Then you go away with your lemon top ice cream and just barf on it with flies all over the place.

Paul: There was loads of chickens around as well. It was brilliant.

Christian: I've got this sucralose-based sugar. I had a quick look, it says it gives leukaemia to mice. Now, that's not great. Or I can use aspartame-based which gives cancer to rats. So, which one's worse for me and which one's better? I mean, clearly both have side effects to rats and mice. But which one are you pulling for?

Paul: Well, I'd go for the first one.

Christian: Are you suggesting I'm more rat like? Well, I brought in two, so I'm going to use both. The more you read up on this, and we're talking about dieting and checking your calories as the main reasons for changing to these artificial sweeteners, evidence still points to sugar being better. As strange as that sounds, you know, it rots your teeth and it causes obesity and cancers, obviously too much sugar. But they're still saying it doesn't have half the problems that they don't know about with these non-calorific sweeteners long term. It's a more complex structure than natural sugars with plenty of chemicals, some nasty. I guess the alternative is honey. Or how about diabetic's urine, that's apparently sweet.

Paul: I don't know I've never drank diabetics wee. I'm not a pervert.

Christian: Okay, what if it were a diabetic woman's wee?

Paul: Oh, that makes it perfectly alright.

Christian: Listen to this news. *Hackers could order sex robots to kill their owners.* Wow. Now that's got you scared. *Hacking into the robots would be far simpler than accessing more sophisticated devices like smartphones.* But the sex robot only does one thing, so you know how it's going to kill you.

A psychologist has shared a seven-step formula that can turn anyone into a morning person. It involves sleeping on the left side of the bed and wearing yellow. How is that science? When did science become something stupid? *Behavioural psychologist, Jo Hemmings has devised a scientific backed formula by becoming a morning person including doing a five-minute burst of exercise and then a two-minute handstand.* Let me tell you, if he got me out of bed and said, 'Come on, quickly do a handstand,' he'd be getting a smack, even if I was a morning person to begin with.

Can you learn while you nap?

Paul: Yeah, I'm going to call fake news on that. I frequently fall asleep while I'm sad, I watch tutorials about electronics on YouTube and I fall

asleep to them and I know nothing about
electronics.

Christian: And when you wake up, you're drooling, holding
your house keys, soaked in some rusty rainwater
leaking from your pants.

Paul: I couldn't even work out how to open a door lock,
never mind rewire a plug.

Christian: *A revolutionary eye test can detect the early signs
of dementia. Scientists at University of
Pennsylvania School of Medicine found eye
changes may signal Frontotemporal dementia.*
That's an amazing breakthrough, because you
know my Nanna bless her, has dementia. She's in
an Alzheimer's care home. I went to see her on
Friday and sat there with my son. I said, 'Oh, we've
had a great holiday Nanna,' and another patient
came over and went, 'You're a liar. You're a liar.
You're full of-.' And he was swearing. And
swearing a lot.

I did think, 'Maybe he knows.' 'Okay Nanna, it
might not have been a great holiday, but it was still
a holiday.' I don't know if he was Irish. I think
sometimes when the dementia kicks in, they go
back to their mother tongue. You may no longer
speak English with no one understanding you. I
could understand him. He was swearing at me a
lot. And it went on for about five minutes, literally,
with him standing behind me just effing and
blinding.

So, I went to a member of the care staff and said,
'There's this guy, he's full of expletives.' And the
carer started to lecture me, not in a bad way, but
maybe I came across wrong. He said, 'You do
know that he's in here for the same reasons as your

Nanna. And his own family and wife are absolutely devastated as well. In fact, if he knew he was like this, he'd probably rather be dead.' The amount of guilt that was tipped onto me was huge. And as much as I knew that it really was more to do with the fact, I couldn't speak with my Nanna and enjoy any conversation. I went to visit her and instead I'm listening to a stranger shouting. And so, I think he got where I was coming from and offered me a family room, which was great, and that's where my story ends.

I think I'd be devastated if I became a foul-mouthed resident. I always think about being in front of my Nanna, and I've never ever let any rude words slip out. I do know there are certain people out there that can't operate on those two levels. If you always use that language, you always use it, and it's very difficult for you to keep polite society from blushing, but thankfully I've never had that problem. Never had it. My Nanna even with her condition, I've not heard her curse. She did say to the gentleman who was swearing, 'Will you please go away.' But he wouldn't. I think it was more when my Nanna was getting a bit upset, that I wanted to intervene because to me it wasn't the be all and end all, I was fine to ignore him, but my Nanna was getting agitated, and I wanted her to be happy.

The man on a mission to save declining bee populations by extracting the insect's semen with his own hands and artificially inseminating the Queen. This is Michael Waite 53 from Castle Douglas in Scotland. Have you ever inseminated a queen? There's a man who would choose honey over diabetic's urine, that's for sure.

Jennifer Lawrence claims that the recent spate of deadly hurricanes Harvey and Irma are the revenge that Mother Nature's thrown upon everyone because they elected President Trump. I like the science to that. Mother Nature always pays particular interest to the US elections. And she's thinking, 'I'm gonna have a really big storm for those Trump supporters.' And incredibly this idiot actress still has a job, unlike Hillary.

Firemen have been ordered to carry out blood pressure tests for the NHS. I noticed machines in supermarkets to do this. I was at South Bank, an area of Middlesbrough. We were doing part of the Teesdale Way when we arrived in Southbank. From Newport bridge, you can walk to Redcar in 11 and a half miles, which took us about 16. Joanne didn't have a Fitbit on, so she's been gutted. We got as far as Southbank station and the rest of the Teesdale Way was cut off with a fence just opposite Dorman Long tower. Shouldn't that be a public right of access? So, we had to go on to the Trunk Road which added those extra miles.

But we did find Asda in Southbank, and noticed they were telling people to go get their smear tests and to get their cholesterol checked. I don't know if this was happening in any other supermarkets or whether they'd noticed industrial areas had more people not engaging with the doctors and their own health. So, the NHS staff went out into the local community to do this. But is it really the fireman's job to promote healthy living choices? But I suppose, if they're not putting out fires, what else are they doing?

Paul: Checking smoke alarms.

Christian: It's a proactive approach for the firemen to check
              the chunk rats weight, that's what I say. Calculate
              their BMI to see if they could be carried out of a
              burning building. The firemen could do that in
              Asda. Sling the chunk rat over their back and see if
              they can scale a ladder. If they drop them, they can
              say, 'Look, you're too fat. That's what'll happen
              with a chip pan fire.' Because you don't need to be
              Poirot to know they'll be eating chips. It's what
              they like, it's part of their culture.

              '*You're so vein.*' I've only mentioned this because
              they've spelt vain, as in Carly Simons classic hit,
              as 'vein' because it's about blood, '*a pound of
              blood that's ready to use in an instant.*' Is there an
              award ceremony where they give out 'headline of
              the year'? Because I want that nominated.

              Is it safe to sit all day? That's the question.

Paul: I suppose drivers do and people working in an
              office.

Christian: Long distance lorry drivers have a much shorter
              life expectancy.

Paul: Then, 'No!' It's not safe.

Christian: The study says, the way you sit is more important
              than the length of time. You could set an alarm to
              go off every half hour, so you'll stand up and
              move. It could be one of those audio alarms,
              'Move or you'll die! Move or you'll die!' It
              doesn't say how long you have to move or whether
              you just stand up and then sit back down again.
              Not sure it's as simple as that, just get the legs
              moving. I mean, you must have done it where
              you've been on a long car journey. And you get out
              the car. It's like Bambi learning to walk on the ice,

you have to get the other leg out of the car and then you think, 'I've got to stand up now.' It's always at these motorway service stations you'll see people getting out of cars, remembering how to walk or at the least not fall over. It's a horrible aching feeling, like listening to this show on a long car journey.

Behavioural scientists up and down the land are saying, 'Play some tunes.' I say, 'Has that been scientifically proven to be the best way to engage with the listener?' And they say, 'No, but If you don't put on any music soon, we'll tune out.' So, we're gonna play music from our friends Skinner and Twitch. I've got their new, and funny song called 'The ageing special agent.' After that John Shuttleworth and 'Can't go back to savory now.'

Last week we talked about Cornish tin miners eating their pasties in the dark, biting into the jam side first, then having to discard the meat and potato side for the same reasons in that song. But I would, if I'd started with dessert, I'd still go back and eat the main savory meal. I hate to see wasted food. Wouldn't trouble me. You told me a joke off air, and I was just wondering, is it possible to yawn on someone else's behalf? It wasn't great, but it's okay, because you didn't share it with the listeners and we're all thankful for that.

Without retelling the gag, you were talking about going to the toilets. Have you ever walked into a public toilet and you can hear a cistern filling up, but you're not sure which trap it belongs to? Because the noise would be emanating from the toilet most recently vacated. Do you think there should be an Amber Alert system? So, it would go from red when it's just been vacated, so you don't make the mistake of walking in and breathing up freshly disturbed faeces particles.

Paul: Phew! What just died in there?

Christian: I love the idea that as a doctor you could say to a
                         stranger who's just dropped their guts, 'Excuse me
                         I couldn't help notice that somethings clearly died
                         inside you. Has a rat crawled up there?' Imagine if
                         it's Richard Gere, well maybe. So, after the first
                         minute it's red, then it drops to amber, if you're
                         willing, brave or desperate enough. You've got to
                         make that decision. But once it's green, it's clear.
                         Let's hear your news.

Paul: *We have got concerns about a Blackburn pet shop
                         after a rat dies two days after being bought.*

Christian: Someone stick it up their bum? We've all got
                         concerns if a celebrity bought the rodent. There's
                         the doctor, 'I think I know the problem just from
                         the smell alone.'

Paul: *The rat was riddled with mites, which died two
                         days later.*

Christian: That's mites, not mice. I could feed them that non
                         calorific sugar and kill them both.

                         There's no movie review this week because I
                         watched an old movie that we've done before, 'Liar
                         Liar' with Jim Carrey. But since all of this STI
                         behaviour, blaming his former dead girlfriend, it's
                         now lost 10 marks. So, it was a good film, but it's
                         now a zero out of ten. I've given one out of ten for
                         my children, who've made their own stop-start
                         motion films. They keep showing me them, and I
                         just think they're awful.

                         It's because they make them too quickly. For
                         instance, Captain America's head rolls across the

carpet in three frames, and then goes onto the Hulks body. And I ask them, 'What was the plot of this?' And they say, 'Oh, well, Captain America lost his head and they swapped it with the Hulk.'

Paul: Isn't that the plot to 'Face off'?

Christian: And then after they've shown me, they go, 'Oh, we've made another hundred films.' I thought, 'Really? The time you've spent on these videos, you could have made a good 10 second film. Instead, you've got a hundred snippets of unconstructed flash photography.'

Paul: I'll tell you what, a challenge for you, why don't you try to make one for your kids.

Christian: Don't say this. I'm a busy person. Look, I'm making this radio show which is pretty much the equivalent of their animation. This is stop-starting throughout the entire production. I shall give my children a ten out of ten for their artistic endeavors that were sadly met with an unappreciative audience.

Paul: Just like ours.

Christian: And the lesson to both my children and us, is to always keep on trying. We'll get there in the end. We're here next week, so until then take care, God bless!

About the Author

Christian Frank is an experienced radio presenter / writer / producer spanning quarter of a century in broadcasting including many freelance hours for local BBC Radio. Since March 1995 he has written and presented a weekly 2-hour show 'The Lemon Circus' which has been nominated for several HBA and Mixcloud Awards. They have attracted a global listenership topping the Comedy, News and Community Radio charts. He made his TV debut by appearing as an extra in the soap opera 'Shortland Street.' His debut novel 'LEAVERS ASSEMBLY' was published in 2020. Christian lives in Teesside, married to Joanne with 5 children.

Also by Christian Frank

Give Pause For... Thanks!   **Leavers Assembly**

'Read two random pages, loved it'.   'I was entertained all the way through.
                                            Brilliant read.'
– Mrs J B Anderson   - Joel Newnham

Both available from Amazon.com

 Remember, it's reviews that help sell - So please do leave one!

**Further Volumes from the 'Life Without A Laughter Track'
series will become available soon.**